OFFICIAL
strategies & secrets

Microsoft®
Train Simulator

David Chong,
Rick Selby, and
Richard Wayne Smith

SYBEX

San Francisco • Paris • Düsseldorf • London

Associate Publisher:	Dan Brodnitz
Contracts and Licensing Manager:	Kristine O'Callaghan
Acquisitions and Developmental Editor:	Dan Brodnitz
Editors:	Howard Jones and Brett Todd
Production Editor:	Kelly Winquist
Proofreader:	Laura Ryan
Book Design:	Diana Van Winkle, Van Winkle Design
Book Production:	Diana Van Winkle, Van Winkle Design
Cover Design:	Richard Miller, Calyx Design
Poster Design:	Diana Van Winkle, Van Winkle Design

Library of Congress Control Number: 2001088238
ISBN: 0-7821-2910-2
Manufactured in the United States of America

10 9 8 7 6 5

For Kate, who heard the trains at night.
—David Chong

Thanks to my wife Melissa for her patience and understanding during my
never-ending list of projects
—Rick Selby

In memory of my Grandfather, Alexander Edgar Smith. He was the C.P.R.
Stationmaster of Scotsguard Sask. from 1914 to 1949.
—Rick Smith

Acknowledgments

Train Simulator is a joy to play thanks to the hardworking and meticulous simulation development team at Microsoft and Kuju Entertainment. Authentic sounds, painstakingly researched realism, and a polished look that was custom built for a ground-level sim make the suspension of disbelief complete, transporting the player into the seats of nine unique locomotives. Thanks go to Mike Geertsen, Kathy Osborne, Claire Dadge, Phil Marley, Paul Astley, Jonathan Newth, Eric Kruske, and everyone else on the *Train Simulator* team who helped make this book as accurate as possible. Thanks also go to the Odakyu Electric Railway Co., Ltd., Japan; the Kyushu Railway Co., Ltd., Japan; Flying Scotsman Railways, England; and Venice Simplon-Orient-Express, England.

My heartfelt thanks go to the entire Sybex team. My co-authors, Rick Selby and Richard Smith, were a pleasure to write with. Dan Brodnitz wore many hats on this project, and he was characteristically masterful in keeping it all on track. Special thanks to Kelly Winquist, who always makes it easy, and to Diana Van Winkle for making it look good, and Laura Ryan for proofreading. Howard Jones did a great job with little time on the copy edit, and the ever-reliable Brett Todd has my sincere gratitude for helping out with the edit at the end of the line. And last but not least, my deepest thanks go to my family, Kate and Maggie, for giving me a wonderful home to write in.

—David Chong

Sincere thanks go out to Mike Geertsen, Rod Fergusson, Shawn Firminger, Kathy Osborne, and Patrick Barker, all from Microsoft Games. Thanks also to the Burlington Northern Santa Fe Railway, Ft. Worth, TX and National Railroad Passenger Corporation (Amtrak), Washington DC.

—Rick Selby

Contents

Part I
Operating the Routes

Chapter 1

Chapter 2

Chapter 6

Chapter 7

Part II
Game Tools

Chapter 8

Chapter 9

Chapter 10

Chapter 11

Appendix

Introduction

Microsoft Train Simulator: Sybex Official Strategies & Secrets will help you operate your virtual railway at maximum efficiency along all points of your engineering career. For the novice, a wealth of train handling basics are offered throughout the book, giving you clear, quick tips on how to get rolling down the line with a minimum of fuss. Old railheads are given invaluable advanced instruction on power assignment and comprehensive tutorials for expanding the simulation. *Microsoft Train Simulator* has been developed with a careful touch to appeal to both the casual gamer and the veteran engineer, and this guide is the perfect companion to your railroading experience from one end of the spectrum to the other.

Train Simulator offers players a unique opportunity to operate a realistically modeled train along a dynamic rail line under authentic conditions. The virtual engineer will be confronted with challenges that mimic the situations that their real world counterparts must face daily. A host of features and comprehensive options for customization and player expansion mark *Train Simulator* as today's leading railroading simulation of today.

As a virtual engineer, you may feel as if you've got to learn a new trade just to play the game. Fortunately, Microsoft tailored *Train Simulator* so that you can configure its depth and difficulty to your precise taste. The game even gives you the opportunity to ride the rails as a passenger, observing the finely detailed scenery and enjoying the trip along your virtual railroad. Several levels of realism can make your job either a push-button operation or a nail-biting flurry of activity.

Game Features

Train Simulator features six unique routes and nine locomotives. Several kinds of rolling stock are available for transport. The game's Explore the Routes play mode allows you to freely conduct your train along the routes, without the concerns of a schedule or other traffic. Numerous Activities are included, ranging from running a train on schedule to switching and problem solving. You can also create your own Activities for new challenges, or download other player's creations from the Internet.

Using This Guide

This strategy guide is an indispensable companion on your journey over the virtual rails of *Train Simulator*. Use the text not only as a manual for study before you begin the game, but also as a quick reference during gameplay. As you run the routes and tackle the game's Activities, you can keep the relevant walkthrough chapter at your side to check your progress and help you out of a crisis if you get stuck. This Introduction and Chapter 1: Basic Train Operating Skills contain valuable information on game controls and universal train handling concepts. They can easily be referenced during play when you forget what a particular gauge does, or when you need to know the optimal speed for descending a 2.5% grade with a heavy intermodal that's behind schedule.

This Introduction contains a summary of essential elements. Of particular importance are the tips on your game settings. Simulators must convey the look, sound, and feel of the experience that they are trying to model, so the proper options settings are of great importance. You'll also find information on what's contained in the game's electronic manual. Since it can be difficult to refer to an Adobe Acrobat file in the middle of a play session, things like train commands, keyboard shortcuts, and basic engineering concepts are covered here for your convenience. Essentially, this is a list of the tools at your disposal in *Train Simulator*.

NOTE If you're a veteran hogger, use the Introduction to familiarize yourself with the controls of the simulator. Then move right to the walkthroughs in Chapters 2 through 7 to get a look at each of the routes in the game. For a slick primer on train operations, turn straight to Chapter 1.

The bulk of this strategy guide is divided into two parts, each consisting of several chapters of specialized instruction. The first part, written by David Chong and Rick Selby, is called Operating the Routes. It presents everything from tutorials on operating the various engines provided with the game to specific coverage of the game's six routes. Chapter 1 provides you with in-depth instructions for operating each category of engine in the game and explanations of basic and advanced train handling. Chapters 2 through 7 offer in-depth examinations of each route in the game. Players of all experience levels will find useful information in these chapters, which point out areas of special concern on each route and offer tips for running every leg of each line.

Part II of this guide, authored by Richard Wayne Smith, offers a detailed overview of the editing tools available in *Train Simulator*. Programmed with the user in mind, *Train Simulator* allows you to create new routes, and import scenery, engines, and rolling stock into the game. These chapters walk you through using the Activity Editor, Route Editor, and Route Geometry Extractor.

Finally, the Appendix contains a discussion of several unique websites that offer various add-ons and supplements. Here you can find places to download custom objects and routes that others have created, and share your own creations with the rest of the world.

At the Station

Before setting out on your first run, configure the game to operate at optimum performance on your computer and familiarize yourself with the controls. The splendid graphics engine in *Train Simulator* has been created specifically for this game because, unlike a flight simulator, you'll be very close to the scenery as you pass it by. Still, the game manages to keep its minimum system requirements fairly low, and this means that there is a wide range of detail options available to you.

Fine Tuning Your Settings

The game automatically detects your computer's hardware and adjusts the game settings to match your processing power. It can be somewhat conservative, however, leaving room for you to fine-tune your settings to provide you with the best simulation experience you can achieve on your desktop. First, go to the main screen and choose Japan's Tokyo-Hakone line using a standard Series 2000 consist and set out from the default station. This route is a good test bed for your computer's performance, because it is a dense metropolitan area with a long train—meaning that there are plenty of things to test the game's rendering muscle.

WARNING Be sure you aren't multitasking while playing Train Simulator in order to get the best performance you can out of your computer. Check for other programs running by looking at your taskbar in Windows or by pressing Ctrl-Alt-Del once. Close all other programs before you play.

Obviously, it's desirable to have as high a framerate as possible. Since your computing power is finite, however, some of that speed can be traded for quality in the appearance of the world and the objects in it. A good target is around 20 frames per second at high speeds. Never accept fewer than 10, and if you are getting more than 30 frames per second you might want to turn up the graphic quality a little.

Hit Shift-Z in the game to display the number of frames that your computer is displaying per second in the lower right corner of the screen. Accelerate your train to about 60 mph (it may help to turn off derailing while tailoring your settings). If your framerate stays above 15, you're doing great! If your number drops too low, turn down some of your settings. Use the four Objects Quality bars at the bottom of the Advanced Display menu coupled with the Visibility distance slider to get in the right ballpark.

Game Controls

You should have an understanding of the controls for making the train move and stop before leaving the station. Keep the game's reference card by your side and make use of the command summaries in the game as you begin playing. *Train Simulator* is almost completely controllable with the active mouse interface, which allows you to manipulate everything with your cursor just as if you were using your hands.

NOTE You can call up a complete listing of the in-game key commands by pressing FII. If you can't find what you're looking for in the command list, or you want more detailed information, press FI for on-screen help.

Keyboard shortcuts also exist to make your virtual engineering life easier. The following tables list all of the default key controls to help you run your trains with maximum efficiency. Note that not all of these controls work on all engines. For specific instructions on how to use these controls, refer to Chapter 1, which covers all aspects of basic train handling skills.

Moving Your Train

SIMPLE MODE COMMANDS

KEY	FUNCTION
A	Speed up
D	Slow down
S	Change directions

ENGINE MOTIVE COMMANDS

KEY	FUNCTION
W	Increase reverser (forward)
S	Decrease reverser (back)
D	Increase throttle
A	Decrease throttle
Backspace	Apply emergency braking
E	Speed gear increase
Shift-E	Speed gear decrease
'	Increase train brake
;	Decrease train brake
.	Increase dynamic brake
,	Decrease dynamic brake
]	Increase locomotive brake
[	Decrease locomotive brake
P	Engage engine braking (KIHA 31 only)
/	Bail off train brakes

ADDITIONAL STEAM ENGINE COMMANDS

KEY	FUNCTION
D	Increase regulator
A	Decrease regulator
J	Toggle small ejector/compressor
C	Cylinder cocks open/close
F	Open firebox doors
Shift-F	Close firebox doors
I	Toggle injector I steam
K	Increase injector I water flow
Shift-K	Decrease injector I water flow
M	Increase damper opening
Shift-M	Decrease damper opening N Increase blower
Shift-N	Decrease blower
O	Toggle injector 2 steam
L	Increase injector 2 water flow
Shift-L	Decrease injector 2 water flow
R	Increase coal shoveling rate
Shift-R	Decrease coal shoveling rate
U	Increase steam heat pressure
Shift-U	Decrease steam heat pressure
Y	Toggle water scoop

Viewing the Action

VIEWPOINTS

KEY	FUNCTION
1	Engine cab view
2	External view 1
3	External view 2
4	Trackside view
5	Passenger view
6	Coupler view
7	Yard view

EXTERNAL VIEWS

KEY	FUNCTION
Up Arrow	Zoom in (from cab view in steam trains, this sticks your head out the window looking forward)
Down Arrow	Zoom out (from cab view in steam trains, this sticks your head out the window looking backward)
Left/Right Arrows	Pan view from side to side
Ctrl-Up Arrow	Raise view
Ctrl-Down Arrow	Lower view
Ctrl-Left Arrow	Center view on the next unit in the train
Ctrl-Right Arrow	Center view on the previous unit in the train
Ctrl-Left Arrow	Focus on front coupler (applies only to Coupler view)
Ctrl-Right Arrow	Focus on rear coupler (applies only to Coupler view)

INTERNAL VIEWS

KEY	FUNCTION
Up Arrow	Look up (from cab view in steam trains, this sticks your head out the window looking forward)
Down Arrow	Look down (from cab view in steam trains, this sticks your head out the window looking backward)
Left Arrow	Look left
Right Arrow	Look right

Miscellaneous Commands

DRIVING AIDS

KEY	FUNCTION
F1	Help
F3	Controls and gauges
F4	Track monitor
F5	Cycle HUD display
F6	Station/Siding display
F7	Car number display
F8	Switching
F9	Train Operations menu
F10	Next station display
F11	Operations notebook
F12	Close all driving aids
0	Compass

TRAIN FUNCTIONS

KEY	FUNCTION
Spacebar	Sound horn
B	Bell
G	Throw switch ahead of train
Shift-G	Throw switch behind train
V	Windshield wipers toggle
H	Increase headlight setting
Shift-H	Decrease headlight setting
X	Sanding toggle
Enter	Load/unload passengers
T	Activate fuel pickup
Tab	Request permission to bypass stop signal
Z	Reset/acknowledge alert buzzer
P	Raise/lower pantograph

GAME FUNCTIONS

KEY	FUNCTION
Esc	Pause game
F2	Save game
Print Screen	Save a screenshot to the Train Simulator directory
Shift-Z	Graphic frame rate

On the Rails

Now that you've got your system set up, you can take the controls with your command list close at hand. The Introductory Train Ride from the main menu is just that—a ride. By selecting this option, you are relegated to the position of a passenger aboard a train operated completely by your computer. While this can be an excellent way to show off *Train Simulator* to your friends it's likely that you want to get out on the rails *right now*.

Tutorials

If you'd like to use the tutorial sessions that come with *Train Simulator*, click on the Tutorials button. From the Tutorials menu, choose the engine type of your choice, and then click Start. These tutorials provide you with detailed walk-throughs of the operation of every engine from origin to destination. If you decide to use the tutorials, try to play them in order to maximize their usefulness.

NOTE We strongly recommend using the tutorials provided with the game, as they are a direct way to learn your way around the simulated cab of Train Simulator. If you'd rather skip them, be sure to study Chapter I of this book to get everything you need to know about operating a train.

Bolder engineers have the chance to step into the cab of the locomotive of their choice, free of the constraints of schedules, right of ways, or speed limits. To get started, choose Drive a Train from the main menu, select one of the available routes, and then click on Explore the Route. You can then set up the simulator to your exact tastes, specifying the locomotive you want to drive, the weather and environment, and even the type of train you're going to pull. When you've readied your dream train, click on Start to load the simulation. Use the F11 key to guide you through the beginning process step by step and close the window to unpause the game and begin your journey.

Get used to starting and stopping the train by exploring a route. Pay attention to how far it takes your train to come to a complete halt from different speeds. These skills are essential for proper and efficient stopping at station platforms. Also, use the freedom of Explore the Route to get a feel for the course of the railroad. When you're tackling the Activities, it's important to have a sense of the route you're operating, to avoid being surprised by special speed zones, curves, or grades.

The Activities

Once you've familiarized yourself with the layout of at least one route, it's time to apply your knowledge to the Activities that come with the game. Each route has a number of these challenges, which will require all of your train handling skills to complete successfully.

The object of each Activity is to complete a number of described tasks on schedule. When a railroad goes off schedule, terrible setbacks can occur as trains begin to compete for the route. Since a given stretch of rail can only accommodate one train at a time, schedule delays quickly domino to other trains as they wait for the late train to clear the track. You'll have to be a strong engineer in top form to complete the Activities successfully.

Part I

Operating the Routes

Part 1 provides you with detailed a look at every route in the game. Historical and operational information about the lines gives each setting relevance, adding to the simulation experience. Mile-by-mile tours help you master the challenges peculiar to each route.

You'll also find detailed, step-by-step walkthroughs of each Activity in *Train Simulator* in these chapters. Engineers of all skill levels will find these walkthroughs both informative and entertaining, and will be aided by the tips and recommendations for each leg of the journeys down the track.

Chapter 1

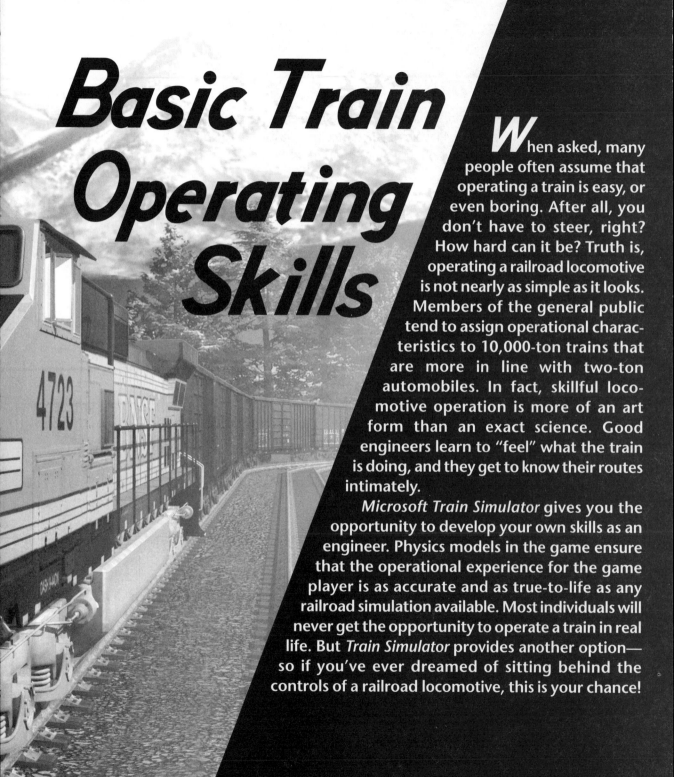

Basic Train Operating Skills

When asked, many people often assume that operating a train is easy, or even boring. After all, you don't have to steer, right? How hard can it be? Truth is, operating a railroad locomotive is not nearly as simple as it looks. Members of the general public tend to assign operational characteristics to 10,000-ton trains that are more in line with two-ton automobiles. In fact, skillful locomotive operation is more of an art form than an exact science. Good engineers learn to "feel" what the train is doing, and they get to know their routes intimately.

Microsoft Train Simulator gives you the opportunity to develop your own skills as an engineer. Physics models in the game ensure that the operational experience for the game player is as accurate and as true-to-life as any railroad simulation available. Most individuals will never get the opportunity to operate a train in real life. But *Train Simulator* provides another option— so if you've ever dreamed of sitting behind the controls of a railroad locomotive, this is your chance!

Train Simulator Routes

The routes in *Train Simulator* provide a nice cross-section of railroad lines from around the globe. Players get a chance to operate steam, diesel, and electric routes that feature both passenger and freight operations. These options include the following:

- Amtrak's Northeast Corridor route between Philadelphia and Washington, D.C.

- England's beautiful Settle and Carlisle line, featuring the Flying Scotsman

- Burlington Northern Santa Fe's route over Marias Pass in Montana

- Japan's Hisatsu Line

- Japan's Tokyo to Hakone Line

- The Orient Express between Innsbruck and St. Anton

Train Simulator Activities

Each route contains between six and 12 game Activities. Think of these Activities as your crew assignments, or definitions of your operating tasks. The operational tasks required to complete the Activities that make up *Train Simulator*'s six routes vary widely. To accomplish all of them demands a variety of train operating skills, for no two trains operate exactly the same.

For example, a short, high-performance passenger train such as the Amtrak Acela is much more responsive than a 50-car freight train chugging over mountain grades. Throw in different cab environments, unique operational requirements for each route, traffic density, and the effects of weather, and one quickly comes to appreciate the skills necessary to safely move 10,000 tons of freight down the tracks.

Terminology

Before you begin experimenting with Activities in the game, you might want to become familiar with common railroad terms. Like most industries, railroads have their own vocabulary of words and phrases, and many of these appear in *Train Simulator* just as they would in a real-world environment.

Common Locomotive Controls

Each locomotive in *Train Simulator* has a unique cab design and control layout. However, all locomotives also have common controls. Table 1.1 describes these controls.

TABLE 1.1: COMMON LOCOMOTIVE CONTROLS

TERM	DEFINITION
Throttle	This mechanism controls the power applied to the driving wheels
Train Brakes	The braking system that activates the brake mechanisms on each car in the train
Locomotive Brakes	The braking system that activates the brakes on just the locomotive. Also called Independent Brakes
Brake Line Pressure Gauge	This is a pressure gauge showing the pressure in the train line (higher pressure equals more available braking capacity)
Ammeter	On diesel and electric locomotives, this instrument shows the amount of current that the traction motors are drawing (too much electrical current drawn for too long can permanently damage traction motors)
Speedometer	Shows the speed of the train
Bell	An audible warning device used to alert passengers and pedestrians of a moving train
Horn	Another warning device used to alert pedestrians and automobile drivers of an approaching train (also used to alert other railroad crew members to impending train movements)

Common Train Types

You will see a number of references to different train types in *Train Simulator*. Table 1.2 describes these train types.

TABLE 1.2: COMMON TRAIN TYPES

TRAIN TYPE	DEFINITION
Mainline Train	A train that operates between distant terminals, often on a daily schedule
Intermodal Train	This is a type of mainline train that carries shipping containers and truck trailers (intermodal trains compete directly with highway trucking companies)
Unit Train	These trains consist of cars carrying the same cargo from a common starting point to a common end point (for example, many coal and grain trains are classified as unit trains)
Mixed Freight	A mainline train that carries general freight, such as lumber, paper, food, chemicals, and other common items
Local Train, Freight	This type of train operates over short distances and typically switches cars at industries and smaller yards while en route
Local Train, Passenger	As above, but serving passengers instead of commercial goods
Express Train	This classification of passenger train makes limited stops along its run and stays on an expedited schedule
Switcher	A term referring to a locomotive that operates in a yard, sorting freight cars

Railroad Slang

As with most industries, railroading has developed many slang terms that workers use to communicate. This list offers a few examples, just in case you want be a hardcore user of *Train Simulator*.

- **Highball:** All clear, proceed ahead ("Highball!")

- **High Green:** A clear signal that refers to the upper position of the green light on certain signal types

- **Color:** Signal indications other than green ("We're catching color from that train ahead of us.")

- **Dump the Air:** Make an emergency brake application ("We need to stop! Dump the air!")

- **Big Hole:** Make an emergency brake application ("He big-holed the train when he saw the red signal.")

- **In the Hole:** In a siding, waiting for an opposing train ("We're in the hole at East Glacier Park waiting for two westbounds.")

- **Running Clean:** A steam locomotive running efficiently, with minimal smoke appearing from the smoke stack ("That crew sure has that steam locomotive running clean.")

- **Stack Talk:** The rhythmic "chuff-chuff" sound that a steam locomotive makes when working hard upgrade ("This class of locomotive sure has some nice stack talk when operating under load.")

- **Unit:** A diesel or electric locomotive ("We're operating with a single unit today.")

- **MU (Multiple Unit):** A collection of diesel or electric locomotives consisting of two or more units ("These four locomotives are MU'd together.")

- **Spot:** To place a car or locomotive on a siding or spur ("Spot these three cars on track 9.")

- **Bend the Rails:** To throw a switch ("Bend the rails for the mill siding so I can spot this freight car.")

- **Dead on the Law:** A crew that has used up their 12-hour crew on-duty limit ("We're dead on the law at Essex, waiting for a relief crew.")

- **Hogger:** The engineer on a train ("That hogger knows how to operate this route!")

- **Hack:** A caboose ("The conductor sits back in the hack.")

- **Crummy:** Also a caboose ("Set out the crummy on track 1.")

Locomotive Types

Train Simulator features three types of locomotives: electric, diesel, and steam. While each pulls a train, they each function in different ways. All three types are fully detailed in the following sections.

Electric Locomotives

Electric locomotives have been in service since the World War I era, not long after electric power became widespread across North America. In the early years, electric locomotives were cheap and reliable to operate. The torque characteristics of their electric motors made them outstanding pullers, and a number of railroads used them to haul heavy freight trains over mountain passes.

The downside to electric locomotives is the extra maintenance required for the overhead catenary systems. These wires in essence double the amount of maintenance needed to keep a rail line in service, for the track crews have to maintain the proper alignment of the wires as well as the rails and ties.

 NOTE In the 1920s, electric locomotives were in use hauling freight throughout the Northeast. They were also used over mountain grades in some western states, where they offered a big advantage over steam power of the day.

How Electric Locomotives Work

Electric locomotives pull electricity directly from overhead wires or from a "third rail" alongside the track. The locomotive's controls route the electricity to the traction motors, which power the wheels.

Figures 1.1, 1.2, 1.3, and 1.4 show the electric locomotives featured in *Train Simulator.*

FIGURE 1.1:

Amtrak's Acela train sets

FIGURE 1.2:

Amtrak's HHP-8 locomotive

FIGURE 1.3:

Odakyu's 2000 Series railcars

FIGURE 1.4:

Odakyu's 7000 Series railcars

Diesel Locomotives

Many people think of diesel locomotives as modern technology, but diesel technology has been around since the early 1930s. Diesel is the most common form of locomotive power today. Its longevity, reliability, and economical operation make it a versatile choice for all sorts of rail operations. Today, diesels come in sizes ranging from several hundred horsepower to as much as 6,000 horsepower.

 NOTE One modern North American locomotive can pull roughly what four 1940's era locomotives could move collectively.

How Diesel Locomotives Work

Diesel locomotives are relatively simple machines. Properly called diesel-electrics or diesel-hydraulics, they use a diesel engine to generate primary mechanical force, which gets converted into secondary electrical or hydro-mechanical force (this in turn powers the wheels).

Diesel-Electric Locomotives

In diesel-electrics, such as the Dash-9 and GP38-2, the engine turns a large electrical generator. This in turn powers large electric motors called traction motors, mounted parallel to the axle between the wheels. The motor output shaft turns a pinion gear, which drives a wheel gear on the axle assembly. Figures 1.5 and 1.6 show the two diesel electric locomotives in *Train Simulator*.

FIGURE 1.5:

The General Electric C44-9W (Dash 9)

FIGURE 1.6:

The Electro-Motive Division (EMD)

Diesel-Hydraulic Locomotives

In diesel-hydraulic locomotives, such as the KIHA 31, the engine drives a hydraulic transmission. Much like an automobile, the hydraulic fluid in the transmission turns a drive shaft that connects to the wheels, causing them to turn. Figure 1.7 shows the KIHA 31.

FIGURE 1.7:

The KIHA 31 diesel-hydraulic railcar

Steam Locomotives

Steam locomotives have been around for over 150 years. The world's first railroads used primitive steam power to move passengers and freight. As the technology progressed, steam locomotives became larger and more potent. High maintenance requirements and overall cost of operation ultimately doomed these elegant machines to secondary status, behind the diesels and electric locomotives that have all but obliterated steam from the rails of the world.

STEAM HOLDOUTS

While steam locomotives are all but gone from revenue service on the world's railroads, there are a few countries where steam still reigns supreme. China is one such country—in select locations in northern China, for example, "modern" steam locomotives manufactured as recently as the 1980s continue to haul freight and passenger trains over remote routes. Even these steam operations can't last forever, though, and there will come a day where the only operating steam locomotives left are those in museums and tourist operations.

How Steam Locomotives Work

Steam locomotives use wood, coal, or oil to heat water into steam. The steam then creates pressure inside the boiler. This steam pressure is used to drive pistons, which are connected to the drive wheels by rods. After being put to use, the steam is expelled out the smokestack at the front of the locomotive.

The engineer controls the train by varying the amount of steam entering the piston. This regulates the power, and in turn, the speed of the locomotive. Steam from the boiler is also used to generate electricity for the headlights and interior lights, and to drive lubrication pumps to keep the heavy drive rods, valve guides, and linkages well lubricated.

Figures 1.8 and 1.9 show the two steam locomotives featured in *Train Simulator*.

FIGURE 1.8:

The UK's Flying Scotsman locomotive

FIGURE 1.9:

The Gölsdorf 380

General Locomotive Controls

The throttle and brakes work independently on diesel locomotives. The techniques you use to move these controls in combination are what lead to smooth train handling. It will take you some time to get familiar with the specific controls in the different locomotives, but generally speaking, the throttle and brake controls have the same effect on every train.

Working the Throttle

Throttles on the *Train Simulator* locomotives have a number of positions, or notches, which correspond to different power settings. Move the throttle one position and the locomotive moves slightly; move the throttle to the last position, and the locomotive leaps into motion.

Most diesel and electric locomotives have throttles that move from 0–100%. Some throttles move in a linear fashion—you can set any percentage you choose—while others move in defined segments, or by notches. The design varies by locomotive type.

Steam locomotives use both a regulator and a reverser to provide power to the drive wheels. The regulator controls the amount of steam leaving the boiler for the pistons, while the reverser adjusts the amount of power that the piston applies to the driving rods, as well as the direction in which the driving rods turn.

Working the Brakes

The brake systems are, by far, the most important control system on a train. The ability to stop thousands of tons quickly and efficiently—and to keep this weight under control on downgrade stretches of track—requires one of three types of brake systems: train air brakes, locomotive (independent) air brakes, and dynamic brakes.

Air Brakes

Train and locomotive brakes control the air brake systems. Train brakes control the brake mechanisms on the entire train; this is the primary brake system you use when operating a train consisting of a locomotive and cars. The locomotive brakes control the air brake mechanism on just the locomotive.

Dynamic Brakes

Dynamic brakes are only available on electric and diesel-electric locomotives in *Train Simulator*. Dynamic brakes essentially "re-wire" the traction motors geared to each wheel, turning them into generators. As you might guess, it takes mechanical force to turn a generator. This mechanical force comes from the momentum of the train. The resistance provided by the motors can work to hold the train in check as it descends a long, downgrade section of track.

Dynamic brakes work well to slow trains in mountainous territory, but there's one byproduct to deal with—electricity! As those turning traction motors slow the train, they also generate lots of electricity. Diesel locomotives don't have any use for this electricity, so it's "wasted" as heat by routing it to large resistor grids on the locomotive's roof. In electric locomotives, instead of wasting this electricity, the brake system routes the electrical power back into the catenary, where it can be used to power other trains.

 NOTE In the Acela, HHP-8, and Series 7000 LSE, dynamic brakes are applied in combination with air brakes to slow the train. There is no separate dynamic brake control.

Cab Tours

The cab of a locomotive is where the action happens. As you tour the cabs of the locomotives in *Train Simulator*, you'll notice that no two are exactly alike. Each one has its own personality and control layout. Let's take a look at the different models, starting with the diesels.

 TIP As you read the following cab descriptions, open up each locomotive in Explore the Routes mode. Use the mouse to manipulate each control so you can get a feel for how it works.

Diesel Locomotives

While diesel locomotives are relatively easy to operate, there are still a number of controls that must be used in combination to operate a train safely.

 TIP All cab interiors offer multiple views; use the arrow keys to look around. On steam locomotives, you can look ahead (along the boiler) by pressing the Up arrow key. You can also look back at your train by using the Down arrow key.

Electro-Motive Division GP38-2 Controls

The GP38-2, shown in Figure 1.10, uses what's called a conventional control stand. It is very similar to the ones used on the first North American diesels back in the 1940s.

FIGURE 1.10:

Looking inside the cab of the GP38-2.

THROTTLE AND REVERSER The throttle on the GP38-2 is located in the middle of the control stand. It has eight positions, Run–1 through Run–8. The reverser handle—which controls the direction that the locomotive travels—is located to the right of the dynamic brake handle.

BRAKE CONTROLS There are two air brake control levers. The green train brake handle controls the brakes on the entire train by varying the pressure in the brake pipe, while the blue independent (or locomotive) brake controls the brakes on just the locomotive. The dynamic brake handle is located above the throttle, and it also has eight positions (B1–B8). The throttle and reverser use an interlock mechanism to prevent movement of the reverser unless the throttle is set to idle.

GENERAL CONTROLS All remaining locomotive controls are located on the control stand. Horn, sand, and bell switches are to the right of the brakes, and headlight controls are to the right of the throttle. Brake pressure gauges can be found above the dynamic brake handle, while the speedometer is on the front cab wall.

TIP As with all Train Simulator locomotives, you can blow the horn on the GP38-2 by using the spacebar.

General Electric Dash 9 Controls

The General Electric Dash 9-44CW (more commonly called the Dash 9) uses a modern desktop control stand. As shown in Figure 1.11, this environment features screens that display critical information to the engineer.

FIGURE 1.11:

A glance inside the cab of the Dash 9.

THROTTLE AND REVERSER The black-handled throttle (also called the combined power handle) and reverser are situated to the left of center on the desktop. It has eight throttle positions (N1–N8) and eight dynamic brake positions (B1–B8). The reverser, with the white handle, controls the direction of the locomotive. The combined power handle and reverser use an interlock mechanism to prevent movement of the reverser unless the throttle position is set to idle.

BRAKE CONTROLS Two brake levers are featured on the Dash 9, one on each side of the brake console on the right side of the desktop. The train brake is the larger handle on the left, while the locomotive brake is on the right.

SECONDARY CONTROLS All remaining Dash 9 controls are on the desktop. Bell, sand, and horn switches are to the left of the throttle and reverser, and headlight controls are to the right of the CRTs (which show train speed, reverser position, power application, throttle position, and brake pressure information).

KIHA 31 Controls

As shown in Figure 1.12, the KIHA 31 railcar cab places everything right in front of the operator. The difference here, as compared to the other diesels mentioned above, is the addition of a gear selector for the hydraulic transmission.

FIGURE 1.12:

Looking at the cab of the KIHA 31.

THROTTLE AND REVERSER The throttle is on the left side of the control stand (it's the lever with the black knob on top). It has six positions that permit increasing power in increments of 20%. The reverser is to the left of the throttle, while the gear selector for the hydraulic transmission is just to the right of the throttle. It has two gear positions (gear 1 and gear 2), plus neutral. The KIHA 31 throttle and gear selector feature an interlock mechanism that prevents gear changes when the throttle is not set to idle.

BRAKE CONTROLS The KIHA features a single brake handle that controls the air brakes for the train. This handle moves through three ranges of positions: release, apply, and hold. Each can be set in ranges from 0–100%. The engine brake is button-operated, and is located right below the headlight switch.

SECONDARY CONTROLS All remaining KIHA controls include the headlight switch and sander button, center, and the speedometer and brake gauges in the console.

Electric Locomotives

Train Simulator features four electric locomotives:

- Amtrak Acela

- Amtrak HHP-8

- Odakyu 2000 Series

- Odakyu 7000 Series

While the two Amtrak locomotives feature almost identical cab controls, the other two locomotives are unique in their design.

Amtrak Acela Controls

Amtrak's Acela features a state-of-the-art operating environment. As shown in Figure 1.13, the controls are easy to use, and the CRTs display information to the engineer.

FIGURE 1.13:

Close up and personal with the Amtrak Acela.

THROTTLE AND REVERSER The throttle on the Acela rests between the two CRT displays. It has a continuous range of movement and can be set from 0–100%. The reverser lever is in front of the left CRT. The combined power handle and reverser use an interlock mechanism to prevent movement of the reverser unless the throttle position is set to idle.

BRAKE CONTROLS The Acela has only one brake lever that controls the train air and dynamic brakes. This lever also has a continuous range of motion from 0–100%. It also has a hold position you can use to keep the train in place while stopped and a release position that frees all brakes and recharges the air system.

SECONDARY CONTROLS Remaining controls are grouped together. The pantograph is on the far left next to the red emergency brake valve button. You can use the emergency brake valve button in case of impending emergency—it automatically applies full brakes. The horn lever is next to the reverser; pull it toward you to operate the horn. The sand, bell, and headlight control switches are located on the right side of the panel. The cab signal display is unique to the Acela and HHL—it shows the indication of the next approaching signal plus the maximum speed that the signal indication permits.

Amtrak HHP-8 Controls

Control systems in the Amtrak HHP-8 cab are virtually identical to those in the Acela. As depicted in Figure 1.14, the only significant difference is the addition of a locomotive brake to the right of the headlight control switch. You can use this brake control when operating the HHP-8 without a train.

FIGURE 1.14:

The interior of the HHP-8.

Odakyu 7000 Series Controls

As shown in Figure 1.15, the Odakyu 7000 Series features a modern control desk and throttle.

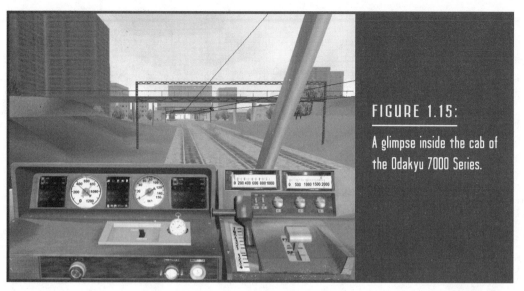

FIGURE 1.15:

A glimpse inside the cab of the Odakyu 7000 Series.

POWER HANDLE AND REVERSER The combined power handle (found to the right of center) controls both the throttle and the brakes. Move it toward you to apply throttle and push it away from you to apply braking force. The reverser handle is the silver handle to the right. Push it away from you to move the locomotive forward and pull it toward you to travel in reverse. The combined power handle and reverser use an interlock mechanism to prevent movement of the reverser unless the throttle position is set to idle.

SECONDARY CONTROLS Only a few other controls of interest are featured in the Odakyu 7000 Series. The pantograph button is on the far lower left of the console, and the headlight switch is located just to the left of the stopwatch. Gauges on the back of the control desk show power and braking system status.

Odakyu 2000 Series Controls

Odakyu 2000 Series railcar cabs—as shown in Figure 1.16—feature a more traditional cab control system as compared to the 7000 Series.

THROTTLE AND REVERSER The throttle is the large black rotary handle just left of center. You rotate it clockwise in order to apply power (this handle moves linearly from 0–100% throttle). The reverser is located at the far left of the cab control stand. Push it forward to travel ahead and pull it back to travel in reverse.

BRAKE CONTROLS You rotate this control on the right side of the cab to apply the brakes. This device also moves from 0–100% brake application.

FIGURE 1.16:

The cab of the Odakyu Series 2000.

SECONDARY CONTROLS The secondary controls for this locomotive are located in the middle of the cab. The pantograph, horn, and headlight switches are in the middle of the panel. Gauges behind the controls convey operational information. They include an ammeter, a brake pressure gauge, a speedometer, and a line voltage indicator.

Steam Locomotives

Steam locomotive cabs are the most complex of all the locomotives included in *Train Simulator*. It's strongly suggested that you follow along in the cab with your mouse as you read the following tours.

LNER No. 4472 Flying Scotsman

The Flying Scotsman cab (see in Figure 1.17) is the easier of the two steam locomotives to operate. However, it will still require some practice to get it right, so read on for a further explanation of how this advanced machine runs.

REGULATOR AND REVERSER The Scotsman's regulator is the vertical red handle. Pull it toward you to apply more power. The reverser is the brass lever right below the regulator. You rotate this handle to set the direction. As you change the handle position, the indicator above changes to show this.

BRAKE CONTROLS Train brake controls are represented by the large red assembly to the right. You move the lever up and down to apply and release the brakes.

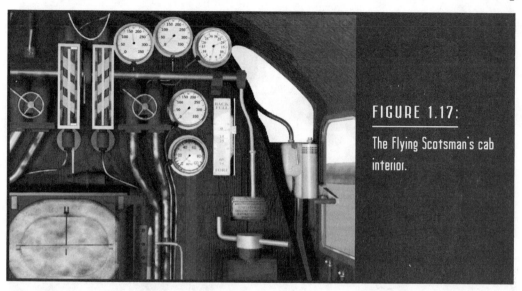

FIGURE 1.17:

The Flying Scotsman's cab interior.

SECONDARY CONTROLS The sander lever is directly above the firebox door. Pull the brass handle toward you to apply sand to the rail. The whistle rope is hanging from the ceiling, just above the water sight glasses. Pull it down to activate the whistle. The rest of the controls are managed by the computer when you have the Fireman option selected. It's impossible to go any further in this limited space on steam locomotives, however, as whole books have been written on operating all the controls on a real steam locomotive. If you want to get adventurous and operate all of the controls on your own, it's recommended that you do some independent research.

Gölsdorf 380

The cab of the Gölsdorf 380 cab is the most complex in all of *Train Simulator* (Figure 1.18). Its bright yellow paint makes it a relatively cheery place to be, however.

REGULATOR AND REVERSER The regulator is the smallish handle in the upper right, just to the right of the cab window. You pull this lever toward you to apply more steam pressure to the cylinders. The reverser is the large white knob in the lower right corner. You turn it to set the direction—clockwise sets the locomotive moving forward, counter-clockwise sets it in reverse. Also, note that the gauge above the firebox changes to show the setting as you move this knob.

BRAKE CONTROL The 380 has both a train brake and a locomotive brake control. The train brake is the red handle to the right of the firebox door, while the locomotive brake is the red handle to the left of the firebox door.

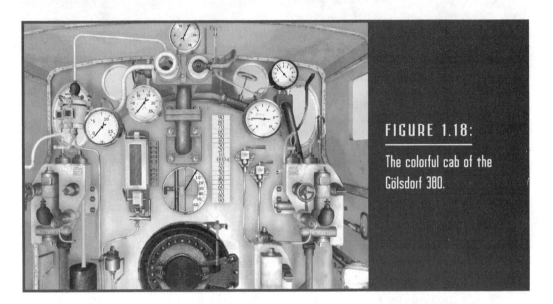

FIGURE 1.18:

The colorful cab of the Gölsdorf 380.

SECONDARY CONTROLS Sander control is located above the train brake control. Pull the silver lever toward you to activate the sanding system. The whistle is the black lever in front of the right cab window; just pull it to blow the whistle. As with the Scotsman, the other controls are covered by the computer as long as you have the Automatic Fireman option selected.

Selecting a Route

Train Simulator's user interface is designed to minimize your time at menus so that you can maximize your time behind the throttle. The menu pages make use of pull-down menus you can use to choose the Activity you want to play—or, when in explore mode, the train you want to run—and the conditions in which you want to run it. Let's take a look at these menu screens.

Home Screen

The Home screen, as shown in Figure 1.19, is where you start when *Train Simulator* is launched. The options on this page allow you to take an introductory train ride, see a tutorial, drive a train, or load a previously saved Activity.

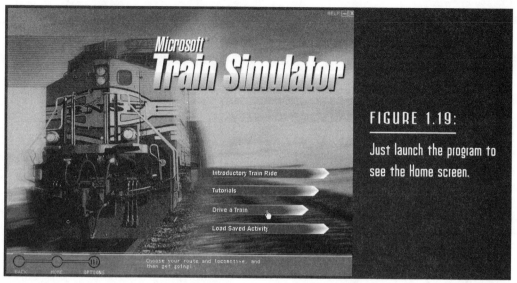

FIGURE 1.19:

Just launch the program to see the Home screen.

Route and Activity Selection

The Route and Activity Selection screen (see Figure 1.20) is where you end up when you choose to drive a train on the Home screen. You use the Routes menu to select the route you want to operate. Make this selection first, and then select the Activity you want to play. If you pick the Explore Route option, you can choose the locomotive, starting and ending location, and weather conditions for your exploration.

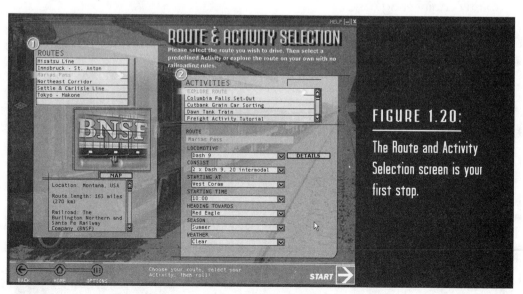

FIGURE 1.20:

The Route and Activity Selection screen is your first stop.

‖‖

 NOTE When you choose an Activity, the route options are pre-selected for you and cannot be changed.

‖‖

Options Screen

From the Route and Activity Selection screen you can also set configuration options for the game. These selections control the quality of the graphical detail and the in-game audio, in addition to keyboard mappings and other gameplay options (see the Introduction to this guide for further details on recommended system requirements).

General Options

Figure 1.21 shows the General Options menu. Here you can tweak a number of realism controls. You can also select the driving aids you want to appear upon starting an Activity.

For those just starting, deselect the Derailments and Alerter options. The Derailments checkbox prevents the train from derailing, regardless of conditions, unless you hit something or run off the end of a track; the Alerter button affects the operation of the crew vigilance systems on locomotives so equipped. These systems require you to manually press the alerter switch in the cab at regular, short intervals, so you'd be best off leaving it deselected until you master engineering basics.

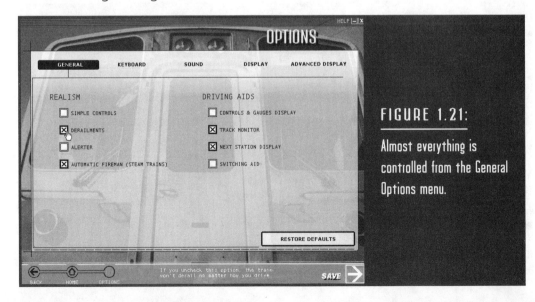

FIGURE 1.21:

Almost everything is controlled from the General Options menu.

WARNING When the alerter option is selected, if you fail to press the alerter button inside the required time limit, the train will automatically make an emergency brake application. The time duration varies from train to train, but it is typically about 45 seconds. On real trains, these systems are intended to prevent crewmembers from falling asleep or from becoming distracted.

Keyboard Options

The Keyboard Options menu allows you to change the default keyboard mappings (see Figure 1.22). Changing the key assignments is easy—simply select the function you want to change and a pop-up message will instruct you to press the new key. As you press the key, the dialogue box is dismissed and the keyboard mapping is changed. As with all Options menus, you must click the Save button in the lower right to save your changes.

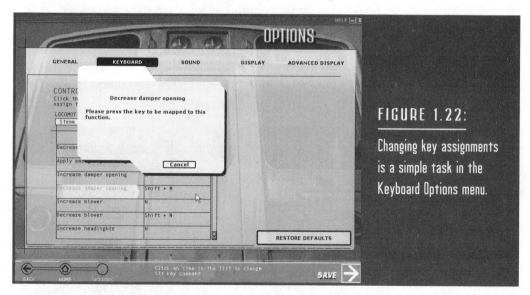

FIGURE 1.22:

Changing key assignments is a simple task in the Keyboard Options menu.

Sound Options

Sound Options (shown in Figure 1.23) allows you to control the amount and volume of all audio effects in the game.

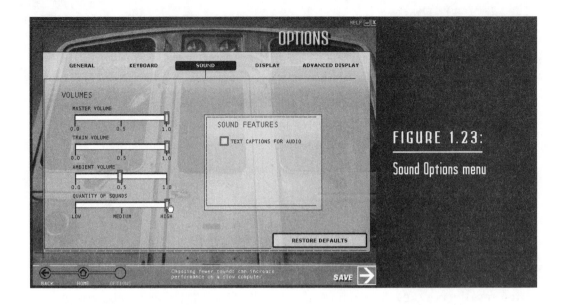

FIGURE 1.23:

Sound Options menu

Display Options

Figure 1.24 depicts the Display Options menu. Here you can select your desired screen resolution and the overall display quality. You should select as high a screen resolution as you can. Of course, the higher your resolution, the better hardware you need to support it. This menu can also affect the quality settings, both here and in Advanced Display Options. A little experimentation is in order to determine the best combination for your system.

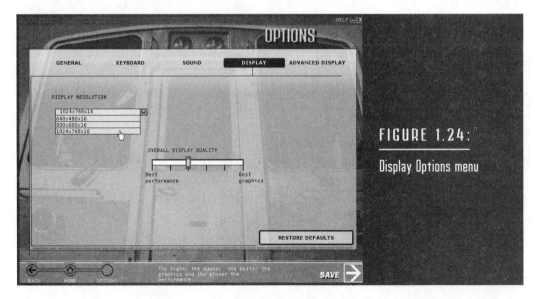

FIGURE 1.24:

Display Options menu

Advanced Display Options

The Advanced Display Options menu, shown in Figure 1.25, allows you to tweak the graphical detail in *Train Simulator*. The ability to max out these settings is directly dependent upon your system configuration. If you're running an older computer with a mediocre video card, think twice before messing with the default settings. Experiment here to determine the best combination of detail and performance for your system.

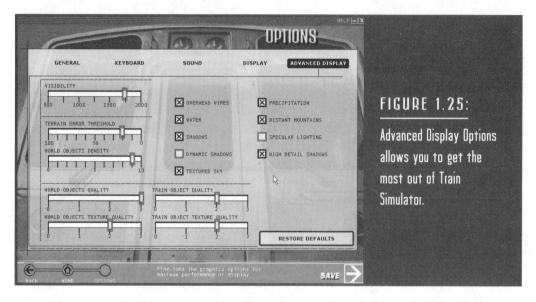

FIGURE 1.25:

Advanced Display Options allows you to get the most out of Train Simulator.

Operating a Train

Now that you know how to select a route and train, let's look at how you actually operate them. *Train Simulator* models the physical properties of each and every car in a train. Each locomotive and car has a number of data points that, when combined together, replicate the physics of a real train quite well.

About Slack

All trains are affected by slack to some degree. Slack is the extra "length" in a train, created by purposely loose tolerances in the coupler assemblies, in each car, and cushion underframe mechanisms in some cars. When a train is stationary, there is no pulling force in the coupler assemblies and underframes; the lack of tension thus allows extra slack to accumulate in the train as the coupler assemblies and cushioned underframes "relax" to their static state.

When starting a train with slack between each car, the train will actually start car by car. In a 50-car train, there may be a collective 50 feet or more of slack. Put another way, this means that the first car must move 50 feet before the last car starts to roll. And when it does, it can do so with a sudden "bang!" as the car gets yanked into motion from the car ahead.

As you start a train and operate it over the route, managing slack action is as important as any other aspect of operation. *Train Simulator* tracks your ability to control slack action. If you get too quick with either the throttle or brakes, you'll get dinged for exceeding passenger comfort levels or freight durability levels, which are tracked as you operate the activity.

Operating Passenger Trains

Generally speaking, passenger trains are easier to operate than freight trains. For starters, they are typically short, most often fewer than 10 cars in length. Second, they tend to weigh less than a typical freight train. They also have a better horse-power to weight ratio in order to allow high-speed operation.

Starting a Train

When you start a train, you should do it in two phases. First, gently get all the passenger cars moving by opening the throttle a little bit—the goal is to take up all slack between the cars. Let the train move at a slow speed until all of the cars are moving. This will generally occur after just a few seconds where a small passenger train is concerned.

With all of the cars in motion, open the throttle several positions so that the train starts accelerating quickly. As the slack is stretched, the entire train will start accelerating at the same time.

Stopping a Train

Train brakes typically apply from the front toward the rear. This means that, as the front of the train starts to slow, the rear cars bunch up. To avoid this becoming a problem, start slowing with a gradual brake application (something in the range of 5%). When the train slows, you can increase the brake setting to add braking force.

A Note about Smoothness

There's one important rule to remember when operating a train: momentum is your friend. The laws of physics apply here—an object in motion really does tend to stay in motion. Translated, this means that you can use the train's own momentum to help maintain its speed.

The Amtrak Acela, for example, can maintain 100+ mph speeds with only 30% throttle. Minor adjustments in throttle settings are usually enough to keep the train moving at a constant speed over long distances. The same rules apply with brake applications—hit the brakes gradually and early so that the train decelerates instead of grinding to a halt.

Operating Freight Trains

When operating a freight train, expect the train to be slow to react to control inputs. The longer the train is, the slower it is likely to respond. This same general rule applies to freight trains in the same way as it does to passenger trains, but more so. Freight trains typically have more slack, and their braking systems tend to be less responsive overall. Smoothness still counts here, as *Train Simulator* also tracks freight durability levels during operation. While you don't have to worry about spilling coffee in the dining car, you do have to worry about damaging that carload of new televisions.

Signals

As displayed in Figure 1.26, *Train Simulator* features a fully operational signal system. Each route has a different type of signal, but each signal type is capable of displaying a common set of signal indications (see Table 1.3).

TABLE 1.3: SIGNAL INDICATIONS

INDICATION	MEANING
Green	Proceed: Block clear
Flashing Yellow	Advanced Approach: Be ready for an approach indication at the next signal; prepare to pass the next signal at a speed of less than 40 mph
Solid Yellow	Approach: Proceed, but be ready to stop at the next signal; speed in block is not to exceed 40 mph
Red	Stop: Don't proceed past this signal without dispatcher permission

FIGURE 1.26:

Each route boasts a fully functional signal system.

You'll see a number of variations of these indications in the different routes. *Train Simulator* comes packaged with a printed signal driving aid that lists these variations. Keep this handy until you're familiar with the signal indications and their meanings.

Ambient Traffic

Train Simulator includes the ability to operate ambient rail traffic on the routes. These AI trains are used to add complexity and variety to the Activities. For example, some Activities require you to meet and pass such AI trains as you operate the route (see Figure 1.27).

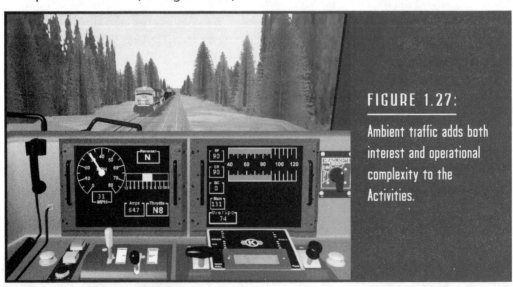

FIGURE 1.27:

Ambient traffic adds both interest and operational complexity to the Activities.

Train Simulator Driving Aids

Real railroad engineers are dependent upon their knowledge of the route and trackside signs and signals to tell them what lies up ahead. *Train Simulator* features these aspects of a railroad man's life, along with several tool driving aids to help you operate the trains.

Control and Gauges Display Tool

The Control and Gauges Display tool serves as a quick reference aide you can use to reference the cab controls inside the locomotives.

TRAIN BRAKE (APPLY 25%)   X

Controls brakes on both the locomotive and attached cars.

Display this tool using the F3 key. Then point to a component in the cab. The name of the component you're pointing to appears, and a short description tells you what the control or gauge does. Use the F3 key again to hide the display when you're done.

Track Monitor Tool

The Track Monitor shows you information about the track ahead. It lists a wealth of information, including the following:

- Signal indications
- Distance to the next signal
- Milepost locations
- Maximum speed limit
- Speed limit changes
- Current speed
- Projected speed
- Temporary speed restrictions
- Station locations
- Track switches

You will find this tool extremely handy as you get to know the different routes in *Train Simulator*. Use the F4 key to toggle this display on and off.

Heads-Up Display

The Heads-Up display lists all of the critical operating parameters for the train you're running. As Figures 1.28 and 1.29 show, this is extremely useful when you want to run the locomotive from an external view.

FIGURE 1.28:

Minimal Heads-Up display data is depicted here.

To display the Heads-Up display, press the F5 key once for basic information and twice for additional (secondary) information.

FIGURE 1.29:

A look at the maximum amount of Heads-Up display information available.

Station/Siding Display Tool

You can display the identification of stations, plus sidings, spurs, and yard tracks, using the F6 key, as depicted in Figure 1.30. Press F6 once to display track names. Press it again to hide the name labels.

FIGURE 1.30:

Tracks can be identified with the F6 key.

Locomotive/Car Identification Tool

The Locomotive/Car Identification tool works just like the above tool, except it uses the F7 key. When you press the F7 key, an ID label pops up above each car (see Figure 1.31).

FIGURE 1.31:

You can display car identification numbers using the F7 key.

Switch Tool

Switch tool allows you to control the position of track switches ahead of and behind your train. It's important to place yourself in the engineer's seat between these arrows when looking at the tool. The upper arrow always corresponds to the switch in front of the locomotive windshield, and the rear arrow always corresponds to the switch behind the locomotive/train, regardless of the direction of movement. Use the F8 key to toggle Switch on and off.

Train Operations Tool

The Train Operations tool allows you to uncouple cars from your train and set the handbrakes on each car. It's useful when operating the Marias Pass freight route (although it can be used anywhere). Use the F9 key to turn this tool on and off.

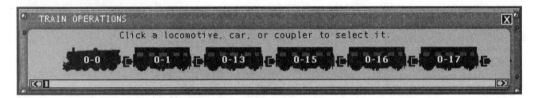

Next Station Tool

Extremely handy when operating passenger routes, the Next Station tool shows the stations that you're scheduled to stop at, the distance away from them in real time, the scheduled arrival time, and the scheduled departure time. This tool is controlled by the F10 key.

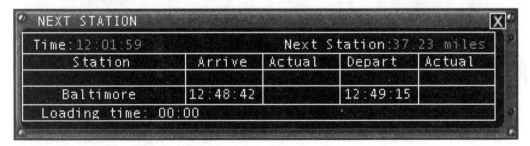

Operations Notebook

The Operations Notebook automatically displays when you start each Activity. You can also display it during operations by pressing the F11 key.

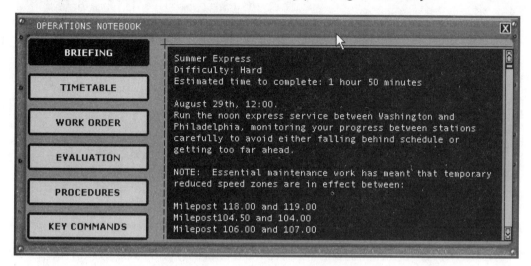

```
OPERATIONS NOTEBOOK                                              X

    BRIEFING          Summer Express
                      Difficulty: Hard
                      Estimated time to complete: 1 hour 50 minutes
    TIMETABLE
                      August 29th, 12:00.
    WORK ORDER        Run the noon express service between Washington and
                      Philadelphia, monitoring your progress between stations
                      carefully to avoid either falling behind schedule or
    EVALUATION        getting too far ahead.

                      NOTE:  Essential maintenance work has meant that temporary
    PROCEDURES        reduced speed zones are in effect between:

                      Milepost 118.00 and 119.00
    KEY COMMANDS      Milepost104.50 and 104.00
                      Milepost 106.00 and 107.00
```

The Operations Notebook reveals the briefing text description, a timetable showing your scheduled work, a work order detailing the locations where you need to pick up and drop off freight cars, an evaluation of your current progress, and procedures and key commands—in case you need a quick refresher while operating.

Switching Activities

Switching freight cars in yards and on industry tracks is a big part of freight railroading. Cars must be spotted into industry tracks to either be loaded or unloaded with freight. These cars then end up in freight yards, where they are switched into groups bound for distant locations. They are then picked up by mainline freight trains and carried on their way. At the same time, these mainline trains leave new cars, and the process starts again.

Switching is very similar to a strategy game—you need to plan your moves well ahead of time to ensure that the cars you need to switch will be in the right place in your train. For example, when you need to set out a car at an industry, you should ideally position this car at the front of your train, just behind the locomotive. As shown in Figure 1.32, *Train Simulator* allows you to experience this component of railroading.

FIGURE 1.32:

Train Simulator allows you to switch the yard at Whitefish on the Marias Pass route.

Coupling Cars and Locomotives

Just as they do on real railroads, *Train Simulator* allows you to couple and uncouple cars. You'll use this feature quite frequently while operating many of the Activities on the Marias Pass route.

Uncoupling Cars

To uncouple a car from an existing train, bring up the Train Operations tool. Then select the coupler that connects the car or cars that you want to uncouple. With the coupler highlighted, double-click it to remove the cars from the train.

Coupling to Cars

Coupling to cars is also straightforward; you simply line up the switch so that you can back your locomotive or train up to the cars (at approximately 2–3 mph). When you hit the coupler on the adjacent car, the cars' couplers will lock together. You'll hear a coupling sound when the cars are successfully locked together.

 WARNING Don't attempt to couple to cars when your train is moving more than 5 mph. If you couple too hard, you run the risk of derailing the cars, which will automatically end your Activity.

COUPLER CAM Use the external coupler cam view (see Figure 1.33) to help gauge distances when coupling to cars. The 6 key displays a direct-down view of the end of the train and the car you're attempting to couple to. You can use the up and down arrows to zoom in on or out on the cars.

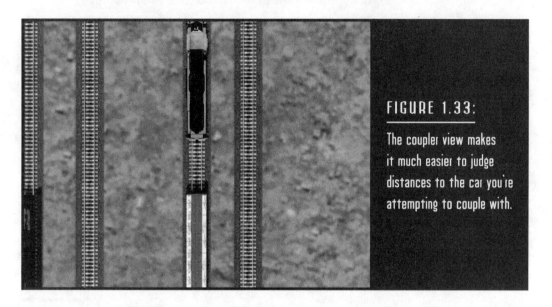

FIGURE 1.33:

The coupler view makes it much easier to judge distances to the car you're attempting to couple with.

OTHER EXTERNAL VIEWS You'll also find the End-of-Train view handy. Use the 3 key to change to this view. The Front-of-Train view can also be useful when performing switching moves. You can switch to this view by hitting the 2 key.

Chapter 2

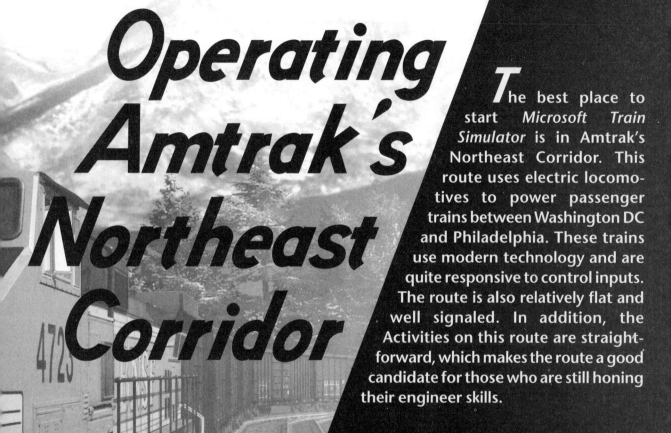

Operating Amtrak's Northeast Corridor

*T*he best place to start *Microsoft Train Simulator* is in Amtrak's Northeast Corridor. This route uses electric locomotives to power passenger trains between Washington DC and Philadelphia. These trains use modern technology and are quite responsive to control inputs. The route is also relatively flat and well signaled. In addition, the Activities on this route are straightforward, which makes the route a good candidate for those who are still honing their engineer skills.

Route Description

Amtrak's Northeast Corridor is considered the premier passenger route in the United States. Home in the past to popular Metroliner trains, this route was a viable transportation alternative for northeast travelers for decades, where short distances between major cities make train travel a popular airplane alternative.

Today, Amtrak offers riders the ability to experience the latest in passenger train technology with the new Acela, shown in Figure 2.1. The Acela, based on European high-speed railroad technology, was designed to compete directly with airplanes in the Northeast. With a top speed of 150 mph, the Acela can literally beat city-to-city travel time for airplanes when one considers the time required for fliers to get into and out of airport terminals.

FIGURE 2.1:

Microsoft Train Simulator features the new Acela high-speed train.

History

The Northeast Corridor route traces its heritage back to one of the great railroads of the US: The Pennsylvania Railroad. The Pennsy, as it was known, was famous for its crack passenger trains and streamlined steam and electric locomotives. For many decades, the Pennsy maintained and operated one of the most admired passenger routes in the country.

NOTE During its heyday, the Pennsylvania Railroad was known as the "Standard Railroad of the World."

As US rail passenger travel waned in the late '60s and '70s, the United States government, in an attempt to salvage America's passenger trains, formed the National Railroad Passenger Corporation, or Amtrak, in 1970. Amtrak experienced a bumpy start, but managed to hang on, in no small part due to the viability and profitability of passenger traffic in the Northeast Corridor.

Today

The track between Washington DC and Philadelphia is the southern section of Amtrak's Northeast Corridor, which continues north to Boston and Providence, Rhode Island. Passenger trains predominate, but many portions of the Northeast Corridor host freight trains, as well as both mainline runs and local trains to service the local industries. In addition, the route is grade separated in most locations, preventing the obvious risks associated with grade crossings on high-speed routes.

NOTE Super-elevated track is banked like the curves on a highway, which allows the trains to negotiate the curves at a faster rate of speed.

Virtually all tracks on this route use concrete ties, heavy rail, and super-elevated track curvature to allow high speeds. This route consists of a minimum of two high-speed mainline tracks at all times. In many places, tracks are signaled for operation in either direction. Dispatchers control rail traffic using a Centralized Traffic Control (CTC) System in Philadelphia.

AMTRAK FUNDING

Funding to support Amtrak has often been a controversial issue. A recent US congressional mandate requires Amtrak to reach operational self-sufficiency by 2002. Simply put, fares have to cover operating costs. To accomplish this, Amtrak began aggressively marketing "less-than-carload" freight shipments on its passenger trains. Over the past several years, this service has proven quite successful. Today, it's common to see Amtrak long-distance passenger trains operating with customized express boxcars behind the coaches, loaded with US Mail or time-sensitive freight materials. The revenue generated by these express boxcars goes a long way toward helping Amtrak meet its revenue goals.

Route Tour: Train Simulator's Northeast Corridor Route

Train Simulator includes the portion of the Northeast Corridor route from Philadelphia to Washington DC (see Figure 2.2). This stretch of the route features minimal grades and lots of high-speed track.

FIGURE 2.2:

Train Simulator includes the portion of Amtrak's Northeast Corridor between Washington DC and Philadelphia.

In *Train Simulator*, the route includes seven passenger stations, as shown in the following table. These stations are the locations where you will stop to load and unload passengers during the game.

STATION NAME	MILEPOST	LOCATION NOTES
Philadelphia	3.00	Northern end of route
Wilmington	26.85	3 platform tracks
Edgewood	81.00	
Baltimore	98.80	Large station
BWI Station	106.40	
New Carrollton	127.10	
Washington DC	134.60	Southern end of route

Let's take a tour of the route as it appears in Microsoft Train Simulator, starting in Philadelphia and heading south to Washington DC.

Philadelphia to Wilmington

As shown in Figure 2.3, we start in Philadelphia, the city of brotherly love. As you leave Philly's 30th Street Station heading south, you negotiate a collection of tracks and crossovers as the station tracks consolidate. The mainline narrows to two main tracks about a mile out of the station before a pair of tracks descends off a flyover to the left, and another pair of tracks appears on the right.

All these tracks come together at the Phil Interlocking plant at MP (milepost) 5.6. Crossovers here allow trains to switch tracks. South of Phil, the mainline narrows to four tracks as the line passes through the Philly suburbs. Speed limit increases to 85 mph through this portion of the route

At MP 14.9, you pass through the interlocking plant at Hook where trains can cross over from track to track. The speed limit through this stretch of track increases to 110 mph. The speed limit markers are somewhat difficult to see on this route (especially at high speeds!), so be sure to use your Track Monitor tool to watch for changes.

NOTE At approximately MP 18.2, your train crosses the state line from Pennsylvania into Delaware.

FIGURE 2.3:

The Acela train, ready to depart from Philadelphia Station

At MP 24.5, you pass the Bell Interlocking plant. Then, at MP 26.85, you arrive at Wilmington Station, as shown in Figure 2.4. Remember, the speed limit through all station platforms is restricted to 30 mph.

FIGURE 2.4:

The Acela at Wilmington Station. There's a third main track to the left of the left-hand platform.

Wilmington to Baltimore

South of Wilmington, the route passes through the Ragan Interlocking at MP 27.7. The speed limit through here is 45 mph. Note the left-hand track— just past the interlocking it veers away from the mainline and ends. This track simulates the connection to the Newcastle Secondary Track. South of the inter-locking, another connection to the Newcastle Secondary appears from the left and parallels the two mainline tracks. These tracks are used to stage AI trains.

Further south, the speed limit increases to 110 mph or greater. The track through here is straight and quick—it's a good place to make up lost time. At MP 41.5, your train passes the interlocking at Iron, where the Delmarva Secondary Track joins the mainline. The speed limit through the interlocking remains at 110 mph.

NOTE At approximately MP 41.4, your train crosses the state line from Delaware to Maryland.

At MP 54.7, you pass the Prince Interlocking, where the three main tracks merge to form a two-track mainline. The speed limit through here is 125 mph; use the Track Monitor tool to watch for speed limit changes, because at MP 56.9 the speed limit drops to 90 mph.

Within a few miles, the speed limit is back to 125 mph. Use the Track Monitor to watch for these speed limit changes, and watch for the speed limit markers on the right side of the track.

NOTE As you cross the Susquehanna River heading south, look to your left to see the pilings from an old railroad bridge. When railroads replace bridges, they typically construct a new bridge parallel to the old one. After the old bridge is dismantled, the support piers often remain in place.

At MP 61.9 you pass through Grace Interlocking. Here, the two-track mainline expands to four tracks. At MP 64.2, you cross a long bridge over the Susquehanna River. The speed limit over this bridge remains at 125 mph.

Just past the river, the tracks enter a sweeping left-hand curve and separate from each other. Beyond this curve a third track branches off from each mainline track. At MP 68.0, you pass through the Wood Interlocking, where a branch line joins the main from the left. Once past MP 71.0, the track straightens out; the speed limit remains at 125 mph.

TIP The bridge at Milepost 77.0, which crosses an inlet from Chesapeake Bay, is over a mile long and offers some interesting views out the side cab windows. Take a moment to look around as you pass by.

The train crosses an inlet from Chesapeake Bay on another long bridge at MP 77.0. Continuing south, you cross a third bridge over another inlet from Chesapeake Bay at MP 84.0

After varying between 110 and 135 mph, the speed limit drops at MP 89.7 as the train nears Baltimore. The limit drops again at MP 91.8 to 60 mph, and again to 45 mph at MP 93.8. Finally, the speed limit drops to 30 mph at MP 95.3 as you begin to enter the station complex. Use the Track Monitor tool here to watch for speed limit reductions and plan ahead—it takes a fair distance to slow your train from 110 mph to 30 mph.

At MP 98.0, you enter the tunnel that takes your train into Baltimore Station, located at MP 98.4. As you enter the tunnel, be ready to make your station stop at the other end. As shown in Figure 2.5, the station is only 0.2 miles past the south tunnel portal, so travel no faster than 30 mph as you exit the tunnel, and be ready to stop adjacent to the Baltimore Station platforms.

FIGURE 2.5:

Baltimore Station lies between two tunnels. The station complex can sneak up on you as you exit the tunnel, so use care.

TIP Use your Next Station Display tool to count down the distance to the station platforms. Slow the train as the counter nears zero. When the Distance to Next Station Display indication reads 00.00, stop the train.

Baltimore to Washington DC

As your train departs Baltimore, it enters the B&P tunnel south of the station. Speed limits here are 75 mph; accelerate to this speed as you leave the station. This tunnel is over a mile long, with several curves in the middle, so be prepared to operate in darkness for a while. As you exit the tunnel, you pass a pair of crossovers, and then enter a very short tunnel only 0.2 miles south. Speed limits increase to 110 once you pass these two tunnels.

The track south of Baltimore is fast and straight. The speed limit is 110 mph or higher for a number of miles. The track encounters a very slight grade heading south, one insignificant enough that it causes no operational difficulties. The speed limit increases to 125 mph at MP 112.3.

NOTE The highest point on the route between Washington DC and Philadelphia is only 141 feet above sea level. Unlike other routes in Microsoft Train Simulator, the Northeast Corridor has very minimal grades. This makes train operation on this route relatively easy.

At MP 126.9, you arrive at the station platform at New Carrollton. Continuing on, the rest of the run into Washington DC is straightforward. Two signals display restrictive indications as you enter the Washington DC Station facility. Watch the Track Monitor, because these signals can sneak up on you when you're traveling at high speed. Slow to 30 mph as you enter the station, and spot your train at the platform, just short of the track bumper. Welcome to Washington DC!

Now that you're familiar with the route, it's time have a seat in the all-important right hand chair inside the Acela cab.

Passenger Activity Tutorial

As with the rest of the routes, the Northeast Corridor contains a simple tutorial Activity. This Activity is the place to start for those who are new to the game.

The tutorial provides pop-up messages that guide you through a short 10-minute Activity (see Figure 2.6). It shows you how to start and stop the Acela and how to use the Track Monitor and Next Station Display tools. It also guides you through a few station stops. If you have yet to run the Acela, start with this Activity first.

FIGURE 2.6:

The Passenger Activity Tutorial provides guidance in pop-up messages to help first-time operators.

Now that you're up to speed with operation basics, let's take a look at each of the Activities for the Northeast Corridor.

Activity Crew Call: Bridge Damage

In this Activity, you'll operate the Acela Express around a damaged bridge. This minor detour has an impact on your schedule.

ACTIVITY SUMMARY

Locomotive/Train:	Acela Express
Starting Point:	Wilmington
Ending Point:	Philadelphia
Time of Day/light:	17:30; dark
Difficulty Level:	Easy
Distance Covered:	Approximately 132 miles
Estimated Duration:	30 minutes

Activity Strategy

The vehicle accident and resulting bridge damage will be a slight hit to your schedule as you operate between stations. The challenge is to negotiate the detour, then attempt to make up time for the remainder of the route. Do your best to operate quickly up to, and through, the speed-restricted detour so that you minimize the delay.

 WARNING Remember, the Acela and HHP-8 cab signal display only shows the maximum authorized speed based on the signal indication. It does not take into account any permanent or temporary speed restrictions on the line. As such, you should treat this number only as a theoretical maximum. Refer to the Track Monitor tool to see the specific speed restrictions.

Playing the Activity

There are two station stops in this Activity, as shown in Figure 2.7. There is one slow order speed restriction due to the bridge damage. It does not appear in the briefing, but the Track Monitor will show you that the 15-mph restriction starts just past MP 24.0. The speed limit is 80 mph between the station and the restricted speed, but don't attempt to get there in the short distance, as you'll reach the slow order long before you reach maximum speed.

FIGURE 2.7:

Bridge Damage Activity timetable

TIP The slow order can be unnerving as you literally creep over a mile and a half of slow trackage. Use care to stay under the speed limit. Find the proper throttle setting (try approximately 2% with no brakes), then keep yourself occupied by playing with the exterior view keys, or sit back in the passenger car for a spell.

The speed restriction routes you around the damaged bridge. At MP 25.0, you cross over to an adjacent track. The slow order is about a mile beyond this switch, just past the apartment building to the left of the tracks, as shown in Figure 2.8. It's a long and slow one—15 mph for over 1.5 miles. Watch your speed carefully through here, for while speeding won't get you a penalty brake application, it will give you a ding on your Activity evaluation.

You'll see a red signal at the end of the slow order. Be sure to stop here, as you need to wait for an AI train operating in the opposite direction to clear. It will take a few minutes for this train to appear, so be patient. The signal will change to green just as soon as this train passes to your left.

WARNING Wet rail in this Activity can limit track adhesion in several locations. Use sand as necessary to keep the locomotive wheels from slipping.

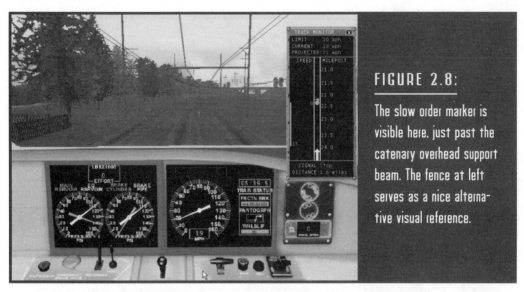

FIGURE 2.8:

The slow order marker is visible here, just past the catenary overhead support beam. The fence at left serves as a nice alternative visual reference.

The remainder of this Activity is straightforward with no surprises, other than a few AI trains. As you proceed after the meet, the speed limit is 80 mph; it quickly increases to 110 mph, and stays this way until you enter the Philly passenger terminal complex at MP 7.5. As you reach the 45-mph speed limit outside Philly, open up your Next Station Display tool to count down the distance to the platform. Spot the train at the platform when the Next Station Display distance reads zero and the nose of the locomotive is just off the bumper, as shown in Figure 2.9.

FIGURE 2.9:

You should spot your train in the Philadelphia Station just short of the bumper post at the end of track.

Activity Crew Call: Morning in Maryland

In this Activity, you will operate an HHP-8-powered train set between Baltimore and Edgewood in a summer rain.

ACTIVITY SUMMARY

Locomotive/Train:	Acela HHP-8
Starting Point:	Baltimore
Ending Point:	Edgewood
Time of Day/light:	8:00; rain
Difficulty Level:	Easy
Distance Covered:	19 miles
Estimated Duration:	30 minutes

Activity Strategy

You need to maintain your schedule as you operate between stations in this Activity. Efficient spotting and loading/unloading of passengers will help you maintain the schedule, so make sure you spot the train correctly at all the station platforms as you arrive. Excess loading/unloading time due to an improper spot can collectively put you significantly behind schedule as the Activity progresses. This Activity has an "Easy" difficulty level; it is pretty straightforward. There is minimum AI traffic to contend with, and there are no speed restrictions to deal with.

Playing the Activity

You only have to make one station stop at Edgewood, as shown in Figure 2.10.

As you leave Baltimore, you enter the tunnel just south of the station. After you clear the platform, the speed limit is 75 mph—accelerate quickly but note that at MP 97.5 the speed limit drops back to 40 mph. Start adjusting your speed soon after exiting the tunnel, and be ready for the 30-mph speed limit at MP 95.3.

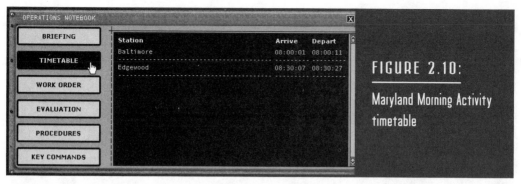

FIGURE 2.10:

Maryland Morning Activity timetable

NOTE The Track Monitor tool is very useful in this Activity: it alerts you to speed limit changes. Use the F4 key to bring it up.

The speed limit increases to 45 mph at MP 94.4, and then again to 60 mph at MP 92.3. As you pass the 45-mph speed limit marker, begin to accelerate to 45 mph, then be ready to increase to 60 mph as soon as your entire train passes the next marker. At MP 90.2, the speed limit increases to 100 mph—accelerate as soon as possible to give you time to make the station stop on or before the timetable listing.

WARNING The rain makes the rail a little slippery, so use care under moderate to hard brake applications to prevent the train from sliding.

The last stretch into Edgewood is quick track; 100–110 mph speeds make the miles pass quickly. At MP 83 you cross a long bridge over an inlet from Chesapeake Bay. As you reach the other end, prepare to slow for your station stop; a yellow signal at MP 82.6 restricts your speed to 45 mph. Reduce the throttle to zero and use a moderate brake application to slow the train. Use your Next Station Display tool to measure the distance to the Edgewood Station. At the southbound signal bridge at MP 81.6, start slowing. Spot the train at the platform using a moderate brake application. As shown in Figure 2.11, Edgewood is a small station; spot the train with the locomotive just past the small station building to the right. The Activity ends when you unload all the passengers.

FIGURE 2.11:

Stop your train adjacent to the parking lot on the left side of the train. The small concrete structure should be adjacent to your first passenger car.

Activity Crew Call: Short Passenger Run

In this Activity, you must operate the Acela train set from Washington DC Station to New Carrollton, which is approximately eight miles north.

ACTIVITY SUMMARY

Locomotive/Train:	Acela Express
Starting Point:	Washington DC
Ending Point:	Beyond New Carrollton
Time of Day/light:	11:00: daylight
Difficulty Level:	Easy
Distance Covered:	Approximately 13 miles
Estimated Duration:	20 minutes

Activity Strategy

To complete this Activity successfully, you need to depart Washington DC as quickly as you can while still obeying the speed limit. Your ability to efficiently manage the train's speed will determine your ability to reach New Carrollton on or before your scheduled time.

Playing the Activity

Your only station stop in this Activity is at New Carrollton. The timetable shown in Figure 2.12 lists your scheduled arrival time.

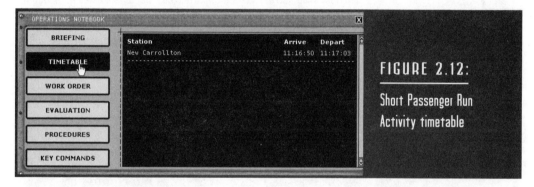

FIGURE 2.12:

Short Passenger Run Activity timetable

There are no other trains on the route to get in your way, so you can make this run as fast as speed limits permit. As you leave Washington DC, the speed limit is 40 mph until you exit the station complex. As soon as you pass the speed limit marker at MP 133.1, start opening the throttle to take advantage of the 85-mph speed limit.

NOTE With departure from Washington DC at 11:00 AM, there is plenty of time to complete this Activity. In fact, if you stick to the speed limits, you should be able to arrive five or more minutes early.

Use your Station Monitor to watch for New Carrollton Station, as it can come up quickly. When the train is a mile out from the station, reduce the throttle to zero and start coasting. When the train reaches 0.6 miles from the station, start applying the brakes with a 5% brake application. Increase the brake setting to bring the train to a stop with the locomotive just past the north end of the platform, as shown in Figure 2.13. The Activity ends when you load/unload your passengers.

 TIP Use liberal doses of throttle to keep the train moving as quickly as possible. Delay your braking for the station stop until the last minute (but be sure to leave enough time to stop!). With an increasingly moderately heavy brake application, you should be able to slow the train from track speed to the station stop in less than one mile without spilling one single drop of coffee in the dining car.

FIGURE 2.13:

Spot the train in New Carrollton with the locomotive just past the north end of the platform.

Activity Crew Call: Train Rescue

In this Activity, you will use an HHP-8 locomotive to rescue a stranded Acela Express train and tow it to the BWI Station.

ACTIVITY SUMMARY

Locomotive/Train:	Acela HHP-8
Starting Point:	Washington DC
Ending Point:	BWI
Time of Day/light:	7:30; dawn
Difficulty Level:	Easy
Distance Covered:	Approximately 29 miles
Estimated Duration:	50 minutes

Activity Strategy

There are two goals to this Activity: get to the stranded train as quickly as you can, and then get the stranded train to the BWI Station as quickly and safely as you can. If you do both well, you'll complete this Activity successfully.

Playing the Activity

Your only scheduled stop in this Activity is at BWI Station after you pick up the stranded train, as shown in Figure 2.14. There are no slow orders in this Activity to worry about. Just pay attention to the speed limit changes along the route.

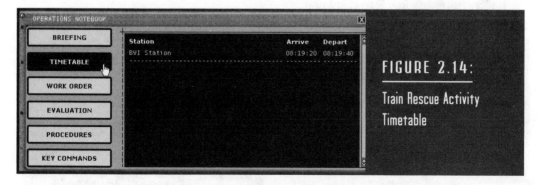

FIGURE 2.14:

Train Rescue Activity Timetable

You will receive a red signal indication just moments after leaving the station track. You must stop at this red signal to wait for an inbound passenger train to clear. The approach signal you pass as you start moving is the warning—the red signal is not far past this, so plan accordingly, otherwise you'll roll through the red signal to end the Activity before you even exit the station complex.

TIP Because you're running with just the locomotive, you can use the locomotive brake to slow the HHP-8, which is the lever on the right side of the control desk.

As you cross over to the right-hand main, the speed limit increases to 125 mph. Don't get too carried away with the throttle, though, as the train you need to pick up is in a siding a short distance ahead, just prior to the New Carrollton Station platform (if you reach the platform, you've gone too far). Don't bother throttling up to the maximum speed, or you will only succeed in blowing right by your waiting train. Even a light locomotive takes a significant distance to stop from 100+ mph. Start slowing as you proceed through the switch.

NOTE When you're operating the light engine move from Washington DC to the stranded train, take advantage of the fact that you have no train to pull to make maximum track speed. Relatively speaking, this single engine will respond like a scalded cat to even minimal throttle and brake inputs.

Once stopped past the switch, as shown in Figure 2.15, use the Switch tool to line the locomotive back to the train. You may find the rear-train external view handy here; use key 3 to display it.

FIGURE 2.15:

Use the external views to back your locomotive into the siding to pick up the passenger train.

Use just a little throttle to back into the siding, and be ready with the brakes so that you don't couple to the cars too hard. Use the Coupler view to go outside the train to couple the locomotive to the cars, as shown in Figure 2.16.

FIGURE 2.16:

The Coupler view makes coupling up to cars much easier. Use the 6 key to display this view.

After picking up the stranded train, the remainder of the run into BWI is uneventful. 110-mph trackage allows you to make good time into the station. You'll see a 45-mph approach signal about five miles out, and then a 30-mph approach signal only two miles out from the station. Again, use your Next Station Display tool to monitor the distance from the platform and spot the train in the proper location. The Activity ends when you finish loading/unloading passengers.

TIP Use care when backing up to couple to the stranded train. Remember to use the Coupler view by pressing the 6 key, as this places you right over the end of the locomotive. Couple to the train at 3 mph or less—anything faster can damage the equipment, not to mention the clothes of those drinking their morning coffee in the dining car.

Activity Crew Call: After the Storm

In this Activity you operate the Acela Express between Baltimore and New Carrollton. It sounds easy at first, but there's a catch—numerous slow order speed restrictions. And, because the railroad is surveying track damage from the storm, you may not know about some of them until you are only a mile or two away.

ACTIVITY SUMMARY

Locomotive/Train:	Acela Express
Starting Point:	Baltimore
Ending Point:	New Carrollton
Time of Day/light:	16:30; dusk, rain
Difficulty Level:	Medium
Distance Covered:	Approximately 29 miles
Estimated Duration:	30 minutes

Activity Strategy

This Activity requires you to pay attention for "surprise" slow orders and speed restrictions. Keep focused, and make liberal use of your Track Monitor to ensure you don't accidentally blow through a speed restriction.

These slow orders will play havoc with your timetable schedule, so be ready to maximize your time at track speed between these restrictions. Even so, you're likely to be late, but try to minimize your tardiness.

Playing the Activity

You must complete three station stops in this Activity, as shown in Figure 2.17.

FIGURE 2.17:

After the Storm Activity timetable

There are a few speed restrictions to deal with as you operate the route. Although they're not identified in the briefing, we can identify them here.

Temporary Speed Restrictions

- **Restriction #1:** 15 mph speed restriction, MP 99.50 to 99.55
- **Restriction #2:** 15 mph speed restriction, MP 112.50 to 112.70
- **Restriction #3:** 15 mph speed restriction, MP 112.85 to 113.20

Remember, as you leave Baltimore, the speed limit through the station complex is only 30 mph. You can accelerate to track speed once your train clears the station. However, note that your first speed restriction is less than a mile up the track, just past the tunnel. You will receive an alert message informing you of this message as you pass through the tunnel.

The first speed restriction is short at only 0.1 mile, where the train crosses over to the left-hand track, only to immediately cross back over to the right-hand track. Once you pass through the restricted area, open the throttle to accelerate the train to track speed, which is 110 mph.

Alert messages also appear as you approach the speed restrictions. Watch for a quick-appearing 45-mph approach signal at MP 103.4—it's really easy to find yourself staring at this 45-mph signal when you're traveling at 110 mph. If you pass it, your train will get stabbed with an automatic emergency brake application.

Your first station is at MP 106.3. As you pass the second 45-mph approach signal, move the throttle to zero, bring up the Next Station Display tool, and prepare to slow the train for the platform stop. Load your passengers quickly and continue on your way.

TIP Watch for the end of the speed restrictions—work the throttle so that, right as the last car in your train passes the end of the restriction, the train is already accelerating back to track speed under full throttle.

Soon after leaving the first station, you'll receive another Alert message warning you about the next two slow orders, as shown in Figure 2.18. You have about four miles to slow for the first one, so don't panic immediately. Maintain track speed for as long as possible to keep on time; start slowing about 1.25 miles before the slow order. You'll find that 1% throttle is enough to keep your train moving at the 15-mph speed limit in these restrictions.

Once past the restrictions, you get a number of miles of 125-mph track before you see two 45-mph approach signals about four miles prior to the New Carrollton Station. Slow to 45 mph for these signals, and after the second one, you've got a few miles of 45-mph track before you need to slow for the station. The Activity ends when you finish loading/unloading your passengers.

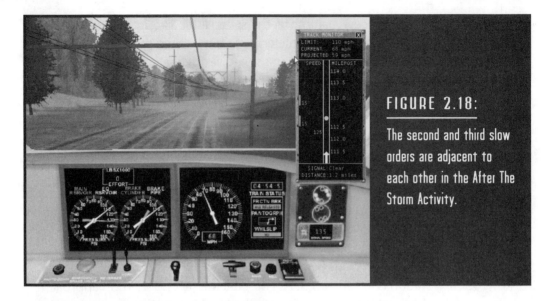

FIGURE 2.18:

The second and third slow orders are adjacent to each other in the After The Storm Activity.

Activity Crew Call: Riding the Yellows

This Activity gives you a chance to experience all the trials and tribulations that come with running trains on a busy stretch of railroad. Traffic ahead of your train will prevent you from making maximum track speed for much of the route.

ACTIVITY SUMMARY

Locomotive/Train:	Acela Express
Starting Point:	New Carrollton
Ending Point:	Baltimore
Time of Day/light:	14:30; overcast with snow
Difficulty Level:	Medium
Distance Covered:	Approximately 29 miles
Estimated Duration:	30 minutes

Activity Strategy

The slower rail traffic ahead of your train is causing you delays, but the dispatcher has no other options but to let you follow the trains ahead. As a

result, yellow approach signals will dog your train as you travel this route. If you get too close to the train ahead, you may get a red signal and have to stop, losing precious time both stopping and moving again once the signal changes.

Playing the Activity

You must make three station stops in this Activity, as shown in Figure 2.19.

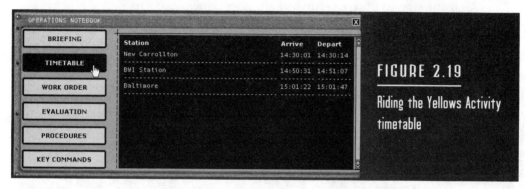

OPERATIONS NOTEBOOK			
Station		**Arrive**	**Depart**
New Carrollton		14:30:01	14:30:14
BWI Station		14:50:31	14:51:07
Baltimore		15:01:22	15:01:47

BRIEFING · TIMETABLE · WORK ORDER · EVALUATION · PROCEDURES · KEY COMMANDS

FIGURE 2.19

Riding the Yellows Activity timetable

The catch here is that you're following slower train traffic ahead, which is causing you to see yellow blocks as you operate your train. As you start, the first signal you'll come to will be yellow. However, if you make a nice, gradual start, this signal will turn green before you reach it.

TIP Basically, you're stuck behind the slower traffic ahead, so stay far enough behind the other train to avoid the need to stop at red signals. If you do this correctly, you will, at a minimum, see nothing but approach signals, and you can at least keep your train moving.

The key to this Activity is to allow enough distance between you and the train ahead. Don't be right at the speed limit as you pass each yellow signal. Instead, operate your train at around 40 mph. As you progress, the train ahead of you will get far enough ahead that you can start seeing green signals instead of yellow. Much of the track north of New Carrollton is 45 mph anyway, so extra speed isn't going to get you anywhere. The worst thing you can do is operate too fast and have to stop at red signals—the process of stopping and starting your train will cost you significant time.

If you follow this technique, you should see green signals. Operate your train between 80 and 90 mph instead of 110, and, if your timing is correct, you should see several green signals before you reach BWI. At this point, you'll have an easy, uneventful run right up to the station platform.

The only exception to this will be the slow orders, as mentioned previously. All of these slow orders are between New Carrollton and just north of BWI Station. Watch for the trackside speed restriction markers, and use the Track Monitor so that you will have advanced warning. Remember, it takes time to slow to 15 mph from triple-digit speeds.

After the stop at BWI, the run to Baltimore allows you a few clear blocks of triple-digit speed before you need to slow for approach signals again. Pass through the tunnel south of the station under the 30-mph speed limit, and be ready to spot your train at the platform, as shown in Figure 2.20.

FIGURE 2.20:

Ah, Baltimore in the wintertime! Spot the Acela with the locomotive just before the end of the platform.

Activity Crew Call: Summer Express

In this Activity, you get the chance to operate the entire route from Washington DC to Philadelphia. During your run, you get the opportunity to experience station stops, other trains, and slow orders—in short, everything a real railroad engineer faces on a daily basis.

ACTIVITY SUMMARY

Locomotive/Train:	Acela Express
Starting Point:	Washington DC
Ending Point:	Philadelphia
Time of Day/light:	12:00: daylight
Difficulty Level:	Hard
Distance Covered:	Approximately 132 miles
Estimated Duration:	90 minutes

Activity Strategy

This Activity is the most difficult one for the Northeast Corridor route due to its length. You do have an advantage, however, for if you've played the rest of the Activities you should be familiar enough with much of the route to know what to look for.

Regardless, this Activity will take some time to complete as you operate the entire route from Washington DC and Philly. Pay attention to your signals and slow orders, and you shouldn't find it any more difficult than the other Activities.

Playing the Activity

In this Activity, operate your train based on signal indications and speed limits. Stop at each station along the route to load and unload passengers—be sure to hit Enter to start the loading/unloading process as soon as you stop. You have four station stops in this Activity, as shown in Figure 2.21.

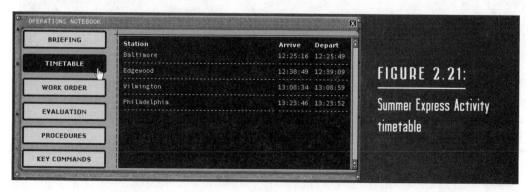

OPERATIONS NOTEBOOK

BRIEFING

TIMETABLE

WORK ORDER

EVALUATION

PROCEDURES

KEY COMMANDS

Station	Arrive	Depart
Baltimore	12:25:16	12:25:49
Edgewood	12:38:49	12:39:09
Wilmington	13:08:34	13:08:59
Philadelphia	13:23:46	13:23:52

FIGURE 2.21:

Summer Express Activity timetable

You also have four slow order speed restrictions in this Activity.

Temporary Speed Restrictions

- **Restriction #1:** 15 mph speed restriction, MP 118.00 to 119.00

- **Restriction #2:** 15 mph speed restriction, MP 109.00 to 109.109.

- **Restriction #3:** 15 mph speed restriction, MP 106.00 to 107.00

- **Restriction #4:** 15 mph speed restriction, MP 104.50 to 104.00

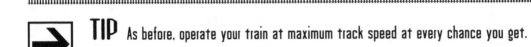

TIP As before, operate your train at maximum track speed at every chance you get.

The route is uneventful from Washington DC north; with the exception of the speed restrictions noted above, the track is clear, and you can operate at maximum track speed. You will see nothing but clear signals until a few miles south of Baltimore. First you will see two approach signals, and then finally a red signal just before you enter the tunnel at the south end of the station. Stop at the red signal and wait for a minute or two—the signal will clear to green and allow you to proceed into Baltimore Station, as shown in Figure 2.22.

FIGURE 2.22:

Baltimore can be a busy place at times. Here's the Acela train along with two other trains at the station platforms

As you leave Baltimore Station, you will navigate through some 45-mph trackage north of the depot. From there, you can operate at track speed until MP 84.7, where you receive an approach signal in advance of a red stop signal.

As shown in Figure 2.23, the 30-mph approach signal is located on a bridge over a portion of Chesapeake Bay. If you arrive at the red signal quickly enough, you'll see an AI train clear the track ahead of you. If you ease up to the red block, the signal may clear to green before you need to stop completely.

 TIP Use the Track Monitor and Next Station Display tools so you have advanced warning of approaching signals and stations.

FIGURE 2.23:

The route between Edgewood and Wilmington contains three large bridges. This bridge crosses an inlet from Chesapeake Bay north of Edgewood.

The station stops at Edgewood and Wilmington are uneventful, as shown in Figure 2.23. Use the Track Monitor to watch for occasional approach signals and the upcoming stations. The rest of the run into Philadelphia is an opportunity for fast travel time, as you'll see only a few yellow signals until you reach the Philadelphia Station complex, just a few miles south of the station proper. The Activity ends when you load and unload your passengers.

Off Duty

At this point you have hopefully completed all the Northeast Corridor Activities. If you feel things have been easy, continue on to Chapter 3. After a turn in a steam locomotive, you'll begin to understand first-hand why diesels and electrics have replaced steam on virtually all railroads around the globe.

Chapter 3

Operating England's Settle-Carlisle Route

*T*he Settle-Carlisle route offers you the opportunity to climb aboard the famous Flying Scotsman, arguably the world's best-known locomotive. Steam locomotives are much more challenging to operate than today's automated electrics and diesels. With boiler pressure, water levels, injectors, dampers, a firebox, and a host of other complexities to manage, steam engines force you to think about running the locomotive in addition to running the route! This chapter will help you get up and running in the cab of a legendary locomotive.

Route Description

Train Simulator models the Settle & Carlisle line as it was in its heyday in the late 1920s. At the time, the route was operated by the Midland Railway Company, offering passenger service from England to Scotland. It was the last great main-line railway to be built in England, and as such it benefited from nearly half-a-century of railroading experience. Seventeen major viaducts and 14 tunnels lie along the scenic route as it passes through rural farm fields, lush moors, and glorious wilderness in areas that are now national parks.

NOTE "The legend and appeal of LNER A3 Pacific No. 4472 Flying Scotsman has long since transcended the boundaries of railway enthusiasm. For a sizeable contingent of the population, the name now encapsulates everything to do with the now-distant dream time of the golden age of steam."—Robin Jones, Heritage Railway Magazine

The legendary Flying Scotsman (see Figure 3.1) is the only locomotive available on the Settle-Carlisle route. The distinctive, apple-green engine held two world records, was the subject of the first feature-length motion picture with sound, toured on three continents, and grew to be a national icon of Great Britain. It's also very fast, as the first steam engine to be officially clocked at over 100 mph.

FIGURE 3.1:

The Flying Scotsman is the most famous steam locomotive in the world.

History

The Settle & Carlisle Railway was originally built by the Midland Railway Company to extend Great Britain's mainline rail service to Scotland. Completed in 1876, the route took over six years to build as the result of the challenging landscape and Midland's specification of grades no more than 1% over the line (which would insure fast operation). Being far removed from the population centers of nineteenth century England, the workers that built the line lived out a harsh existence in mobile shantytowns next to the roadbed. Many lost their lives along the way, with the 104-foot high Batty Moss (now Ribbleshead) viaduct taking the greatest toll.

RUNNING CLEAN

Learning how to run clean in a steam engine is one of the hardest (and most important) skills to master as a steam engineer. More art than science, this proficiency is primarily based on sound. A steam locomotive will make a pulsing, rhythmic choo-choo sound when running most efficiently, and there will be little steam coming from the pistons or stack (lending it the term "running clean").

Fine tuning your regulator and reverser is truly an acquired touch. Since it is the product of multiple controls, it's not easily taught.

Besides sound, you can use the external cameras to help you keep track of your efficiency. Always avoid spinning the wheels, because you waste boiler pressure and momentum for little effect—spinning wheels have almost no traction on the rails. Set up an external camera to provide you with a zoomed-in view of your locomotive's drive wheels at all times, and use the other external camera for all your sightseeing. If the wheels are spinning faster than the rails are passing under them, you have wheelslip and you'll need to throttle down immediately to regain traction.

When complete, the Settle-Carlisle route was (and still is) advertised as the most scenic railway in England, and the Victorian public quickly embraced the line as its preferred route to Scotland. In the early 1920s the line was revitalized with express service. Here began the service of the legendary Flying Scotsman.

Engine No. 4472 was the first locomotive to bear the apple-green livery that was to become a trademark of the designers at the London and North Eastern Railway (LNER). Designed by Sir Nigel Gresley, then the LNER's chief mechanical and electrical engineer, the Flying Scotsman was shown off in 1924 and 1925 at Wembley's British Empire Exhibitions as representing the latest in transportation technology. It was fitted with a special corridor tender, giving it the endurance to make the first non-stop run from King's Cross to Edinburgh in 1928.

The LNER rebuilt the Flying Scotsman in 1947 and again in 1959, improving its operating performance with new technologies each time. After 40 years of service, the locomotive was decommissioned in 1963. Over 70 locomotives of its class were summarily scrapped, leaving No. 4472 as the only remaining example of the A1 Pacifics. Railway enthusiast Alan Pegler purchased the old engine, and carefully preserved and maintained it in working order.

The Flying Scotsman toured the USA from 1969 to 1972, introducing North Americans to its beauty and appeal. Following its tour abroad, it ran special excursion trains on its old route. It also participated in Australia's 1988 and 1989 bicentennial celebration, travelling across the country under its own power. While in Australia, No. 4472 set the world record for a non-stop steam locomotive run, hauling a train for 422 miles from Parkes to Broken Hill in New South Wales.

Today

Today, the Settle-Carlisle line is operated by Railtrack. The route remains known as the most scenic railway in all of England, attracting tourists not only for its destinations served, but also for the trip itself. The Flying Scotsman was purchased in 1996 by Dr. Tony Marchington. The engine had a cracked firebox and was not operational, but even with repairs it would no longer be fit for mainline service. Following Dr. Marchington's investment of over a million US dollars, the engine made its return to the rails on July 4, 1999, on a re-inaugural run from King's Cross to York. It now conducts regular legacy runs, drawing fans from all over the world eager for a chance to ride behind the world's most famous steam locomotive.

 NOTE Railtrack has spent 18.2 million pounds since 1999 refurbishing the Settle-Carlisle line, including re-laying 17 miles of track and shoring up hillsides to prevent landslides (like those that have caused two serious derailments since 1996).

Route Tour: Train Simulator's Settle-Carlisle Route

Settle-Carlisle consists of 72 miles of track, hosting 17 major viaducts and 14 tunnels (Figure 3.2). The grades are no steeper than one foot of rise over 100 feet of run (1%), but even that can be challenging in a steam engine during the frequent rains and storms of northern Britain. The scenic route passes through compelling historic townships and beautiful moors, dales, and valleys. As if in testament to the line's beauty, it borders two national parks along its length.

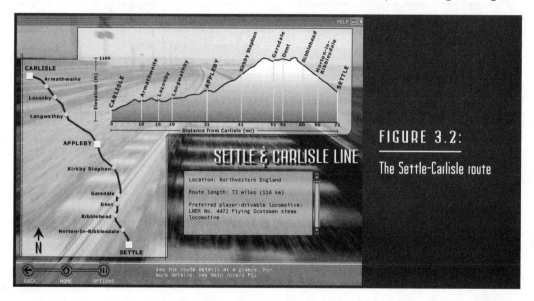

FIGURE 3.2:

The Settle-Carlisle route

The route's southern end is anchored in the bustling market town of Settle, nestled in the scenic Yorkshire Dales. This area includes Yorkshire Dales National Park, known for its scenic beauty and historic villages. Limestone forms much of the bedrock in the area, resulting in expansive underground labyrinths of caves, massive sinkholes, and craggy ravines on the surface. At the northern end of the line lies the city of Carlisle, capital of Cumbria. The Lake District National Park is also in this vicinity, beginning just outside Lazonby and extending to the south and west.

STATION NAME	MILEPOST LOCATION	NOTES
Settle	236.4	Southern end of route
Horton-In-Ribblesdale	242.42	—
Ribblehead	247.2	Ribblehead viaduct
Dent	253.32	—
Garsdale	256.53	Ais Gill summit
Kirkby Stephen	266.47	St. Stephen's Church
Crosby Garrett	270	—
Ormside	275	—
Appleby	277.22	Appleby Castle
Long Martin	280.15	—
Langwathby	288.23	—
Little Salkeld	289.56	—
Lazonby	292.5	St. Nicholas' Church
Armathwaite	298.09	—
Carlisle	308	Northern end of route

North Yorkshire

Your route begins in the town of Settle, in the foothills of the Pennines Mountains. Overlooking the town itself is the largest outcropping of limestone in Britain. The town draws tourists as a jump-off point for visiting the Yorkshire Dales National Park. Northward, the line climbs up a steady grade as it loosely follows the Ribble River.

Horton Station is a whistle stop just inside the park, serving a quaint rural village. The route is fairly straight all the way through to Ribblehead. A curve at MP 248 requires a speed of less than 60 mph to be safely negotiated. Beyond this turn lies the Ribbleshead viaduct, a massive bridge composed of 24 sweeping stone arches (see Figure 3.3). The viaduct runs 1,320 feet across Batty Moss, a peaty moor unsuitable for supporting a mainline roadbed. At its highest point, the viaduct is 165 feet above the moor.

FIGURE 3.3:

The Ribblehead viaduct is an impressive feat of nineteenth century engineering.

The line continues within the boundaries of Yorkshire Dales National Park beyond the Ais Gill summit. Similar views of placid meadows and moors abound along the route within the park. You will even sometimes see some of the park wildlife on the tracks. Just north of the viaduct itself, the line crosses into Cumbria.

Cumbria

The northern end of the route runs from the Yorkshire Dales to the city of Carlisle. It loosely follows the Eden River out of the Pennine Mountains through Westmorland, winding down the grade from Garsdale Station. The towns along the way are characterized by their medieval churches, some of which date back to the twelfth century and earlier.

Numerous curves down the grade can be found here, owing to Midland's specification of no more than a 1% grade along the line. All of the turns are safe at 60 mph, but beware if you are trying to set a speed record or make up time between stations. On average, roughly three miles of relatively straight track are followed by a 60–70 mph turn throughout the Cumbria descent into Carlisle.

TIP Try the steam tutorial before attempting the Settle-Carlisle route. Operating a steam locomotive is much more difficult than today's modern engines, and this straight-forward lesson can help you through the basics.

Appleby is the largest station between the line's ends. Situated in the Eden Valley, the city developed as the market town of Westmorland after the Norman Conquest. Impressive Appleby Castle stands guard over the town, and St. Lawrence's church in the downtown area is visible from the rails (see Figure 3.4). Northward out of Appleby lie many small, historic villages with rudimentary platforms and station facilities.

FIGURE 3.4:

Several landmarks are visible from the mainline in the town of Appleby.

Carlisle is at the northern end of the line. The largest station on the route, Carlisle was also the second largest rail hub in Britain during the time portrayed in *Train Simulator* (behind only London in terms of routes serving the city and daily scheduled service). Just south of the station is the Scotby grade, the steepest on the entire route. Ramp up in the valley if you are on your way up, or conversely go easy on your speed and run with a hand on the brakes if you're coming down.

Passenger Activity Tutorial

You can learn how to operate the Flying Scotsman with the help of this tutorial, so it's worth trying out just for the sake of the steam locomotive lessons. The Activity gives you an easy scheduled run between Kirkby Stephen and Appleby on a clear spring morning. The 15-minute Activity will teach you how to start and stop the Flying Scotsman through the use of pop-up messages that guide you through a few station stops.

Activity Crew Call: Local Service

A string of mechanical breakdowns leaves the durable Flying Scotsman as the only locomotive available to conduct local passenger service along the Settle-Carlisle line.

ACTIVITY SUMMARY

Locomotive/Train:	Flying Scotsman
Starting Point:	Settle
Ending Point:	Carlisle
Time of Day/light:	9:00; spring/clear
Difficulty Level:	Easy
Distance Covered:	71.6 miles
Estimated Duration:	Two hours, 10 minutes

Activity Strategy

Despite the Easy rating, this activity is actually one of the most difficult and longest available on the route, so it may not be the best choice for a first run. On the other hand, it's a great way to get familiar with the line, as you'll be covering every single inch of its rails. If you're coming in cold, be sure to save often along the way. This will help you avoid going all the way back to the beginning if you underestimate a turn and derail on the downgrade. This Activity is made very hard by the numerous starts you have to make with the engine, which is arguably the single most difficult task in a steam locomotive.

Playing the Activity

The run begins with the climb out of Settle toward the Yorkshire Dales. Ease the Flying Scotsman into motion and bring down your regulator until you are efficiently accelerating to track speed. Remember to avoid wheelslip as you start, using your external camera to watch your wheels for traction.

A straight section of the line marks the first two station stops, but your starts require a bit of care at each station to avoid wheelslip on the grades. Open up your regulator before you release the brakes, and slide your reverser forward as you let off the brake pressure to execute a nice, smooth start. You won't have to worry about the sharp turn just north of Ribblehead, since you'll be stopping at the station and won't be moving very fast by the time you encounter it. Enjoy the view from the Ribbleshead viaduct (see Figure 3.5) and make sure you're on schedule when you arrive in Dent.

FIGURE 3.5:

The viaduct offers one of the most spectacular views in the game.

You can make up a little time with a fast start out of Dent if you're running behind, as the grade is much more relaxed on this portion of the line. Remember your stop in Garsdale and run a little hot as you ascend to the Ais Gill summit about two miles north of the platform. From here on out, it's a downhill run. You can be a little easier on the steam pressure to maintain speed, and allow your fireman to ease up on shoveling. The station calls are almost all two or three miles apart, so you can get up to a respectable speed before slowing approximately 0.15 miles outside of each stop.

TIP Starting up efficiently at each station is the greatest challenge in this Activity. Try to establish a rhythm on the uphill leg of regulator—reverser—brakes, and brakes—regulator—reverser on the downhill leg. Don't be afraid to use the external view to watch your wheels for slippage. Soon, you should have a good feel for starting the Flying Scotsman by sound alone.

The first portion of the downhill line is the best place to make sure that you're on schedule, as the stations are up to five miles apart. This spacing allows you to push your speed a little if you're running late. Be careful of the turns, which should be taken at approximately 60 mph. Your next opportunities to make up time are between Little Sakeld and Lazonby, and between Armathwaite and Carlisle. As long as you don't overshoot any stations, you should be able to maintain your schedule fairly easily. Be sure to develop your ear for No. 4472's stack talk along the way.

Activity Crew Call: Short Passenger Run

This activity allows you to practice your steam locomotive operating skills by conducting a short passenger run from Horton-In-Ribblesdale to Dent, with a stop in Ribblehead along the way.

ACTIVITY SUMMARY

Locomotive/Train:	Flying Scotsman
Starting Point:	Horton
Ending Point:	Dent
Time of Day/light:	8:35; summer/clear
Difficulty Level:	Easy
Distance Covered:	10.9 miles
Estimated Duration:	20 minutes

Activity Strategy

This is the best choice for a first run on the Settle-Carlisle route, with an easily met timetable over three station stops. The run is uphill the entire way, so go easy on your starts to avoid wheelslip. Let off your brakes only after you've opened up your regulator and set a little forward reverser.

Playing the Activity

Don't ease up on the brakes until you've got your steam up in Horton. The old stations on this line don't offer level grades at the platforms, so you can start rolling backwards very quickly after you release your brakes if you're not under pressure from your drive pistons. Accelerate to 60 mph up the grade, using steadily increasing reverser application and matching the settings with your regulator.

You don't have to slow for Ribblehead until about 0.08 miles out, because of the uphill grade and your relatively low speed. Ease into the brakes and bring the train to a gentle stop at the edge of the platform. If you use the mouse to control your brakes, you can use a "brake waggle" to alternate between maintaining your brake pressure and letting it go (see Figure 3.6). This technique provides you with more precise control of your speed than a single brake percentage.

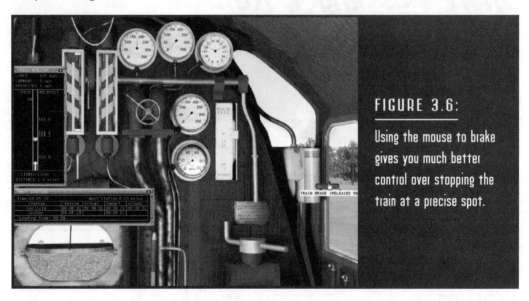

FIGURE 3.6:

Using the mouse to brake gives you much better control over stopping the train at a precise spot.

Start carefully after you hear the all-clear signal from the conductor, easing up the regulator pressure and gently applying the reverser as you let off the brakes. Sound is more important than settings—make sure that you hear the rate of your chugging increasing, and the pitch slowly climbing. Naturally, a look out the window should tell you that you're beginning to roll forward and away from the platform.

WARNING If you start rolling backwards, don't try to compensate with more reverser—you'll only work against your drive piston and compound the problem. Reapply the brakes and try your start again.

The station in Dent requires you to decelerate a bit earlier, as it's on relatively flat ground. Start slowing down while about 0.10 miles out, or earlier if you pushed your speed up on the straight before the station. As long as you manage to avoid the temptation of stopping on the viaduct to enjoy the view, you should be able to meet your schedule and complete the Activity flawlessly.

Activity Crew Call: After the Storm

Gale-force winds have brought down trees and debris along the line, and torrential rains may have caused undercutting of the roadbed. Despite these challenges, you must try to keep your scheduled passenger run to Armathwaite.

ACTIVITY SUMMARY

Locomotive/Train:	Flying Scotsman
Starting Point:	Garsdale
Ending Point:	Armathwaite
Time of Day/light:	15:00; autumn/clear
Difficulty Level:	Medium
Distance Covered:	41.5 miles
Estimated Duration:	One hour, 20 minutes

Activity Strategy

You have nine scheduled stops along your route, and you'll have to endure two particularly slow restricted speed zones due to track damage. In addition, failed signals will require you to stop and radio dispatch for permission to pass. Animals will be on the line with greater frequency due to damaged fences, so spend as much time as possible looking ahead of the engine from either the window or exterior views.

Special speed zones:

- 15 between Mileposts 259.4 and 263.3

- 15 between Mileposts 295.2 and 297.2

Playing the Activity

Run up the first leg of the hill as fast as you can in anticipation of the slow order zone near MP 260. The restrictions are in place for several miles, so this will severely impact your average speed over this portion of the run. Maintain a speed of 14 mph through the slow order zone as best as you can without exceeding the speed limit. Remember that the track monitor does not indicate fractions, so even if you show 15 mph you may in fact be going 15.9 mph, which will result in a poor evaluation due to operating in excess of the speed limit.

WARNING Failed signals are extremely important to observe. Blowing a signal is a major operational error that results in the immediate end of the Activity.

The slow order zone ends a few miles south of Kirkby. Accelerate to maximum speed as soon as you clear the zone, and maintain it until you're just outside of the station. Approximately 0.1 miles out, begin applying your brakes. Use the Next Station Display to coordinate your approach from within the cab. This will allow the mouse to regulate your brake pressure and stop at 0.0 miles to the platform (see Figure 3.7).

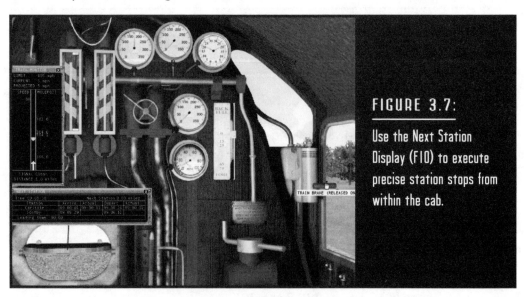

FIGURE 3.7:

Use the Next Station Display (F10) to execute precise station stops from within the cab.

You may encounter one or two failed signals along the rest of the route. These will be brought to your attention through a pop-up dialogue, so you can't overlook them. As you approach, you'll see a gray circle in the Track Monitor where the signals are indicated. Treat it as a red signal, and hit Tab to request permission to pass as soon as you reach a full stop. Be sure to halt before the signal itself, but approach to within about 0.02 miles.

The last slow order zone is just before your destination station. Unfortunately, this means that you'll have no opportunity to make up time at the far end of the restricted zone. Therefore, make sure that you head into the zone on time. Keep your speed up until just before the zone begins. Treat it as you would a station stop, but release your brakes at 15 mph to avoid coming to a complete standstill. Once again, maintain a speed of 14 mph throughout the zone, cranking things up only after you clear the far side for a short run into Carlisle.

Activity Crew Call: Medical Emergency

In the middle of a routine run, one of your passengers goes into labor aboard the train! Your remaining station stops are cancelled, and you must rush the expectant mother down the grade to the hospital in Carlisle.

ACTIVITY SUMMARY

Locomotive/Train:	Flying Scotsman
Starting Point:	Appleby
Ending Point:	Carlisle
Time of Day/light:	10:15; winter/clear
Difficulty Level:	Medium
Distance Covered:	40.8 miles
Estimated Duration:	45 minutes

Activity Strategy

Although set in the winter, the track is clear and dry, allowing maximum speed. The line is open all the way into Carlisle, allowing you to really push your train to the limit in order to make the best time to the maternity ward.

Playing the Activity

This run is all about speed. Pay attention to your stack talk, working to get your piston to drive the wheels at maximum efficiency. After the Long Martin Station, run it wide open until MP 289. There, slow to 60 mph in preparation for the turns after Little Salkeld Station. Unfortunately, you'll have to remain at that speed through Cotehill, where the turns open up a bit on approach to Carlisle. You can gain a little bit of time in the straights after Mileposts 291, 294, and 298, but each of these ends in a turn after approximately two miles (see Figure 3.8).

FIGURE 3.8:

Be sure to slow down in time for the turns, or there'll be a lot more passengers headed for the hospital.

If you push your speed a little bit, you should actually be able to arrive early in Carlisle, helping to add to the legend of the mighty Flying Scotsman as the fastest locomotive of its day.

Activity Crew Call: Low Water

Water shortages along the route force you to make the trip from Settle to Carlisle with only limited waterings in Garsdale and Appleby. Conserve your water by operating efficiently to reach Carlisle.

ACTIVITY SUMMARY

Locomotive/Train:	Flying Scotsman
Starting Point:	Settle
Ending Point:	Carlisle
Time of Day/light:	12:00; summer/clear
Difficulty Level:	Hard
Distance Covered:	27.9 miles
Estimated Duration:	Two hours, 10 minutes

Activity Strategy

You'll have to use your regulator economically if you're going to make it all the way to Carlisle without running dry. The route is the same one described in the Local Service walkthrough of this chapter, so for general route strategies refer to that section. Despite the water shortage, you still have to make all of your stops along the line, so be vigilant for the entire run.

Playing the Activity

Run this one just like the Local Passenger Service Activity, but be extremely sparing with the regulator. Most people use more pressure than they need, since it isn't as obvious as having too little pressure. Running it too high wastes water, and if you do it too much you won't have enough to reach Carlisle.

TIP Back off the regulator as you run, tapping it back up just as you see your projected speed begin to drop off.

Your job here is complicated by frequent station stops. You'll take on water on this run from a trough and from a tower, which are both actions unique to this Activity. Rather than reiterate the details of the run (which can be found in the Local Passenger Service walkthrough), we'll examine the process of watering.

The Garsdale Trough

Water at Garsdale is located in a trough between the rails. The train picks up water by lowering a scoop into the trough, and ramming it up into the tank via the train's momentum. You need to be traveling at least 25 mph to have enough speed to collect the water. Press Y to lower your scoop and begin taking on water. The trough begins just after a viaduct crosses over the mainline above the station, and continues for a few hundred miles (see Figure 3.9). Be sure to retract your scoop by pressing Y again before the end of the trough, or you'll ram it into the ground and cause damage.

FIGURE 3.9:

The trough is clearly visible as a blue-colored area between the rails.

You won't get very much water at Garsdale, owing to the local drought. Therefore, be sure to remain in conservation mode all the way over the summit and into Appleby.

 TIP The trough operation can be tricky, so save the game on your way into Garsdale. If you fail to take on water, reload the Activity and try it again.

The Appleby Tower

Taking on water from the Appleby tower is different than using the trough at Garsdale. Stop so that your tender is directly underneath the tower's spigot (see Figure 3.10). Once you're in position, hold down the T key to transfer water into your tender. Water will continue to flow as long as you hold the key down, but since water is scarce on the route, the Activity calls for you to use as little as possible in consideration of the other trains. Switch to the cab view and watch your tender water level meter (the vertical bar on the right, in the upper center of the screen). When it fills with blue up to the center, let go of the T key and get underway.

FIGURE 3.10:

Taking on water from a tower is much easier than using a trough.

The hardest part of this Activity is the front end, where you must climb the grade with your tender down to a quarter of its water capacity. By using the regulator efficiently, you can make it to your watering stop in Garsdale both on time and with water. You can't make it to Appleby without a successful run at the trough, so reload a saved game if you miss the trough. If you make it, you should have no trouble reaching Carlisle!

Off Duty

The Activities on the Settle-Carlisle line are very challenging in their own right, let alone with the additional difficulty of operating a steam engine manually. If you have too much trouble with these Activities, you can lower the difficulty by activating the Automatic Fireman, or even enabling Simple Mode. This will greatly reduce the complexity of running the engine, allowing you to focus on running the route.

On the other end of the spectrum, veteran hoggers can find some of the greatest challenges in the game in the cab of a steam engine with the automatic fireman turned off. Regardless of what settings you use, conquering the Settle-Carlisle route is a great accomplishment. And in doing so you'll capture a taste of a privilege few people alive today have known—operating a steam locomotive.

Chapter 4

Operating the Burlington Northern Santa Fe's Marias Pass Route

Now that you've had a taste of passenger operations, it's time to try your hand at moving heavy freight trains over mountain passes, switching freight yards, and operating local trains to serve industries. The diesel locomotives in this route are relatively simple to operate, but the sheer weight of the trains behind them adds a whole new set of challenges.

The Marias Pass Route

The route over Marias Pass is an exciting, dynamic stretch of railroad. The line is operated by the Burlington Northern Santa Fe Railroad Company (BNSF), and is well known to railfans. This busy northern transcontinental mainline moves traffic between Pacific Northwest cities and the Great Lakes Region of the United States. Officially named the Hi-Line Subdivision of the Montana Division of the BNSF, this route carries a large amount of intermodal traffic, lumber from Pacific Northwest lumber mills, coal for western power plants, and general freight traffic.

History

The Marias Pass route traces its history to James Hill's Great Northern (GN) Railway, part of the Hill railroad empire. The GN was the first route to forge a northern transcontinental route from Minneapolis to the Puget Sound. Hill's GN was the dominant route for decades until it, along with several other roads, were merged to form the Burlington Northern Railroad in 1970. BN itself merged with the Santa Fe Railway to form the Burlington Northern Santa Fe, or BNSF.

Today

As shown in Figure 4.1, today's Marias Pass is but one of the BNSF's transcontinental routes from the west coast. Operated by one of the premier rail carriers in the US today, Marias Pass represents a modern, fully equipped, high volume freight rail route.

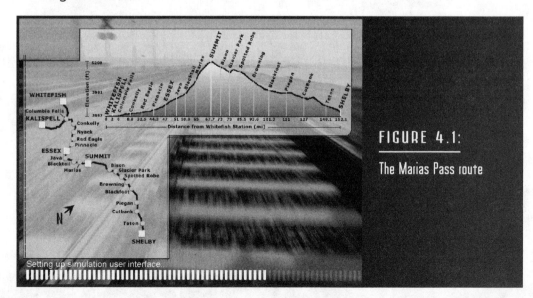

FIGURE 4.1:

The Marias Pass route

Route Tour: Train Simulator's Marias Pass Route

The main line between Whitefish at the west end of the route and Shelby at the east end sees approximately 30 trains a day. Traffic includes anything from mixed freight, to intermodal trains, to coal or grain trains, to Amtrak's Empire Builder train from Seattle to Chicago.

Most of the track on this route uses concrete ties, as they have proven more reliable under high volumes of traffic. The line is equipped with a Centralized Traffic Control system (CTC), which allows a dispatcher in Fort Worth, Texas, to control all train movements

Let's take a look at the line from Whitefish to Shelby as it travels from east to west.

The West End: Flathead Valley

The west end of the Marias Route is where most of the local activities are set. Whitefish Yard, at MP 1217.5, marks the western end of the simulated world in Microsoft *Train Simulator*. The yard in Whitefish has a total of 11-yard tracks, plus other spurs for defective rolling stock. It also features the restored Amtrak station, as shown in Figure 4.2.

FIGURE 4.2:

The Whitefish Depot is a local landmark in the upper Flathead Valley.

Columbia Falls, at MP 1211, is where the Kalispell branch line departs the mainline for the town of Kalispell. Columbia Falls features a number of industrial sidings to serve lumber mills and other local industries. The main line through Whitefish is double track from Whitefish to MP 1208 just east of Conkelly, where it drops to single track as the route enters the Flathead River canyon. Be sure to slow down here, as you run the risk of derailing the train on the tight turns.

The West Slope: Conkelly to Essex

The route east of Conkelly can get tricky: it has numerous slow curves as the track starts winding its way up the river canyon. Keep your train speed under control, especially when eastbound. Excess speed on the East Conkelly switch or the first few curves will almost certainly derail your train.

When heading east just before MP 1203, the speed limit increases to 60 mph. The track straightens out, so go ahead and notch out the throttle to get the train moving. About a mile east, you cross the Flathead River on a large bridge—plan ahead to leave yourself time to enjoy the view.

At MP 1203 you enter Coram, with its signaled passing track and setout spur. Coram is the first location east of Conkelly where you can meet and pass another train. The speed limit past Coram siding drops to 55 mph, and approximately two miles past the east end of Coram, the grade increases significantly to climb a short rise. The track flattens out at the top of this short grade, but only for a short distance before heading upgrade again.

The next siding is Belton, at approximately MP 1197. Belton marks the western boundary of Glacier National Park. As you enter Belton, the speed limit drops to 45 mph, so monitor your speed closely. Past the east switch at Belton, you pass through a number of tunnels as the grade increases slightly. Pay attention to your throttle and brake settings through this stretch.

Next is the location of Red Eagle, which has a signaled passing siding and a through siding for car setouts. Next comes Pinnacle, then Essex Pit as you near the town of Essex proper. A few additional miles and you arrive at Essex at approximately MP 1169. Essex contains a small yard, a siding off the double-track mainline, and a wye track

The Pass: Essex to East Glacier

Things are literally all uphill from Essex to Summit. Uphill trains need a liberal amount of throttle to ascend the long, almost-constant grade, and downhill trains must use both dynamic brakes and air brakes to maintain westbound train speed. Watch the throttle carefully as you ascend the grade to ensure you don't exceed the 30-mph speed limit before you reach Summit

Summit features a siding and a balloon track, which is simply a loop of track used to turn trains and equipment. At Summit, the grade flattens out and the speed limit increases to 40 mph. However, just east of Summit is False Summit, which, as its name implies, creates one last uphill stretch for eastbound trains. Past False Summit, the speed limit increases to 50 mph.

At Bison, the speed limit drops from 50 mph to 35 mph. Be ready to slow your train to 35 mph as you pass the west end of Bison siding, as there's a steep descent down the east side of the pass. The speed limit varies between 35 and 45 mph for the rest of the trip down to East Glacier Park, which marks the end of serious mountain grades. At Glacier Park, there is a signaled passing track as well as two sidings and a wye track.

The East End: East Glacier to Shelby

As trains pass the switch at East Glacier, they cross the spectacular Two Medicine Bridge, the longest and highest bridge on the featured route. Less than a mile east of the bridge is the siding of Grizzly, which can serve as a meeting place for passing trains. Track speed limit here jumps to 65 mph, so go ahead and throttle up eastbound trains to take advantage.

Then, at approximately MP 1123.5, trains cross under Highway 2 overpass. Just east of the overpass is a section of snow fences, used to keep snow off the tracks during winter months. These snow fences mark the approach of the town of Browning.

The next siding east of Browning is Blackfoot. West Blackfoot marks the beginning of double track, and it includes a through siding and a wye track you can use to turn locomotives.

Just west of Cutbank, the double track returns to single track as the railroad crosses over Cutbank Creek Bridge. As you enter Cutbank, the speed limit drops sharply to 30 mph. Start slowing as you approach the bridge; time your deceleration so that you roll across the bridge into the town of Cutbank at the speed limit.

The remainder of the route into Shelby is comprised of fast track. Aside from a few short stretches of grade, both eastbound and westbound trains can make good time on this track.

The Branch Line: Columbia Falls to Kalispell

Train Simulator also includes the branch line south from Columbia Falls to Kalispell. Departing the mainline at the mill complex, the Kalispell Branch heads south through the Flathead Valley to serve industries north of the town of Kalispell. Several lumber mill spurs leave the branch in the Columbia Falls area.

South of Columbia Falls, the single track branch line heads toward Kalispell. Airport Siding, a through siding is used to store cars, but the remainder of the sidings on the branch serve industries. Kalispell Yard includes three stub tracks, a run-around track, and several industry tracks. A wye track just south of town is large enough to turn an entire branch line train of typical length.

The branch is restricted to 4-axle locomotives, which means GP38-2s only— no Dash 9's allowed. Maximum speed on the branch line is 30 mph. The branch line has minimal grades, so moving the typically short trains up and down the branch trackage is straightforward.

Freight Activity Tutorial

The freight Activity tutorial is a good exercise for those who have not yet had the chance to switch cars in sidings. As shown in Figure 4.3, the tutorial walks you through the process of making a simple setout and pickup on two sidings on the Kalispell branch.

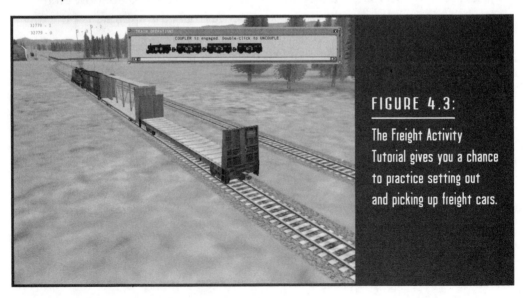

FIGURE 4.3:

The Freight Activity Tutorial gives you a chance to practice setting out and picking up freight cars.

This tutorial gives you a chance to get used to using the coupling views, and helps you get familiar with the work order in your operations notebook. Once you've mastered the art of setting out and picking up cars from sidings, you're ready to tackle the activities for the Marias Pass route.

Activity Crew Call: Columbia Falls Setout

In this Activity, you get to haul a few freight cars to Columbia Falls and set them out in a lumber mill siding. This is an easy Activity designed to allow you to get your feet wet switching cars.

ACTIVITY SUMMARY

Locomotive/Train:	GP38-2
Starting Point:	Whitefish
Ending Point:	Columbia Falls
Time of Day/light:	8:00; daylight
Difficulty Level:	Easy
Distance Covered:	Approximately 8 miles
Estimated Duration:	25 minutes

Activity Strategy

You're tasked with hauling four boxcars from the Whitefish Yard to Columbia Falls, where you will set two of them out at a mill siding. After you set out the cars, you will continue south down the branch line to terminate the Activity.

Playing the Activity

There is only one setout in this Activity, as shown in the work order in Figure 4.4. This Activity starts with your train, already assembled, in the Whitefish Yard. Run your train through the yard to the east end, where you enter the main line, as shown in Figure 4.5. Remember, the yard speed limit is only 15 mph.

FIGURE 4.4:

Columbia Falls Setout work order

FIGURE 4.5:

The signal at the east end yard lead grants you permission to enter the mainline.

The single GP38-2 on your train will have no problem moving the cars down the mainline at track speed. As you exit the yard and proceed through the crossover to the right-hand main, notch out the throttle, a couple positions at a time, until your train nears track speed. Set the throttle back notch by notch until you reach idle; once you crest the short grade east of the yard, you can easily maintain track speed using only the first one or two throttle positions.

Soon after leaving Whitefish you'll see an advanced approach (flashing yellow) signal, warning you of an approach signal a mile ahead. This is the indication that you are approaching Columbia Falls. When you pass under the overpass, prepare to slow for the branch line switch. You should negotiate this switch at no more than 30 mph. The spur for your boxcars is just past this switch; you will see an alert as soon as you enter the branch.

TIP Remember to keep your speed to 10 mph or less as you navigate through the mill complex at Columbia Falls.

The last two cars in your train need to be dropped off, so you can pull the entire train past the siding, and then back them into the spur, as shown in Figure 4.6. Use the rear-of-train view to make sure the last car in your train is past the Columbia Falls Plywood siding switch. Display track IDs using the F7 key if you are unsure which track you are supposed to use.

TIP Once south of the four-lane highway, you can resume maximum speed on the branch, which is 40 mph.

FIGURE 4.6:

Spot the last two cars in your train in the Columbia Falls Plywood spur.

NOTE It's good railroad practice to reset a track switch for the main route after using it. While there is no penalty in Train Simulator for failing to line a switch, you should try to make it a habit, just like the real crews do.

With the cars in the siding, use the Train Operations tool to uncouple the last two cars. Reverse the locomotive direction, and then proceed out of the siding and down the branch line. The Activity ends when you exit Columbia Falls to the south.

Activity Crew Call: Cutbank Grain Car Sorting

In this Activity, you get to expand your switching responsibilities considerably. You also have to navigate several sidings and other tracks to complete your switching moves.

ACTIVITY SUMMARY

Locomotive/Train:	GP38-2, two locos
Starting Point:	West of Cutbank
Ending Point:	East of Cutbank
Time of Day/light:	13:00; daylight
Difficulty Level:	Easy
Distance Covered:	Approximately 4 miles
Estimated Duration:	25 minutes

Activity Strategy

In this Activity, you operate the local train on the east end of the route near Cutbank. You need to spot a cut of grain cars at an elevator, spot a boxcar on the team track, then cross the mainline to pick up a loaded cut of train cars. Your setouts are shown in the work order, seen in Figure 4.7. Once you gather up these cars, you will proceed east toward Shelby.

FIGURE 4.7:

Cutbank Grain Car Sorting Activity work order

Playing the Activity

As the Activity starts, your train is in Run-3 moving at 25 mph as it approaches a red signal at the west end of Cutbank. Bring the train to a stop at the red signal, because you must wait for an AI train to clear the single track over the Dry Creek Bridge before proceeding into town. If you time your approach right, you can slow as the AI train clears without having to stop completely. Watch the Track Monitor for the clear signal indication.

WARNING The most difficult part of this Activity is determining the appropriate track for your car setouts. Thankfully, all the switches are lined for the appropriate tracks as you approach them. Use the F6 key to display the siding names on the screen.

As shown in Figure 4.8, you see a diverging advanced approach signal as you approach West Cutbank, indicating your train is lined into the siding. Make sure your speed is less than 30 mph.

FIGURE 4.8:

Cutbank Bridge

TIP Watch your speed on the sidings; remember most industrial tracks have a speed limit of 15 mph.

The switches are already lined for your train to enter the Cutbank Grain Elevator 1 siding, which is the destination for your grain cars. As shown in Figure 4.9, enter the siding and, with the grain cars in the clear at each end, uncouple them from the train. Proceed out of the east end of the siding, stop, line the switch behind the train to run around the grain cars, then push the boxcar straight back to the Team Track. Uncouple the boxcar and spot it on this track.

FIGURE 4.9:

Spot the grain cars between switches on the Cutbank Grain Elevator 1 siding.

With the boxcar spotted, you now need to cross over the mainline to pick up the other cut of grain cars. Proceed back down the South Siding 1 track to the east end of Cutbank, where you reenter the mainline. The crossovers at the east end of Cutbank are already lined to route your locomotives to the westbound main. Once through the crossover, pull past the opposing signals, stop, then reverse back toward Cutbank.

Your grain cars are waiting on the North Elevator 3 track; couple up to the cars, reverse direction, and proceed east out of the siding. The Activity ends when you get east of Cutbank.

Activity Crew Call: Dawn Tank Train

In this Activity, you operate a train of 23 tank cars down through Glacier Park, across the Two Medicine Bridge, and up to Spotted Robe. You must navigate a slow order speed restriction along the way.

ACTIVITY SUMMARY

Locomotive/Train:	Dash 9, two locos
Starting Point:	Glacier Park
Ending Point:	Spotted Robe
Time of Day/light:	7:10; dawn
Difficulty Level:	Easy
Distance Covered:	Approximately 5 miles
Estimated Duration:	20 minutes

Activity Strategy

The downgrade through Glacier Park is the primary challenge in this activity. Your train is stopped when you begin, so you must start the train and operate it across the bridge and east to Spotted Robe. Use your Track Monitor to watch for the temporary speed restriction.

Playing the Activity

The Activity begins with the train stopped in the west end of the siding at Glacier Park. Start the train moving toward the east end of the siding, but keep the speed below 30 mph until you are back on the mainline. Watch for deer; they seem to be in abundance this morning.

After you cross the Two Medicine Bridge you will come up to a diverging advanced approach signal at the west end of Spotted Robe. The dispatcher has lined your train into the siding so you need to proceed through the west switch no faster than 30 mph.

At MP 1134.4 you enter the slow order speed restriction. Make sure you don't exceed 15 mph through this section of track. Use the Track Monitor to watch for the upcoming restriction, and also keep watch for the yellow flag as shown in Figure 4.10. This flag indicates the start of the speed restriction.

 WARNING The uphill grade prior to the speed restriction makes it difficult to gain too much speed, but the track actually changes to downgrade during the speed restriction, making it easy for your train to accelerate past 15 mph.

FIGURE 4.10:

This yellow marker indicates the beginning of the speed restriction.

Use your dynamic brakes to keep the train speed in check as you proceed through the speed restriction. The green speed board sign, just past the signals in Figure 4.11, marks the end of the speed restriction. You must wait for your last car to exit the speed restriction before you accelerate past 15 mph. As you approach Spotted Robe, the Activity ends.

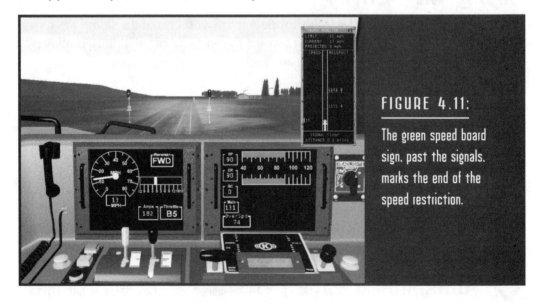

FIGURE 4.11:

The green speed board sign, past the signals, marks the end of the speed restriction.

Activity Crew Call: Grain Train through the Night

In this Activity, you simply need to take an eastbound grain train the remaining 7 miles into Essex where a relief crew is waiting. Sounds easy, right? Well, the snowy darkness adds a new twist to train operations.

ACTIVITY SUMMARY

Locomotive/Train:	Dash 9, two locos
Starting Point:	MP 1177.6, east of Red Eagle
Ending Point:	Essex
Time of Day/light:	20:30; nighttime
Difficulty Level:	Easy
Distance Covered:	Approximately 7 miles
Estimated Duration:	20 minutes

Activity Strategy

The snow and darkness make this Activity a bit more challenging—be sure to turn your headlight to bright to illuminate the track ahead. And be ready with the horn as you proceed—the wildlife does tend to come out at night, after all.

Playing the Activity

The Activity begins with your train rolling toward the end of double track at MP 1177. The signal ahead is red; as the Activity starts, you have 0.7 miles to stop your train from 21 mph. As Figure 4.12 shows, you must meet a westbound train coming off the single track before you can proceed past the red signal.

As your train proceeds onto the single track, notch out the throttle several positions to keep your speed up. The speed limit here is 40 mph; even though your train is heavy, it doesn't take long to reach maximum track speed. Throttle position N3 should be about all you need as you upgrade your speed through the tunnels.

FIGURE 4.12:

This AI train is responsible for the red signal about 0.2 miles ahead of the train.

When you near Essex you will see an advanced approach signal. Keep your speed to 40 mph as you pass this signal. As you reenter a double track railroad, you will operate down the left-hand main in preparation for your stop at Essex. You may need some extra power once you pass the signal; don't be afraid to notch the throttle out to N6 or higher to keep your train moving. Just remember, don't apply the throttle all at once or you risk slipping your wheels on the snowy rails.

 TIP The uphill grade varies as you approach Essex, so keep your eye on your speed to ensure you're making good time up the hill. Use Track Monitor to help manage your speed while moving upgrade.

Use the sander controls to help traction on the snowy track. Press the blue button on the console, just ahead of the horn button. A yellow indicator appears in the right CRT when the sand is activated.

You pass another advanced approach signal just west of Essex. Do not pass this signal moving faster than 40 mph. In fact, you should start slowing for the Essex yard switch, for as with all yards, the speed limit in the Essex Yard is 15 mph.

NOTE As you proceed through the yard, look out the cab to your left and you'll see several cabooses perched atop the hill across the tracks. These cabooses are part of the Essex Lodge, which rents them out as deluxe rooms for visiting guests.

Run your train to the east end of the yard. Stop the train before the trailing point switch. If you go past the switch, as shown in Figure 4.13, you've gone too far and the Activity won't end. If you accidentally pass this switch, simply move the reverser to the reverse position and back the train up. When you stop in the proper place, the Activity will end.

TIP Make sure you spot the train in the proper location in Essex Yard. Use Track Monitor—the dark blue line indicates the proper location to stop your train.

FIGURE 4.13:

If you get this close to the lodge, you've gone too far, as you need to spot your train west of the last yard switch.

Activity Crew Call: Morning Intermodal

In this short Activity you operate a mainline intermodal train approximately nine miles from Conkelly to Whitefish Yard. Your single locomotive should have no difficulty handling the intermodal train through the Flathead Valley.

ACTIVITY SUMMARY

Locomotive/Train:	Dash 9
Starting Point:	Conkelly
Ending Point:	Whitefish
Time of Day/light:	9:00; daylight
Difficulty Level:	Easy
Distance Covered:	Approximately 9 miles
Estimated Duration:	20 minutes

Activity Strategy

This Activity allows you to run an intermodal double-stack train the short distance between Columbia Falls and Whitefish. This is a pretty straightforward Activity, making it perfect for those without much time in the right-hand seat of the Dash 9. While playing, practice the use of the throttle and brakes and experiment with the dynamic brakes to get a sense for how they work.

Playing the Activity

You start this activity at rest on the eastbound main track, just east of the aluminum plant at Conkelly. Start your train gradually and accelerate to track speed. You will see green signals all the way into Whitefish yard, as the only opposing traffic is several eastbound AI trains on the eastbound main.

TIP Use Track Monitor to watch for changing limits. as the route between Columbia and Whitefish varies between 45 mph and 70 mph.

While operating this train, watch for the white W signs alongside the track, as shown in Figure 4.14. These indicate that you are approaching a road crossing, and you should prepare to sound the required warning signal with the horn. When you see these W signs it means you're approximately 0.25 miles away from the roadway. At track speed, the crossings appear quickly, so be ready.

 TIP Open the throttle as much as necessary to maintain track speed. without exceeding the speed limits.

FIGURE 4.14:

These W signs mean your train is approaching a road crossing. and you should prepare to blow the horn as a warning.

This required signal consists of two long blasts, one short blast, and then one long blast that should not end before you pass through the crossing, as shown in Figure 4.15.

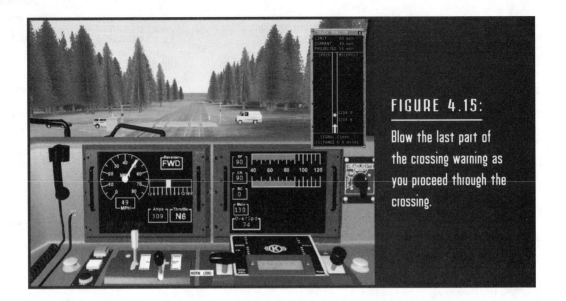

FIGURE 4.15:

Blow the last part of the crossing warning as you proceed through the crossing.

 TIP By using the space bar to blow the horn, you can quickly learn to sound the required two longs, a short, and a long as you pass over the road crossings.

You will see an approach signal as you approach Whitefish, restricting your speed to 40 mph. Slow to 30 mph as you pass this signal, then be prepared to slow your train to 15 mph as you enter Whitefish Yard.

Once at Whitefish, you need to spot your train on Whitefish Siding 1 in the Whitefish Yard. Use the Switch tool to line the switches for Siding 1, which is the furthest track from the mainline. Pull the train all the way into this yard track and stop the train, and the Activity ends.

Activity Crew Call: Setting Out Westbound Pickup

So you say you're getting the hang of mainline train operations? Well, then this Activity gives you a chance to try something different—switching cars in Whitefish Yard.

ACTIVITY SUMMARY

Locomotive/Train:	GP38-2
Starting Point:	Whitefish Yard
Ending Point:	Whitefish Yard
Time of Day/light:	11:00; daylight
Difficulty Level:	Easy
Distance Covered:	None (yard Activity)
Estimated Duration:	15 minutes

Activity Strategy

In this Activity, you spend your time switching cars in the Whitefish Yard. Here you get a chance to use the Work Order data and practice your switching techniques to sort cars onto the appropriate tracks. This Activity requires some strategic thinking about how to complete all the moves in the most efficient manner.

Playing the Activity

As with most yard activities, there is no one correct way to complete this Activity, but the instructions that follow provide a logical, valid approach. Feel free to experiment with other options.

The Activity starts with your train on the Whitefish Siding 4 track in the Whitefish Yard. Read the Activity briefing carefully, because it clearly explains the work you need to do. Your work order also states the cars you need to move, and the destinations for these cars, as shown in Figure 4.16.

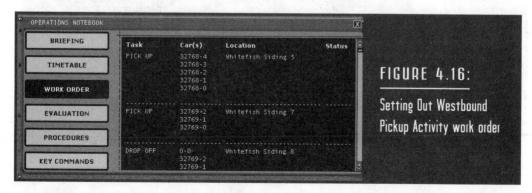

FIGURE 4.16:

Setting Out Westbound Pickup Activity work order

Run down to the west end of the yard. This is the end from which you will work this switching move. Pull the cars on track 5 first. Back into this track from the yard lead, then gently roll back to the cars and couple up.

WARNING Do not attempt to couple to the cars moving faster than 2—3 mph. If you couple too hard, you run the risk of derailing the cars. A derailment is a critical error and will cause the Activity to end.

Once coupled to the cars on Track 5, pull them back out to the yard lead and past the switch for Track 8. Once past the switch, stop the train, throw the switch, and back the entire cut into Track 8, toward the second cut of cars.

WARNING Remember, keep your speed below 15 mph at all times.

Again, use care to couple the train together. Use the Coupler view (key 6) to better gauge the distance to the standing cars. Pull both cuts, now combined, back out to the yard lead. Pull past the switch for Track 8, then stop the train. Throw the switch, then back the entire cut into Track 8, as shown in Figure 4.17.

FIGURE 4.17:

Back the combined cut of cars into Whitefish Siding 8, aka Track 8.

As you push all the cars past the yard lead switch, the Activity ends.

Activity Crew Call: Building and Sorting Outbound Cuts

The switching activities continue with a more elaborate Activity in Whitefish. This time, instead of a single cut of cars, you need to spot a collection of cars, mixed in the middle of other cars, on a track for pickup by a mainline train.

ACTIVITY SUMMARY

Locomotive/Train:	GP38-2
Starting Point:	Whitefish Yard
Ending Point:	Whitefish Yard
Time of Day/light:	15:00; rain
Difficulty Level:	Easy
Distance Covered:	None (yard Activity)
Estimated Duration:	20 minutes

Activity Strategy

In this Activity, you must pull cars from three separate tracks and assemble them on one track for pickup by a mainline train. This Activity will require you to sort out the cars you need to spot from other cars in the yard.

Playing the Activity

The Activity starts with your locomotive spotted on Track 4. The work order, shown in Figure 4.18, shows the cars you need to pick up, and the destination track they need to be spotted to.

‖‖

 TIP You may find it easier to keep the Switch tool up on screen throughout this Activity.

‖‖

FIGURE 4.18:

Building and Sorting Outbound Cuts Activity work order

First, pick up the empty bulkhead flat log car from Track 1. This car can go along for the ride while you switch out the remaining cars. Next, operate your locomotive and the log car down Track 3 to pick up the next cars.

The cars you need from Track 3 are buried in the middle of the cut. To access them, couple your locomotive and the log car onto the front of the cut. You need cars 32771-2 and 32771-3 (two green Burlington Northern boxcars). Open the Train Operations tool and uncouple the cut between cars 32771-3 and 32771-4. Pull the cars from Track 11, as shown in Figure 4.19.

 TIP Use the Coupler View (key 6) when attempting to select the proper yard track.

FIGURE 4.19:

Pull the first four cars off the cut on Track 3.

Next, pull past the Track 4 switch, throw the switch, and back your two boxcars into track four. Uncouple them, then pull the red center beam and tank car back out onto the yard lead. Throw the Track 4 switch again, back the two cars onto Track 3, and uncouple them, as shown in Figure 4.20. Then go back and couple up to the two boxcars on Track 4. At the end of this move, you should have the bulkhead flatcar and the two BN boxcars.

FIGURE 4.20:

Drop the unneeded cars back on Track 3.

Drop the three outbound cars behind your locomotive in Track 8. Uncouple them, then proceed to Track 5 to retrieve the remaining cars. Pull the entire five-car cut to the yard lead, reverse the locomotive, and back the last car, a gondola, into Track 4. Uncouple the gondola and pull forward. Push the rest of the cars back into Track 5; drop cars 32770-1 through 32770-4 back on Track 5, but keep car 32770-0. Pull this car back to the yard lead, back into Track 4 to pick up car 32770-5, then pull both down to Track 8 to spot with the others. The Activity ends when you get all five outbound cars on Track 8.

Activity Crew Call: Kalispell Setout and Pickup

In this Activity, you will drop off and pick up cars from a siding on the Kalispell Branch. This siding, used to store cars for local industries, is south of Columbia Falls.

ACTIVITY SUMMARY

Locomotive/Train:	GP38-2, two locos
Starting Point:	Columbia Falls (MP 1213.45)
Ending Point:	Kalispell Branch
Time of Day/light:	13:00; rain
Difficulty Level:	Medium
Distance Covered:	Approximately 5 miles
Estimated Duration:	25 minutes

Activity Strategy

In this Activity you need to drop off two cars and pick up two others. There are several approaches for this; the following Activity description will walk you through the most logical one.

Playing the Activity

As the Activity starts, your train is operating down the Kalispell Branch, just south of Columbia Falls. You have several miles to go before you reach the Airport Siding, where your cars are waiting.

When you approach the siding you pass your cars to be picked up, as seen in Figure 4.21. You should work this siding from the south end; this means you should pull the entire train south of the siding. Back your locomotive and two center beam cars into the siding and couple up to the cars.

 WARNING Make sure you pull the cars you need from the siding before you attempt to spot the empty center beam cars. Otherwise, you will find it rather difficult to head south with all the cars you need.

You only need the first two boxcars, and the first five woodchip cars. Use the Train Operations tool to uncouple the remaining cars. Pull the two boxcars and five woodchip cars back out onto the branch line. Once you clear the switch, back them north past the road crossing.

FIGURE 4.21:

The cars you need to pick up at Airport Siding are seen to the right of the train.

NOTE It is generally not good practice to block road crossings unless absolutely necessary. In fact, in some locations it is actually illegal for railroads to do so. Always try to spot cars clear of road crossings.

Next, uncouple the two center beam cars that came down with your locomotive from Columbia Falls, as shown in Figure 4.22. Pull these center beam cars south of the siding switch, throw the switch, then back them into the clear in the siding. Uncouple the locomotive, return to your train, and you are ready to proceed south.

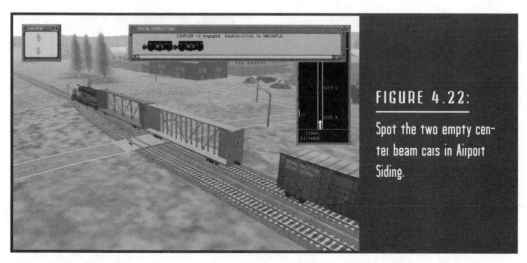

FIGURE 4.22:

Spot the two empty center beam cars in Airport Siding.

Note the slow order speed restriction just south of the Airport Siding. You need to maintain 15 mph or less while traveling through this slow order. Once you successfully pass the slow order and proceed several miles down the track, the Activity ends.

Activity Crew Call: Running with Hotbox

In this Activity, you get to deal with defective equipment, which requires you to slowly operate your train downgrade until you reach the location where you can safely set out the defective car.

ACTIVITY SUMMARY

Locomotive/Train:	Dash 9, three locos
Starting Point:	MP 1140.0
Ending Point:	Spotted Robe
Time of Day/light:	16:30; daylight
Difficulty Level:	Medium
Distance Covered:	None (yard Activity)
Estimated Duration:	30 minutes

Activity Strategy

In this Activity, you're operating a train that has developed a hotbox on the thirty-fifth axle in the train, which translates into the sixth car. Proper procedure for moving a car with a hotbox is to proceed at no more than restricted speed to the nearest setout point. In this case, that is the Hole Track at East Glacier Park.

Once you complete the setout, you will operate the train east to Spotted Robe, where the Activity ends.

HOTBOX 101

A hotbox is a railroad slang term for an overheated wheel bearing on a railcar. The term dates back to the days when freight and passenger cars used friction bearings, which consisted of bronze axle ends and bushings bathed in oil inside the truck's journal box. Friction bearings were notorious for overheating, for they were dependent upon sufficient oil in the journal box to stay lubricated. Yard crews were responsible for checking each car's journal boxes before a freight train departed a yard to ensure it had sufficient journal lubrication.

Today, virtually all North American freight cars use roller bearing trucks, which are much more resistant to overheating. But hotboxes still occur. Axle loadings on modern freight cars approach 35 tons per axle. When the bearings in either axle end stop functioning, the bearing assembly starts generating massive amounts of heat due to the friction of metal wearing on metal. If operation in this condition continues, the bearing assembly generates enough heat to start melting. As the metal melts, the truck assembly disintegrates to the point where the wheel set drops out of the truck assembly. In all but rare cases this causes a derailment as the axle wedges under adjoining car superstructures. Damage in a hotbox-induced derailment is usually severe.

Railroads have always used a number of techniques to prevent hotboxes. One of the main purposes of the conductor in a caboose was to watch for smoke from a car. This, along with the telltale odor, was solid evidence that something was amiss. Today, automatic trackside detectors watch for hotboxes using infrared heat sensing equipment. If the detector identifies an overheat condition, it broadcasts a computerized voice over the railroad road frequency channel alerting the crew and dispatcher to stop the train immediately.

Playing the Activity

When the Activity begins your train is moving at 35 mph. As soon as the game starts, slow the train down as quickly as you can to 15 mph or less. Use smooth applications of the brake—a 10-pound reduction is sufficient to slow the train. Don't make a full brake application, as you'll just vent your brake pipe air unnecessarily.

To operate at a steady downhill speed you can use the locomotive's dynamic brakes. Set the brakes to B3 or B4 to retard the train's downhill momentum. Another option is to set a five-pound air reduction on the train brakes. This will start slowing the train. Advance the throttle to N1. This sets up a situation where the locomotive is dragging the train down the grade. This "drag-braking" technique is generally frowned on because it consumes excess fuel. But in this case, with the hotbox condition, it is an acceptable way to safely bring the train down the hill.

Operate the train into Glacier Park. As shown in Figure 4.23, when you app-roach the west switch at Glacier Park, you'll see a diverging advanced approach signal, indicating that your train is lined into the siding. An AI train is waiting on the main to continue its westward journey, as shown in Figure 4.24. Operate at restricted speed down to the west side of the Glacier Park Hole Track switch.

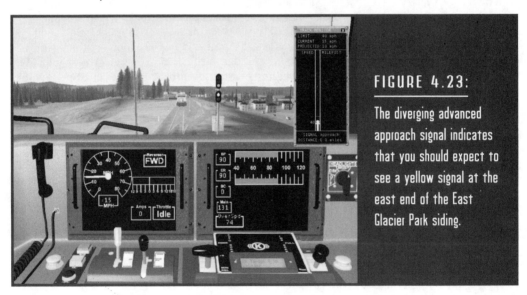

FIGURE 4.23:

The diverging advanced approach signal indicates that you should expect to see a yellow signal at the east end of the East Glacier Park siding.

Once there, cut the train between the sixth and seventh auto rack car. Pull the front portion of your train past the switch, line the switch for the Hole Track, then push the defective autorack into the siding. Spot the car in the spur, uncouple it, then pull forward back to the siding. Reassemble your train and head east.

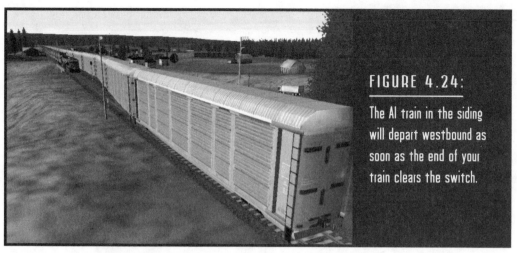

FIGURE 4.24:

The AI train in the siding will depart westbound as soon as the end of your train clears the switch.

Beyond East Glacier, you operate the train across Two Medicine Bridge and up to the Spotted Robe siding. Once you arrive at Spotted Robe, the Activity ends.

Activity Crew Call:
Auto Train with Setout

In this Activity you have another hotbox to deal with as your train descends the west slope of Marias Pass.

ACTIVITY SUMMARY

Locomotive/Train:	Dash 9, two locos
Starting Point:	West Java
Ending Point:	Coram
Time of Day/light:	10:00; rain
Difficulty Level:	Hard
Distance Covered:	Approximately 31 miles
Estimated Duration:	30 minutes

Activity Strategy

In this Activity, you have another auto rack with a hotbox. This time, you will operate this car downgrade to Essex, where you need to set it out in the yard. After you set the car out, you'll reassemble your train and continue west to Coram.

Playing the Activity

The Activity starts with your train headed downgrade from West Java toward Essex. The dispatcher has already lined you into the Essex Yard so you can set out the defective auto rack. Slow to 15 mph as you approach the switch into Essex Yard, so that you don't exceed the speed limit.

Once you enter Essex Yard, pull your train down to the west end of the yard. Stop the train at the west end, then cut off the first 16 cars. Pull these cars ahead, past the switch to Essex Siding 2, then back the train into this siding. Spot the car between the wye track legs, adjacent to the Essex Siding 2 label, as shown in Figure 4.25.

 WARNING Use care when switching the auto racks. Due to their expensive cargo, these cars have a low freight durability level and are subject to damage if handled too abruptly.

FIGURE 4.25:

Spot car 0-16 on Essex Siding 2, between the wye tracks as shown.

Reassemble your train and then depart Essex westbound, minding the downgrade. The rest of the trip down to Coram is uneventful. Use care as you operate the train down the west side of the pass; use dynamic brakes and air brakes in combination, as necessary, to keep the train in check. The Activity ends when you reach Coram.

Activity Crew Call: Noon Mixed Freight

In this Activity you get to operate a mainline mixed freight over Marias Pass and down the west slope into Pinnacle. This Activity gives you a great opportunity to test your throttle and brake skills as you attempt to keep your heavy train in check on the mountain pass.

ACTIVITY SUMMARY

Locomotive/Train:	Dash 9, two locos
Starting Point:	Glacier Park
Ending Point:	MP 1177.6
Time of Day/light:	12:00; snow
Difficulty Level:	Hard
Distance Covered:	Approximately 42 miles
Estimated Duration:	90 minutes

Activity Strategy

In this Activity you need to stay engaged as your train operates up and over the pass. The east approach is generally uphill, but there are a few downgrade stretches as well, so be alert. The descent down the west slope is long and steep; you'll need both your dynamic brakes and air brakes to safely navigate this stretch of track.

Playing the Activity

As the Activity starts, your train is just starting up the grade from East Glacier Park. The throttle is set to N1 and the train is only moving approximately 10 mph. Notch the throttle out to N6 to keep the train moving upgrade near track speed.

WARNING The train has a tendency to run away down the west slope—a minute or less of inattention can leave your train out of control. Watch your projected speed in Track Monitor to help keep things in check.

You will need to use the combined power handle to apply both throttle and dynamic brakes to successfully ascend the east slope of the pass. The majority of the route is upgrade, but there are the occasional sags where the train wants to pick up speed. To use the dynamics, place the handle in SETUP until you see a yellow current reading, then move the handle to a brake position.

At MP 1142.2, you enter the siding with a diverging advanced approach signal. As you enter the siding, notch the throttle out to N8 because you will need full throttle to move your train up the upcoming grade. You soon traverse a stretch of downhill track—don't be deceived, you are not yet at the summit. Use dynamic brakes to keep the train in check in this stretch. You'll pass an AI train along the way, as shown in Figure 4.26.

FIGURE 4.26:

An AI train waits in the siding at East Summit.

 TIP You will see green signals all the way down the hill, so there is no need to worry about sudden stops for other trains.

The descent west of Summit has no surprises, but you still need to pay attention here. Use your dynamic brakes to keep train speed in check. The speed limit on the west slope is 25 mph; you may need some air brakes as well as dynamics to keep the train speed below the limit. It's a long, downhill run, and there are some stretches where you really need to stay alert to keep your train under control.

At Essex you need to set out the third locomotive in your consist in Whitefish Siding 2. Use the Train Operations tool to uncouple the locomotive, then re-assemble your train and head west. The Activity ends when you pull onto the westbound main track at MP 1177.6, stopping your train with the last car clear of the switch, as shown in Figure 4.27.

FIGURE 4.27:

Spot your train clear of the switch to end the Activity.

Activity Crew Call: Whitefish Yard Switching

In this Activity, you get to experience the life of the Whitefish yard crew as they sort cars in the yard. This Activity will take some time—plan for longer than the stated time in the Activity summary.

ACTIVITY SUMMARY

Locomotive/Train:	GP38-2
Starting Point:	Whitefish Yard
Ending Point:	Whitefish Yard
Time of Day/light:	17:00; late afternoon
Difficulty Level:	Hard
Distance Covered:	None (yard Activity)
Estimated Duration:	60 minutes

Activity Strategy

You are trying to accomplish two objectives:

- Sort inbound cars off the Kalispell and Columbia Falls local trains so they can be picked up by mainline trains. You will assemble an eastbound cut and a westbound cut, per the cars' destination out of Whitefish Yard

- Sort inbound cars off mainline trains for the two locals the next day. You need to build the Kalispell Local and the Columbia Falls Local.

As shown in the timetable in Figure 4.28, there are a lot of cars to switch out in Whitefish.

FIGURE 4.28:

Whitefish Yard Activity work order

Playing the Activity

There is no one "right" way to play this yard Activity. As in real life, there are a large number of switching moves necessary to sort all the cars in the yard. Make sure you take time to look around before you begin switching. Use the Track ID and Car ID views, as shown in Figure 4.29.

FIGURE 4.29:

Use the Track ID view (F6) and the Car ID view (F7) to determine the location of all the tracks and cars.

There are some suggested approaches for completing this Activity, though. First, work one track at a time. Sort all the relevant cars off that one track to their appropriate destination tracks. Work this entire track until you have all the cars on that track sorted, then move on to the remaining tracks. You have two GP38-2s at your disposal, so don't hesitate pulling entire cuts of cars from a yard track.

There are two cars that are destined for the "rip track" for repair—32771-3 and 32771-4. These cars are damaged and in need of repairs before they can continue on their way. There is also a tank car (32770-15) that is destined for the fuel rack at the engine facility, across the main line. You need to spot your locomotives at the engine facility when you're done, so save this tank car for last.

Off Duty

Hopefully by now you have completed all of the Marias Pass route activities. Freight activities are difficult—heavy trains often seem to have a mind of their own. In the next chapter you get to operate passenger trains again, this time on Japan's Hisatsu route.

After your stint on Marias, the visit to Japan will be a nice change.

Chapter 5

Operating Japan's Hisatsu Line

*T*he Hisatsu Line is one of the more challenging routes in Train Simulator. The KIHA 31 is more difficult to operate than the other modern locomotives, and the route is very challenging, with steep grades, switchbacks, and tight turns. It's quite easy to derail your train if you don't manage your speed carefully on these mountain curves! Both sightseeing and commuter passenger service are offered in this route's Activities. The terrain itself makes this difficult route a joy to operate.

Route Description

The historic Hisatsu line offers scenic passenger excursion service on the island of Kyushu, the third largest of the Japanese Islands. Located off the southernmost tip of the main island, Honshu, Kyushu enjoys a lush landscape with a slightly more temperate climate than that of Honshu. Like all of the Japanese islands, the landscape is defined by the volcanic mountaintops at its center. The Hisatsu line cuts through the very heart of those mountains (see Figure 5.1) on a direct route to the protected southern port of Kagoshima. This route gives the line a staggering 537-meter rise along its 100-km length, much of it over the 40 km-long mountain portion. To accomplish this, the line makes use of two switchbacks and one loop to help trains handle the grade. Even so, your train will frequently struggle up the steep grades, and you'll get very good with the brake bar.

FIGURE 5.1:

It's easy to see why the route offers sightseeing excursions, with wonderful views all along its length.

The special KIHA 31 excursion locomotive is the only engine (or consist, for that matter) normally available on the Hisatsu route. These workhorses are true diesels, with a physical drive system instead of electric motive power. The Engine Brake is exclusive to this engine type in *Train Simulator*, and it can help keep speed under control on the long downgrades.

History

The Hisatsu Line was constructed at great financial and human cost. Laid in the first decade of the twentieth century, the line served as the main overland connection to the southern end of the island. The treacherous alpine cliffs and numerous tunnels required for the roadbed claimed the lives of many builders, and plaques on either end of the impressive Yatake Tunnel commemorate the hardships of the route's construction.

NOTE Trains on the Hisatsu Line are nicknamed for the Yatake Tunnel plaque they face on their run, after the men who placed them. Southbound trains are named "Isaburo" after Isaburo Yamagata, and northbound trains are named "Shinpei" after Shinpei Goto.

The Japanese National Railway operated the Hisatsu Line up until the national rail system's privatization in 1987. Steam engines plied the steep grades with regular passenger and freight service for many decades. Eventually, the longer but flatter JR Kagoshima coastal line superceded the Hisatsu route, as modern high-speed trains overcame the extra mileage.

Today

With 13 round trips per day, the JR Kagoshima Line has taken over passenger through service from Kumamoto to Kagoshima and the south coast. JR Kyushu continues to operate local commuter service between Yatsushiro and Hitoyoshi. The company also operates scenic tours and excursion trips up the winding Mountain Line, and even runs occasional historic steam train tours on the route for tourists and rail enthusiasts alike. The Isaburo/Shinpei sightseeing train makes extra long stops at scenic vistas, allowing passengers to get out and take a look before moving on. The route is credited with one of the three best railroad views in all of Japan's proud rail network.

Route Tour: Train Simulator's Hisatsu Route

Train Simulator models the JR Hisatsu Line from its origin in Yatsushiro in the north to the city of Yoshimatsu in the south, nestled in the mountains above Kagoshima Bay (Figure 5.2). Daunting grades make work for the engineer going up and coming down, and several station stops on the northern half of the route offer you the chance to experience passenger commuter service in a true diesel locomotive.

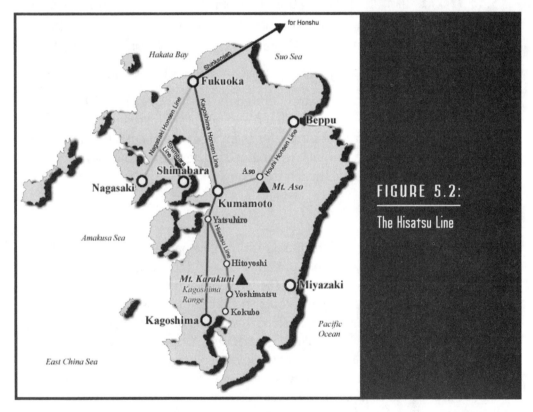

FIGURE 5.2:

The Hisatsu Line

The Hisatsu Line is traditionally divided into two distinct halves, the first of which is the River Line, north of Hitoyoshi, which snakes alongside the Kuma river. South of Hitoyoshi the route is called the Mountain Line because of the steep grades that climb more than 300 meters over a run of just 23 km! The following sections provide you with an overview of the route from north to south, divided into its two distinct segments. The stations on the line are summarized in the following table.

STATION NAME	MILEPOST LOCATION	NOTES
Yatsushiro	0.5	Northern end of route
Dan	7.2	—
Sakamoto	12.6	Several sidings
Haki	15.9	—
Kamase	19.3	—
Setoishi	21.8	Includes siding
Kaiji	23.5	—
Yoshio	25.8	—
Shiroishi	29.4	Small through yard
Kyusendo	34.6	—
Isshochi	40.3	Includes siding
Naraguchi	42.7	—
Watari	45.7	Includes siding
Nishihitoyoshi	49	—
Hitoyoshi	52.5	Border between River and Mountain sections
Okoba	62	Switchback and loop
Yatake	71.9	Highest point on route: Yatake Tunnel
Masaki	77.2	Switchback
Yoshimatsu	85	Southern end of route

The River Line

The northern half of the Hisatsu Line winds along the floor of the Kuma River Valley on its way up the Kagoshima Mountain Range. The River Line has no less than 24 tunnels along its 51 km route between Yatsushiro and Hitoyoshi—about one tunnel every mile! This attractive river valley is beautifully modeled in *Train Simulator*, and is a strong candidate for some of the best photo opportunities in the game courtesy of the Print Screen key.

NOTE If you choose to take screenshots with Train Simulator's built-in screenshot key, be sure to examine and save your work as soon as you leave the game (or even immediately after taking the shot, by hitting Alt-Tab). Every game session, Train Simulator starts its screenshots over with the number 0, overwriting any previously captured shots.

The River Line originates in the seaside town of Yatsushiro, on a bay facing the East China Sea (see Figure 5.3). After leaving the flat river delta, there's an overall gradual climb headed south from Yatsushiro. Small villages are served by open-air platforms along the line, separated by tunnels and trestles as the roadbed winds up the valley. The speed limit is 85 throughout the River Line, but many of the curves require a prudent speed as low as 50 km/h to negotiate safely. The first tight turns are between Mileposts 10 and 11, so watch for signs recommending lower speeds.

FIGURE 5.3:

Looking due east from Yatsushiro toward the volcanic Kagoshima Mountain Range.

At about MP 15, just north of Haki, a short downgrade can catch new crews unawares, so check your throttle after departing Haki. Conversely, ramp up for the incline if you're headed northbound from Kamase. The line is very straight through Kamase Station, allowing high-speed operation, but be ready for the sharp turn just after the station. Another pair of short curves follows a kilometer down the line, north of Setoishi.

TIP Sound your horn as you approach tunnel entrances and exits to warn any people or animals that happen to be on the tracks. You'll frequently encounter deer on the tracks on the Hisatsu Line, because it traverses rural and unsettled areas for its entire length. Be sure to operate your headlight even during the day to provide illumination in the tunnels.

MP 25, outside of Yoshio, marks the next stretch of straight track. Gentle curves for the next 10 km enable high-speed operation all the way to Kyusendo. There, slow for an S-curve at MP 35.5, but you may then run fast again through MP 40, just before Isshochi. The leg between Isshochi and Naraguchi stations has some of the sharpest curves on the River Line, and requires careful speed management. Once clear, however, it's fast running all the way to the Hitoyoshi approach (see Figure 5.4).

FIGURE 5.4:

The town of Hitoyoshi is the largest stop between Yatsushiro and Yoshimatsu.

The steep grades of the Mountain Line begin even before you reach Hitoyoshi. Sometimes, the grade may require downshifting to first gear if you cannot maintain 50 km/h in second. A sharp curve just before the station requires prudent speeds from through trains; even if you are not stopping in Hitoyoshi, slow to 50 km/h for the turn. Once you pass the station in Hitoyoshi, you're on the mountain section of the line.

The Mountain Line

The Hisatsu Mountain Line is all up, and all down. A 300-meter rise over approximately 20 kilometers means an average 1.3% grade over the entire distance, which is quite steep for a railroad. The stations between Hitoyoshi and the end of the line are primarily switching stations, in place only to service the route at critical points. The small community of Yatake is at the line's summit (see Figure 5.5), but it consists mostly of vacation homes and small resort facilities.

FIGURE 5.5:

The village of Yatake, just north of the historic tunnel of the same name

The Okoba station is nestled in a small saddle overlooking the Kyushu countryside; it is a popular stop for the sightseers. The station oversees the operation of the route's northern switchback, and includes a loop that helps distribute the particularly steep grade on this leg.

At the line's summit is the historic Yatake Tunnel, which is over 2 km long. Constructing the tunnel took a painstaking three years and two months to build, and many workers lost their lives completing it. Just south of the long Yatake Tunnel is a fantastic scenic stop, overlooking a beautiful valley in the heart of the mountain range. Sightseeing trains often have scheduled stops on this lookout, even though there are no improvements or a platform.

On the southern slope, the Masaki switchback lies in a secluded alpine valley. Scenic stops are usually scheduled at the platform before continuing down the southern slope to the town of Yoshimatsu. The end of the line has maintenance facilities and two sidings, and also serves as a junction with a branch railroad with service to Miyakonjo and Shibushi to the south.

Passenger Activity Tutorial

The Hisatsu tutorial offers you a good introduction to passenger operations on the mountainous Hisatsu line. The true diesel KIHA 31 is a unique engine, so it's worthwhile to go through the short introductory ride to get a feel for the controls. The programmed instruction will walk you through a short passenger run with pop-up windows describing every step of the action.

Activity Crew Call: Quake Damaged Track

A minor earthquake has caused some damage to the line. Several slow order zones are in effect while maintenance crews inspect and repair the affected areas, forcing you to use caution along your evening run.

ACTIVITY SUMMARY

Locomotive/Train:	KIHA 31
Starting Point:	Sakamoto
Ending Point:	Shiroishi
Time of Day/light:	18:28; spring/clear
Difficulty Level:	Easy
Distance Covered:	16.8 km
Estimated Duration:	30 minutes

Activity Strategy

Some areas of the track are still being assessed, so you may receive notification of emergency reduced speed zones while en route. You'll have to maintain high speeds on the unrestricted portions of the line to help make up for time lost.

Special speed zones:

- 25 between Mileposts 13.9 and 15.1

- 25 between Mileposts 19.7 and 20.8

Playing the Activity

It's dusk, so turn on your headlight to full illumination by hitting the H key twice, or clicking the switch with your mouse cursor. Driving the KIHA 31 is a lot like driving a car, with two gears, a throttle, and brakes. Remember that the unique drive system in the KIHA 31 gives you a few more control considerations, as you can leave the transmission in gear on descents and use the crankshaft to slow your train.

Some of the platforms are slightly in front of the point indicated by your Next Station Display on this route, so stop a little earlier than you normally would. Aim for the center of each platform, using your views more than your Next Station Display for reference. Pull off the siding you start on and head for your first station call at Haki. Get up to speed, transitioning to 100% throttle in first gear, and shifting to second gear at around 45 km/h, which should be before the first tunnel (see Figure 5.6). Idle the engine and begin to slow as soon as you exit the first tunnel in preparation for the first emergency slow order zone. Leave the engine in second gear and press P to activate the engine brake, assisting your deceleration.

FIGURE 5.6:

The first emergency zone is on the far side of the first tunnel.

Alternating between 20% and 40% throttle in first gear should maintain 25 km/h throughout the slow order zone. Be sure to stay at 24 or less to allow yourself time to react in case your train starts accelerating down a grade. After you clear the slow order zone, accelerate until you're approximately 0.35 km away from the Haki station. Cut the throttle, but stay in gear, which helps the KIHA 31 slow down. Apply your brakes smoothly, and settle to a stop beside the platform.

Accelerate up to track speed quickly after you depart Haki. You can maintain a speed close to the 85 limit all the way through MP 19 at 80% to 100% throttle in second gear. Use engine braking to help your train slow for the platform, applying brakes when you're within about 0.2 km. Another emergency zone lies beyond the station (see Figure 5.7), so you won't be able to reach track speed before slowing down again; get up to about 35 before applying the engine brake to negotiate the slow order zone under 25.

FIGURE 5.7:

The second slow order zone begins on the far side of this bridge, at the mouth of the tunnel beyond.

Accelerate to 80 after the speed restriction is lifted, but remember your next stop at Setoishi. Your last stops are uneventful; use 60% to 80% throttle to maintain 80 on the straightaways between stations, using engine braking to drop down to 70 before the turns. If you stay under the speed limit in the emergency zones, you should complete this Activity without trouble.

Activity Crew Call: Short Passenger Run

This simple Activity puts you on a three-stop commuter run from Watari to Isshochi under normal operating conditions.

ACTIVITY SUMMARY

Locomotive/Train:	KIHA 31
Starting Point:	Watari
Ending Point:	Isshochi
Time of Day/light:	18:30: spring/clear
Difficulty Level:	Easy
Distance Covered:	5.4 km
Estimated Duration:	15 minutes

Activity Strategy

The run from Watari to Isshochi is fast at the front end and very tight at the back, which will help hone your speed management skills for the much steeper grades and sharper turns on the Mountain Line. Your schedule is somewhat tight, so use full throttle to get up to track speed. Stay close to the speed limit between the first two stations, as this portion of the line is relatively straight. The last leg requires braking to avoid derailment on the tight turns.

Playing the Activity

Get up to speed as soon as you start the Activity to make your scheduled arrival at Watari. Getting a KIHA 31 running is the most complicated task of all the modern locomotives—only steam engines require more work. Turn on your headlights, throw the reverser forward, release your brakes, put it in gear, and throttle up. Shift into second gear as soon as you're past 40 km/h, and maintain 100% throttle until you're at 80 km/h.

WARNING The KIHA 31 brakes much slower than you'd expect from a two-unit consist, so apply brakes early, as if you were operating at the head of a much longer train.

Get up to track speed quickly on the way to the next station. Just as you claw your way up to 80 km/h, you'll encounter a downgrade (see Figure 5.8) that can put you overspeed quickly if you don't back off the throttle. Use the throttle to maintain a speed of about 83 until you're just 0.3 km away from Naraguchi, then cut your throttle and prepare to brake. Apply 100% brakes just before you reach a distance of 0.2 km, bringing you to a stop at the platform for an on-time arrival.

FIGURE 5.8:

Watch your speed as you traverse this bridge, which is in the middle of the downgrade just north of Watari.

The last leg of your journey is more complicated, because the track curves are tighter, forcing lower speeds. Accelerate to a speed of 70 out of Naraguchi in anticipation of the turns. Although the track speed limit is 80, you'll see a sign at the beginning of the first tunnel recommending 50. As with any signage, take it seriously—apply engine braking to drop down to 50. If you aren't below 60 by the next tunnel, you'll run the risk of a tunnel derailment, which is an especially devastating accident.

You can open up again for a few hundred meters after the tunnel turn, but slow down as you approach MP 41. Another tight turn requires a speed under 50, and your destination station of Isshochi lies at the far end of the bend. Apply your brakes 0.14 km away from the platform, as it requires less distance to brake from the moderate speed of 50. Settle to a stop at the end of the platform for a successful run!

Activity Crew Call: Isaburo

In this Activity, you'll be operating the Isaburo sightseeing train up the Mountain Line. Long passenger stops at your station calls allow the tourists to get out and enjoy the view, so bring a book! A few slow speed zones are in effect along the route.

ACTIVITY SUMMARY

Locomotive/Train:	KIHA 31 Isaburo/Shinpei
Starting Point:	Hitoyoshi
Ending Point:	Yoshimatsu
Time of Day/light:	13:30; summer/clear
Difficulty Level:	Medium
Distance Covered:	33 km
Estimated Duration:	1 hour

Activity Strategy

You're operating a sightseeing train, so your objective is somewhat different than commuter runs, which are scheduled to get passengers to their destinations as quickly as possible. The Isaburo is more about the trip itself than the destination, so your timetable is scheduled to allow for a leisurely pace between stations. Your target track speed is about 55 km/h, or slightly more if you need to make up time between stations.

Special speed zones:

- 25 between Mileposts 72.3 and 73

- 25 between Mileposts 81.2 and 82

Playing the Activity

Hitoyoshi is situated in a large mountain valley, and you will actually encounter downgrades for the first several kilometers of your run up the mountain. Accelerate to 55 km/h when you hear the all-clear buzzer. Watch your projected speed in the Track Monitor to dictate your throttle settings. Because you have plenty of time to get between stations and you won't be pressing the speed limit, you won't have to apply brakes. If you coast to 65, just make it up by spending some time at 50 or so on one of the more scenic stretches of the line.

The stop at Okoba encompasses many of the unique features of the Mountain Line. The panoramic view to the north of the station is typical of the fantastic scenes visible from the line, and switchbacks like the one at this station are unique to the Hisatsu route in *Train Simulator*. When you complete your passenger service at the platform, you'll have to back up to use the switchback. This is indicated by the white arrow that reverses upon itself in the Track Monitor.

To reverse the train, make sure the engine is idling and out of gear, then toggle the reverser. Use a light touch on the throttle to start rolling downhill, then go back to idle again, relying on gravity to keep you going. Use the train brake to keep your speed under 25 while you roll on the switchback.

 TIP For a better view of your switching activities, press 2 and rotate the view with the arrow keys until you're looking toward the rear of the train.

As soon as you've cleared the switch, apply 50% brakes. Because you're probably out of the cab view, use the keyboard shortcut keys (the ; and ' keys) to apply the brakes. Note that the keyboard gives you much finer control of the brakes, which really means it takes a lot longer to change brake settings than it does when you're using the mouse in the cab. This means you must start your braking early. You should stop about 50 meters back from the switch, as shown in Figure 5.9. Note the white reversing arrow in the figure describing the maneuver.

When the signal turns green at the siding, you may proceed up the pass. Use first gear if you drop below 45 km/h on the way up. Make your scheduled station call in Yatake, and use a light touch on the throttle on your departure. The grade switches to a downhill slope here, so use gravity to pull you along.

FIGURE 5.9:

Use the exterior view to see where you're going as you move in reverse to navigate the switch.

Immediately after the station, you'll hit a slow order zone at the mouth of the Yatake Tunnel, so get on your brakes to keep your speed down. The speed zone ends within the tunnel, so keep an eye on the Track Monitor in anticipation of the end of the zone. You can operate at up to 60 km/h for the remainder of the way toward Masaki, where you must stop and navigate the switchback.

After Masaki, you should maintain 65 km/h on the straightaways in anticipation of the slow order zone at the end of the line. This will cost you precious time at the end of your run, after which you will not be able to make up time. Stack up a buffer in front of the restricted zone by being a little faster on the descent from the Masaki switchback. If you can get down the mountain relatively quickly, you should have no trouble making your scheduled arrival at the end of the line in Yoshimatsu.

Activity Crew Call: Low Fuel

A malfunction in the fueling system at Yoshimatsu has prevented you from refueling your train on the southern end of the line. You'll have to operate very efficiently if you are to make it to Hitoyoshi without running out of fuel.

ACTIVITY SUMMARY

Locomotive/Train:	KIHA 31 Isaburo/Shinpei
Starting Point:	Yoshimatsu
Ending Point:	Hitoyoshi
Time of Day/light:	15:25: autumn/clear
Difficulty Level:	Medium
Distance Covered:	33 km
Estimated Duration:	55 minutes

Activity Strategy

You can complete this activity successfully by using minimal throttle applications, and coasting whenever possible. Use 20% throttle to get rolling, and use gravity on the downhill portions of the route instead of throttle to accelerate. Use second gear whenever under light load, and make use of first gear when ascending grades, even though that means suffering low speeds. Your only station stop is at your destination, so focus on running the line with a maximum conservation of momentum.

Playing the Activity

Start with 20% throttle out of Yoshimatsu Station, and accelerate to 35 km/h in first gear. Every 8 seconds or so, notch up the throttle by 20% until you are at 100%. The timing is right if you're throttling up just after your projected speed begins to drop below your current speed. Although you should usually shift to second gear at about 45, do it early at 35—40 to trade acceleration for efficiency. Continue to accelerate to 80 on the gentle grade on the way out of Yoshimatsu.

NOTE Operating efficiently means spending fuel to maintain your speed instead of spending it to accelerate. It's hard to get a train going, but it takes much less energy to keep it rolling once it's started.

Throttle down to 80% to maintain speed once you've accelerated. Don't go to 100% again, even if that means letting your speed drop down to 70. You should be able to maintain 70–80 with a throttle of 60% to 80%. Throttle down to 60% whenever your projected speed is more than 15 km/h faster than your current speed (wasting fuel accelerating quickly). Conversely, throttle up to 80% if your projected speed drops more than 10 km/h below your current speed (wasting fuel by letting go of too much momentum).

Around MP 80, the grade becomes steeper, and you'll need 80% throttle all the time. Even still, you'll slowly drop off toward 60 km/h. Once you are slower than 60, *cut* your throttle to 40%. You'll be approaching the first switchback by this time, and you will have wasted no fuel if you hardly have to apply any brakes to stop at the turnaround. When you reach a speed of 35, shift into first gear, but maintain 60% throttle. Despite the indications of your projected speed, you should be able to maintain 30–35 at this setting.

You should be at about 25 by the time you reach the Masaki platform. Cut your throttle as soon as you pass the switch before the station (see Figure 5.10), shift into neutral, and apply your brakes. After you come to a complete stop, release your brakes and allow the train to roll back the other way to begin the switchback (you may have to throw the reverser and give the throttle a quick 20% bump to get rolling). Apply 20% brakes at 20 km/h, then increase to full brakes when your nose hits the northbound mainline.

FIGURE 5.10:

The switchback at Masaki Station, in the shadow of the Kagoshima Mountains

Come to a complete stop, then release your brakes and gently accelerate northward again (remember to throw the reverser if you put it in reverse for the switch). 80% throttle will only get you 40 km/h in first gear on the next stretch of track, and the grade is too steep to use second gear. Don't fight it; just park the controls in first at 80% throttle and approach the summit at Yatake at 40 km/h. At around MP 75 you'll be able to drop down to 60% throttle and maintain your speed thanks to a reduced grade.

At the summit, the Activity's challenge shifts from throttle management to brake management. Shift into second gear as you pass through Yatake Station, and drop your throttle to idle as soon as you begin the descent down the northern slope of the line, which begins just after the station platform. Using light brake applications and releases, keep the train at about 65 km/h down the slope.

Brake to 60 for the S-curve north of MP 69. Decelerate all the way down to 50 as you approach MP 66, as one of the sharpest S-curves on the line lies over the next kilometer. Stay slow after the turn, because the Okoba loop is another kilometer down the hill. Negotiate the loop under 40 km/h, slowing to a yard speed of 20 by the time you sight the station, just after MP 63. After you run the Okoba switchback, you can roll all the way into Hitoyoshi at up to 75 km/h if you have to make up time. You may have to apply some power beginning at MP 55. Pull into the station gently, and pat yourself on the back for making the run over the mountain and back without refueling!

Activity Crew Call: Shinpei

Guide the Shinpei sightseeing train down the Mountain Line from Yoshimatsu, making sightseeing stops along the way. Temporary reduced speed zones along the way require careful brake management.

ACTIVITY SUMMARY

Locomotive/Train:	KIHA 31 Isaburo/Shinpei
Starting Point:	Yoshimatsu
Ending Point:	Hitoyoshi
Time of Day/light:	15:25; summer/clear
Difficulty Level:	Medium
Distance Covered:	33 km
Estimated Duration:	One hour, 25 minutes

Activity Strategy

Like the Isaburo Activity, you want to maintain a leisurely pace on this route, allowing the passengers to take in the landscape as it passes by. There are, however, three temporary slow order zones in effect on the line, so you'll want to run a little faster than usual—up to 70 km/h on the straightaways, as your schedule dictates.

Special stops:

- Stop for two minutes between Mileposts 64.2 and 64.3
- Stop for two minutes between Mileposts 74.4 and 74.5

Special speed zones:

- 25 between Mileposts 56.7 and 59.4
- 25 between Mileposts 64.6 and 69.3
- 25 between Mileposts 78.1 and 81.9

Playing the Activity

Because you are traveling over the same exact route as the Low Fuel Activity, you can refer to that walkthrough for a step-by-step account of the line between Yoshimatsu and Hitoyoshi. However, with a full tank of diesel, you're free to use liberal throttle applications to maintain your schedule. You'll also be making two station calls along the way, at each of the switchback platforms, in addition to your sightseeing stops.

 TIP Use F6 to display the precise location of the scenic overlooks in the simulator, and come to a full stop within the specified zone.

Your only other considerations are the slow order zones on the route, which will cost you some time. The first two are easy to observe, because they are centered around the switchbacks. The first restricted zone is at Masaki on the uphill grade, which will help you slow your train. Be sure to slow early for the second two zones, which are on the downhill grade. The second slow zone is just before Okoba Station (see Figure 5.11), so brake a little early for the Okoba loop. The last slow order zone is at the end of the mountain pass as you emerge into the Hitoyoshi valley.

FIGURE 5.11:

The second slow order zone is centered around scenic Okoba Station.

Pay close attention to the time as you approach each station, comparing distance to station with the current time. You have an average of about two and a half minutes per kilometer on this Activity, so if you're 5 km away from Okoba and you're supposed to be there in 10 minutes, you know you're running behind. Pick up your speed between stops to make up time, but be careful not to jar the passengers with sudden acceleration or stops—they are on this route for a relaxing excursion, after all! If you can manage to avoid being delayed too much by the slow order zones (particularly the last one), you can pull into Hitoyoshi right on time.

Activity Crew Call: Westbound River View in the Spring

This challenging scenario puts you on an evening commuter run on the northern end of the line. Several signals have failed along the way, and slow order zones are in effect while maintenance crews work on the problem.

ACTIVITY SUMMARY

Locomotive/Train:	KIHA 31
Starting Point:	Nishi-Hitoyoshi
Ending Point:	Yatsushiru
Time of Day/light:	20:20
Difficulty Level:	Hard
Distance Covered:	49 km
Estimated Duration:	One hour, 20 minutes

Activity Strategy

A tight evening schedule, two reduced speed zones, and two signal failures spell a hard night's work for you on this commuter run down the length of the River Line. Come to a complete stop before the failed signals, and press Tab to request permission to pass. This activity requires strong train handling skills, as you've got a triple challenge. Use full throttle and full brakes in and out of the stations to maintain your tight schedule, and be careful to observe the failed signals.

Signal failures:

- At MP 41.3

- At MP 2.6

Special speed zones:

- 25 between Mileposts 28.0 and 26.9

- 25 between Mileposts 24.5 and 22.4

Playing the Activity

Begin by smoothly accelerating away from the Nishihitoyoshi platform using 100% throttle applied in stages. Use the downgrade to help you accelerate to 80 before braking when you are 0.3 km above Watari Station. Accelerate hard again on departure, and brake at MP 43 for the stop at Naraguchi. You'll have to stay below 40 for the next leg of the route, stopping before the tunnel to observe the broken signal at MP 41.3. This comes up rather quickly after the first turn below Naraguchi Station, so be prepared for it.

WARNING Failure to stop at a failed or stop signal immediately ends the activity, so be sure you stop!

Once you get permission to pass (see Figure 5.12), open up the throttle and speed down the line at 75 km/h until you pass MP 37.5. Cut the throttle and brake down to 50 before negotiating the turns above Kyusendo. Don't bother accelerating again after the turn; glide your way into the station for your scheduled stop.

FIGURE 5.12:

Passing the broken signal below Naraguchi Station.

You can run your train fast again through Shiroishi station at MP 29.4, but be prepared for the slow order zone immediately beyond the station. This extends through what is normally a high speed zone to Yoshio station, but you'll only be able to accelerate to about 40 before braking again for the station when you are about 0.16 km away from the platform. Another slow order zone is on the other side of Yoshio, so don't accelerate above 40 upon departure. You'll have about a kilometer and a half to accelerate and then slow down again, and the speed sign comes up somewhat unexpectedly around the turn.

The rest of the run is a standard trip down the River Line until you reach the JR Kagoshima junction, on the approach to Yatsushiro. The signal at the junction is also malfunctioning, and you will have to wait for a mainline train to clear the track before receiving permission to proceed. Wait for the train to pass, then press Tab again to ask for permission. When you get it, move into the station and finish the Activity!

Off Duty

You deserve a break after completing the challenges on the Hisatsu Line. The Mountain Line offers the most difficult turn- and grade-related challenges in the game. The Activities also gave you a taste of short-distance light commuter service on the River Line. For a more difficult passenger challenge, try Chapter 6, where you'll be operating in the very heart of Tokyo! You'll take the controls of high-speed commuter trains, helping speed workday commuters, holiday travelers, tourists, and shoppers along one of Japan's busiest routes.

Chapter 6

Operating Japan's Tokyo-Hakone Railway

*T*he Tokyo-Hakone route provides you with excellent challenges no matter where you are on the learning curve of train handling. Beginning engineers will find that the powerful, straightforward Odakyu 2000 Series engines are easy to manage on the relatively flat line. The graceful 7000 Series "Romance Trains" running down to Hakone are fast, powerful, and beautiful. Veteran hoggers will find that the route grows with them, as precise speed management must be demonstrated to complete the commuter Activities on schedule.

Activities on the Tokyo-Hakone route offer a mix of local and express passenger service. The challenges range from heavy traffic to severe weather conditions, including storm damage and winter effects. Walk-throughs in this chapter will help you meet your timetables in each of the Activities on the Odakyu Electric Railway.

Route Description

The Odakyu Electric Railway Company offers commuter and resort passenger service in the Kanto District of Japan, including the heart of Tokyo. At the other end of the line is scenic Fuji-Hakone-Izu National Park. The park is home to the majestic Mt. Fuji, one of Japan's national icons. Almost two million people ride these rails every day, either commuting between Tokyo and the suburban areas to the south or heading out of the city to the world-class resort of Hakone. The island of Enoshima, home of Japan's most famous oceanside resort, is also served by a branch of the mainline.

This line offers you two different locomotives: the 2000 Series for hard-working commuter service, and the 7000 LSE Series at the head of the luxurious Hakone Express (see Figure 6.1). The latter offers passengers the luxurious accommodations of the Romance Car on its way to the resorts. Computer-controlled trains on the route will be headed by the 30000 EXE Series engines.

FIGURE 6.1:

The Romance Car captures the spirit of the Tokyo-Hakone route.

History

The Japanese commuter rail system is among the finest railways in the world. (With over 34,000 people per square mile in Tokyo, it has to be!) The Japanese National Railway (JNR) has a proud tradition of efficiency and safety, with an on-time record of 99% and the absence of even a single fatality on the bullet trains after carrying more than three billion passengers over nearly four decades.

Japan's first rail line was constructed along nearly the same route as the one that you'll be operating on. Completed in 1872, the line was built to connect Tokyo with the port of Yokohama. Japan's national railroad soon became a symbol of the nation's progress, mirroring the country's booms and busts through the changes of the Meiji Restoration period, industrialization, and the reconstruction following the Second World War. Because of this national identity, it was with great sadness that the government-run JNR was privatized in 1987, after 115 proud years of operation.

NOTE "In a public ceremony at midnight on April 1, 1987, the president of the JNR, dressed in an engineer's uniform, rode a C-56 steam locomotive in Tokyo and blew the whistle that signaled the end of the 115-year-old national railways. This ceremony marked the closing of the industry that was once regarded as the symbol and backbone of Japan's modernization."—Paul Noguchi, "A Railroad History of Modern Japan"

Six private firms emerged from the ashes of the JNR. The railway tightened its operations, and made the hard decision to cut 83 unprofitable lines. The new railway companies diversified into other businesses to assure their financial stability, and were granted greater freedom from government regulation. Through privatization, the railroads climbed their way toward profitability, ensuring the long-term survival of the industry in Japan.

Today

Today, Japan's railroads total over 21,000 kilometers of track, a quarter of which is double tracked. Approximately half of the nation's tracks are electrified, helping keep pollution down. Japan's rails accommodate 20 million people and 150,000 tons of freight daily. Bullet trains provide high-speed service between all of Japan's major urban areas, promoting business and commerce throughout the country. Certainly, the railroad is an established and integral part of Japanese daily life.

NOTE Shinjuku Station employs white-gloved "pushers," whose job is to literally shove passengers inside the packed trains before the doors close.

The Tokyo-Hakone line includes Japan's single busiest train station, Shinjuku Station. A key rail interchange, it handles more than three million passengers per day! Trains are notoriously overcrowded at this station, and can often be filled to over double their rated capacity. One of the Activities on the route in *Train Simulator* is based upon such an overcrowded day, and you'll experience loading delays. Without a doubt, the Tokyo-Hakone railroad is the definitive line upon which to test your urban train operation skills!

Route Tour: Train Simulator's Tokyo-Hakone Route

You'll find almost all of the Odakyu mainline represented in *Train Simulator* (see Figure 6.2). This route is one of the game's most varied, with landscapes that range from one of the densest cities in the world to the wide-open spaces within Fuji-Hakone-Izu National Park. The southern end of the line features some moderate grades as well, adding a greater challenge.

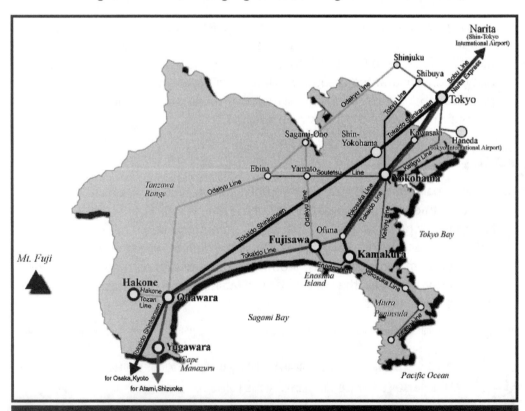

FIGURE 6.2: The Tokyo-Hakone Route

The following sections comprise an overview of the route, starting at busy Shinjuku Station on the northern end of the line. As the track includes metropolitan areas, there are a tremendous number of stations along the way, some separated by a mere fraction of a kilometer. Some of the major stations on the route are noted in the following table.

STATION NAME	MILEPOST LOCATION	NOTES
Shinjuku	0.0	Northern end of route
Yoyogi-Uehara	4.1	—
Shimo-Kitazawa	—	—
Noborito	—	—
Mukogaoka-Yuen	13.5	—
Shin-Yurigaoka	18.8	—
Machida	27.9	—
Sagami-Ono	29.5	—
Ebina	40.8	Large station
Hon-Atsugi	43.1	—
Hadano	56.6	—
Shin-Matsuda	67.2	—
Odawara	82.8	Large station
Hakone-Yumoto	87.9	Southern end of route

The Metro Area

This route is decidedly urban at its northern end, originating in the heart of Tokyo itself. Shinjuku Station is the single busiest point in Japan's entire railway system. A substantial switching yard is situated to the immediate north of the main line, but it isn't connected. The platform is actually enclosed within the gigantic Shinjuku Center, a multi-level transit hub for several commuting services.

TIP The switching yard at Shinjuku Station is an excellent candidate for hosting custom Activities involving switching or assembling a consist. If you get really ambitious, you can even use the Route Editor to connect the yard to the main line, and then take your assembled trains down the Odakyu line!

All trains are restricted to 40 km/h near the station, so watch your speed on approach and departure. Four quick station stops through MP 2 serve downtown Tokyo traffic, and can often threaten delays with large passenger loads. Throughout the central Tokyo area, you'll find up to four stations per kilometer (see Figure 6.3), so be sure to check the Next Station Display (F10) before setting off (so you don't over-accelerate and miss a stop that's only 0.2 km down the line). Another tight group of stations begins at MP 4 with the Yoyogi-Uehara Station, which is at one end of a short yard.

FIGURE 6.3:

Downtown Tokyo is packed with train stations.

The route between Mileposts 5 and 11 runs comparatively straight. There's no effective speed limit, as 110 km/h is faster than you'd ever want to go. This allows you to make up time on this stretch of track if you're running behind in an Activity; push the throttle by one more notch on your acceleration phases and bump up to 20% or even 30% brakes when you slow for turns. A north-bound spur splits from the mainline at MP 7.4, facilitating switching at the Kyodo throughyard.

The route is quadruple-tracked between Kitami and Izumi Tamagawa Stations. A short southbound spur just north of this area hits the mainline at MP 10.4, serving the Seijo Gakuen Mae siding. Southward lies the Tama River Bridge, and past that the Mukogaoka-Yuen Station (the last platform in downtown Tokyo). Once you pass MP 14, you'll note the presence of more open spaces between fully urbanized areas. For the engineer, this means higher speeds are possible as a result of the more gradual turns.

Yurigaoka to Atsugi

Shin-Yurigaoka at MP 18.8 is the first major Tokyo suburban station. There you'll find quadruple track, northbound and southbound sidings, and a double-tracked southbound setout spur. A shorter northbound spur meets the mainline further south at about MP 19.5. You'll encounter the first notable grades in the line at this point, as you begin a steady climb to this station. Immediately after the station, you'll come across a steep downgrade at MP 19. The line starts climbing again at MP 25.5, and reaches a local high point at Machida, the major station at MP 28.

Sagami-Ono hosts one of the largest stations on the line, centered around MP 30. With a major switching yard to the south and multiple sidings, Sagami-Ono Station is well suited for its role as the interchange with the Odakyu Enoshima line, with service to Kamakura and the Enoshima resort island to the south. The line is very straight through the large Sobudaime Station at MP 33.7 until a sweeping curve at MP 35. Here, the suburbs of Tokyo are thin, and the urban centers are separated by large tracts of lightly populated open space.

TIP The Yurigaoka to Atsugi stretch is a great place to make up time if you're behind schedule, because of the long straightaways and high-radius turns. Be a bit more aggressive with your speed transitions if you need to catch up with your timetable.

After the curve north of Zama Station, the line is straight again through MP 39, where a 90 km/h bend to the right swings the track on a westerly course. After the initial turn, the curve relaxes, allowing you to accelerate back to express speed. Ebina Station is situated at the beginning of the longer curve, with a good switching yard on the west side of the mainline and several sidings.

A pair of slower turns south of the station require you to slow to 75 km/h by the time you cross over the Sagami River Trestle.

You'll find yourself on an elevated railway as you pass through Atsugi, the first city south of the Tokyo suburbs. Two sidings at Hon-Atsugi Station are partially enclosed beneath an elevated bridge and a densely packed downtown area, reminiscent of the right-of-way through downtown Tokyo (see Figure 6.4). Southward, the line returns to ground level, and is accommodated by a lowered trackbed. The line is very straight all the way to MP 48, just before Isehara Station with its three sidings.

FIGURE 6.4:

Atsugi is a large city, with an elevated line through the downtown area.

The Kanagawa Countryside

The route passes through the open countryside of Kanagawa Prefecture south of Atsugi. Long straightaways slice through rural farmland and wilderness on this leg of the railway, and there are longer distances between towns. Tsurumaki Onsen is the first town south of Atsugi, separated by rolling hills to either side of the elevated roadway. Beware of the long, tight left turn at the station, just past MP 51.

A constant ascent toward the highest point on the line begins in this area, so you'll need more throttle on southbound trains. Of course, northbound hoggers may need to keep a hand on the brakes. Tunnels frequently cut through hillsides that were too big to grade or avoid. Be conservative with your speed as you exit tunnels, as some are immediately followed by 55–65 km/h turns. The city of Hadano, just north of the line's summit, is at MP 56, where you'll be subject to a

35-km/h speed zone. Despite tempting straight runs on the line, you'll be limited by a 75-km/h speed zone all the way to MP 61.

South of Hadano is the steepest grade on the route. Get a running start at the grade as soon as you leave the 35-km/h speed zone, moving up to 100% throttle smoothly to keep your passengers comfortable. At the top of the grade is Shibusawa Station, a medium-sized urban center. Anticipate the change to a 15-km/h speed limit at the station. The line is graded beneath the surrounding ground level south of the station, but there are still ample views of the mountainous landscape to the west—on a clear day, you can see Mt. Fuji from this portion of the line (see Figure 6.5).

FIGURE 6.5:

The views from the top of the Odakyu line are glorious.

Following the turns leading up to MP 68, the line is almost completely straight. You won't need much throttle to accelerate, as the line drops 150 meters over about 1.5 km of track. A few sidings complement the mainline around MP 70. The straight run continues all the way to Ashigara Station at MP 80.5. The speed limit is 40 km/h in the vicinity of the station, but the downgrade will make braking more difficult, so brake much earlier than you normally do when southbound. Ashigara is equipped with a switching yard on the west side of the mainline that can be used for setouts.

The Tozan Railway

Nestled on the shore of Sagami-Wan Bay, Odawara Station at MP 82 is the last platform modeled in *Train Simulator* on the Odakyu mainline. To the east of the Odakyu line, you'll see a segment of the Shinkansen bullet train route laid out on its path from Tokyo to Kyoto. If you want to transfer to the scenic Tozan railway to reach the end of the line in *Train Simulator*, you'll have to switch over to the westernmost mainline in Odawara Station (be careful not to switch over all the way to the western siding).

The Tozan Railway cuts through the Fuji-Hakone-Izu National Park, and offers glimpses of Mt. Fuji to the north through the mountainous terrain. The real Tozan line runs all the way to the shoreline of Lake Ashi-no-Ko, but Hakone-Yumoto Station marks the end of the line on *Train Simulator's* Tozan Railway. When you've reached this station, it's time to turn around!

 WARNING The smaller Tozan line isn't as fast as the Odakyu mainline, so watch your speed after you've been screaming down the rails toward Odawara.

Passenger Activity Tutorial

The Tokyo-Hakone tutorial is similar to the tutorials for the other passenger routes. You'll be operating a 2000 Series from Sangubashi to Chitose Funabashi on a clear afternoon. You'll learn how to start and stop the 2000 Series through the use of pop-up messages that will guide you through a few station stops. If you're already familiar with electric locomotive operation, you can skip this tutorial. Otherwise, the short 10-minute Activity is worth the effort to get you up to speed on operating the train.

Activity Crew Call: Shinjuku to Machida in the Winter

This simple Activity is a point-to-point run through the northern half of the Odawara line. Good weather and clear rails leave you to test your handling skills on open track.

ACTIVITY SUMMARY

Locomotive/Train:	2000 Series
Starting Point:	Shinjuku
Ending Point:	Machida
Time of Day/light:	17:00, winter/clear
Difficulty Level:	Easy
Distance Covered:	27.9 km
Estimated Duration:	20 minutes

Activity Strategy

This is a relatively straightforward Activity, with your only station calls at your origin and destination stations. As a result, your primary focus is to observe speed limits and maintain the comfort of your passengers with smooth transitions and appropriate velocity around the curves.

Playing the Activity

You begin the Activity at the southern end of Shinjuku Station (see Figure 6.6). Wait for the highball, and then release the brakes and apply 25% power to bring your train up to speed. It doesn't take long to get up to 40 km/h, so pay attention to your acceleration while you're in the station's restricted speed zone. Slow down to about 30 km/h for the reversing turn that merges you with the mainline just before reaching the Minami Shinjuku Station, before MP 1.

Around the Sangubashi Station, the speed limit opens up to the route's default of 110 km/h. Keep it around 70 km/h, and prepare to use about 10% brakes to get down to 55 to maintain a smooth ride. Watch your track monitor carefully for speed zones ahead, such as the 60-km/h zone beginning at Highashi Kitazawa at MP 4. You can open up the throttle again after the Yoyogi-Uehara Station, but stay under 60 km/h for the turn at MP 5, just past the Shimo-Kitazawa Station.

FIGURE 6.6:

Shinjuku Station is a bustling transit hub.

TIP When you're in low speed zones, alternate between idle and 25% power to maintain a speed of about 2 km/h under the speed limit. Let off the throttle early under acceleration (when you're about 5 km/h under the limit), as the throttle will lag a bit as you reduce power.

After the Setagaya Daita Station, you can accelerate to about 90 km/h for the long straightaway through Kitami Station at MP 11. Once again, apply 10% brakes approximately 100 meters before the turns, and then tap the throttle when the tail end of your train clears the curve. After your train clears the Umi Gaoka platform, apply constant 10% brakes to negotiate the next turn at 60 km/h, increasing to 20% if you aren't slowing fast enough. Another straightaway allows you to accelerate to about 95 km/h until about MP 10, where you should again apply 10% to 20% brakes for the turn after Kitami Station. Take the turn at 55 km/h to ensure the comfort of your passengers.

The speed limit goes back down to 75 km/h at Izumi Tamagawa Station, so watch your track monitor and make sure you're below the limit on the approach. Don't be fooled by the high speed limit following the restricted zone—tight turns can force you to stay at 70 km/h throughout the next portion of the line. You can speed up in the straightaway at MP 13, but slow down by the end of the bridge over the Tama River (see Figure 6.7).

FIGURE 6.7:

Use the river bridge as a landmark for applying your brakes.

Mukogaoka-Yuen is the last station in Tokyo proper, and you can open up the throttle a bit to take advantage of the broader curves in this suburban track. Free of the confines of the urban corridors, the line has more room for high-radius turns, allowing you to travel at a higher speed. As soon as you cross the next river, you'll begin climbing a gentle grade that will require a little more power to maintain velocity.

WARNING You need to hit about 95 km/h at the end of the straightaways before braking in order to maintain your scheduled arrival in Machida, assuming that you obey all speed limits. Don't push the curves though, as a derailment means the difference between getting there a few seconds late and never getting there at all!

Slow down again at MP 17, as the curves get tighter near the suburb of Yurigaoka. Prepare for a dramatic downgrade at MP 19, just after the downtown Shin-Yurigaoka Station. You may need to apply 10% braking to maintain a reasonable speed down the grade. After you clear the downtown area, you'll be in the home stretch all the way to Machida Station. Use 50% power in the straightaways, and then apply 10% brakes approximately one-quarter of a kilometer before the turns at Mileposts 21 and 22.5 to get down to 60 km/h. Note that if you're early or heavy on your throttle, you may need to brake before

Kakio Station to account for your higher speed. The second turn is tighter than the first one, so slow down if you're still fast at MP 21.

Accelerate to 70 km/h up to MP 24, where a pair of tight turns just before Tamagawa Gauken Mae Station requires a little extra braking. Get back up to 70 after the turn and then slow again at MP 25.5, where a grade starts that will help you reduce your speed on the way to your destination. There's a 70-km/h speed zone at Machida, but since you'll be stopping at the platform, you'll be well below it. By MP 26 you should be down to 55 km/h, using 25% throttle to maintain your speed on the uphill. Let the hill slow you down to 50 km/h by the time you pass under the automobile bridge just before the station, and apply 10% brakes from that speed after you pass the end of the siding on the right of the main line. Maintaining 10% brakes should glide you to a stop at the end of the platform. Once you're at a complete stop, hit Enter to unload your passengers and complete the Activity!

Activity Crew Call: Short Passenger Run

This is a quick but challenging commuter run on the northern end of the line. Because of the short duration, it makes an excellent practice run for getting the feel for the 2000 Series trains.

ACTIVITY SUMMARY

Locomotive/Train:	2000 Series
Starting Point:	Shinjuku
Ending Point:	Yoyogi-Uehara
Time of Day/light:	9:00; spring/clear
Difficulty Level:	Easy
Distance Covered:	Approximately 4 km
Estimated Duration:	Five minutes

Activity Strategy

Short doesn't mean easy when you're talking about this Activity! Although the whole episode only takes about five minutes to complete, you have only a little bit over a minute to make it from a full stop at one platform to a full stop at the next one! If you want to arrive on time, you'll have to use 100% throttle on acceleration, and full brakes to slow.

Playing the Activity

Start by releasing your train brake and waiting for your departure time to come around. In this Activity, you need maximum responsiveness from your train brake. Every time that you release it, pull it back to 0% so that you can quickly transition to applied braking when you need it. As soon as you see the 54-second mark, peg your throttle to 100% and keep it there until your speedometer passes 30 km/h. As soon as it does, start tapping your A key to drop your throttle steadily down to 0. There is a bit of lag time between when you make a throttle input and the engine's response, so be sure to throttle down early to avoid going over the speed limit of 40 km/h.

TIP Make sure that your Track Monitor and Next Station Display are both open in this Activity (as they should be with any Activity, really). In this particular assignment, you'll be paying special attention to the speed zones in the Track Monitor, and the distance to station in the Next Station Display.

As soon as your train clears the siding at Shinjuku Station, you're in an unrestricted speed zone. Move your throttle back up to 100% and accelerate until you pass under the road overpass in front of Sangubashi Station, when you should bring the throttle down to 0. Immediately apply 100% brakes when you reach the beginning of the platform, and leave them applied. You should come to a stop precisely at the end of the platform.

Accelerate to full as soon as you hear the highball, and leave your throttle wide open through the second milepost. As soon as you sight the platform at Yoyogi Hachiman Station around the right-hand turn (see Figure 6.8), cut the throttle and apply 100% braking. Zero the brake handle when you've built up the braking pressure, but don't release it until you slow to approximately 55 km/h. Then, release the brake pressure at about 70%, releasing it as soon as you see your train drop below about 47 km/h. Your aim is to spend as much time at speed as possible, and only drop to 45 km/h immediately before the platform, which marks the beginning of the 45 zone.

FIGURE 6.8:

Apply hard brakes as soon as you see the Yoyogi Hachiman platform emerging from around the curve.

From a speed of 45, the 2000 Series train only takes 0.08 km to stop using 100% braking. Right about the time you cross under the pedestrian walkway at the center of the station, you should see 0.09 km or so in your Next Station Display. Zero the brake handle and apply 100% brakes as soon as you hit 0.08 km distance to the platform (too early is better than too late). Once again, you should settle in right at the end of the platform.

Accelerate at a throttle setting of 80% out of the station. By the time you get up to speed, you should be out of the 45-km/h speed zone. This will free you to go to 100% throttle as you approach the Yoyogi-Uehara Station. Let off the throttle when you're about 0.3 km out and lay on the brake at 100% to prepare for the platform's 45-km/h zone. If you get a yellow approach signal, of course you should slow sooner.

Release your brake pressure when you're at 55 km/h, and then nudge it down until you're at 45 by the time you reach the platform. Remember to zero that brake after you use it! Once again, you only need 0.08 km to stop at the end of the platform, so plan your braking accordingly. If you've nailed your acceleration and braking procedures, you should be right on time for a perfect evaluation!

Activity Crew Call: After the Storm

A major storm has hit the Kanto District, and there has been some damage to the rails. Operate the commuter service out on the middle of the route, and try to keep to your schedule despite several slow order zones.

ACTIVITY SUMMARY

Locomotive/Train:	2000 Series
Starting Point:	Ebina
Ending Point:	Shin-Matsuda
Time of Day/light:	9:35: autumn/rain
Difficulty Level:	Medium
Distance Covered:	27.5 km
Estimated Duration:	40 minutes

Activity Strategy

With special speed restrictions in place, it will be hard to maintain your time-table in the middle of this storm. There's nothing you can do about the reduced speed zones, so the best strategy is to try to make up your time in the unrestricted zones after your delays. Use 100% throttle out of the stations to get up to speed as quickly as possible, and go to 100% braking at the last possible moment on approach to the stations.

WARNING Don't try to compress the front end of your route to arrive early at the back end. Being too early is just as bad as being too late—you'll throw off the traffic on the route, fight color at the signals, and miss passengers connecting from other mass transit lines.

Special speed zones:

- 25 between Mileposts 59.2 and 60.4

- 25 between Mileposts 63.4 and 65.2

Playing the Activity

Unlike some Activities, you don't begin at your first station call. As soon as you clear the Operations Notebook, get your train in running order and depart Ebina immediately. Release the brake, throw the reverser, and throttle up to 100%. Accelerate until your train reaches 100 km/h, and then let off on the throttle. You'll have to cut your throttle early to avoid going over 100 km/h for the turn before the station.

Coast until you approach within 0.3 km of the station, shown on the Next Station Display. As soon as you're closer than that magic number (you're shooting for 0.29, to be exact), lay on the brakes at 100%. It takes just a shade under 0.3 km to bring a loaded Series 2000 to a full stop from 100 km/h, so timing your braking with the distance to station aid can put you on the edge of the platform every time.

Hon-Atsugi Station is graded, so don't release your brakes until you hear the all-clear buzzer. Accelerate at 100% to reach 80 km/h, and then coast all the way to the Hon-Atsugi Station approach. You should be at about 75 km/h by the time you're within 0.35 km of the station. When you are 0.25 km/h away, apply 100% brakes.

TIP Constantly monitor the projected speed indicator in your Track Monitor. The greater the difference between your current and projected speeds, the greater your rate of acceleration (or deceleration). Take this into consideration when adjusting your throttle or brake settings.

Downgrades will make braking harder on your way into Aiko-Ishida Station. Accelerate to 100 km/h out of Hon-Atsugi, but let her drift down the steep grades to avoid going overspeed (see Figure 6.9). You'll also have to apply 100% brakes when you're still 0.42 km out of Aiko-Ishida to compensate for the downgrade. Accelerate to 100 km/h again, and maintain your speed for the long straightaway to Isehara.

FIGURE 6.9:

Downgrades south of Hon-Atsugi will increase your acceleration and extend braking distances.

You'll be directed onto track four at Isehara, which means a few tight turns as you enter the station and change tracks. Prepare for this by braking down to 60 km/h while you're still 0.4 kilometers away from the station. Remember to start bailing off on your brakes early! Apply full brakes when you're 0.34 km out to achieve a nice platform stop from a speed of 60.

WARNING Remember, when arriving early, stay at the platform until your scheduled departure time. Your loading will be complete, but you must maintain your position at the platform and depart in accordance with the timetable to avoid an operational error.

As you pull into Isehara, you'll be notified of debris on the line between Mileposts 55 and 56. Climb up to the speed limit and maintain it on the way into Tsurumaki Onsen. Watch the grades, and adjust your throttle as necessary to stay under 110 km/h. Approach the station at 100 km/h and lay on the brakes when you are 0.3 kilometers away.

Accelerate to 100 km/h on the way to Tokai Daigaku Mae, cutting throttle at a distance of 0.4 km and braking at 0.33 km. The extra 30 meters are needed because of the downgrade before the station, which your tail end will still be fighting when you start braking. Dispatch will let you know that the debris has been cleared from the track ahead, but the special speed restriction is still in place as damage crews access the track.

Accelerate to 100 km/h out of Tokai Daigaku Mae, but slow to 90 just before the tunnel entrance to negotiate the jog to the left comfortably. Accelerate up to 90 through the tunnel, but let the grade slow you to about 80 by the time you exit, to ride out a few curves immediately after you emerge. Maintain 80 on approach to MP 55, applying full brakes as you pass the signal just before the restricted zone (see Figure 6.10). Drop your speed below 30, and then fine-tune it with smaller brake and throttle applications.

FIGURE 6.10:

An express train passes northbound as we prepare to slow down at the signal just before MP 55.

The speed zone will require careful operation to negotiate at maximum efficiency. Pay very close attention to your projected speed, because it will change as you ride the varying grades in the zone. Be ready to alternate between 20% throttle and 20% brake constantly. In the last kilometer to Hadano, you'll be able to relax, using momentary 20% throttle inputs to maintain 24 km/h. The restriction lifts about 600 meters before Hadano, so arrive early by speeding up on your way in. Cut throttle when you're at 65 km/h, and apply brakes 0.22 km outside the station.

Mind the 35 limit departing the station. Accelerate to 25, then let your train coast down the hill until you're in the 110 zone. Speed up to 100, and maintain it until you're about half a kilometer from MP 59 (see Figure 6.11). You can simply allow the grade to slow your train to 25, although you should be prepared to throw in a little braking if you're late cutting the throttle. Gauge your approach when you spot the yellow 25 zone sign at the beginning of the right curve at MP 59. Maintain 25 throughout the zone, and then speed up to 75 on approach to Shibusawa. Hit the brakes when you're 0.25 km outside the station, and you should be early again.

FIGURE 6.11:

The 25-km/h speed zone begins at the end of this straightaway, at the edge of the buildings.

The last leg of the journey is more of the same. Speed up until you're within a half kilometer of the restricted speed zone, and then coast, applying light braking if necessary. Maintain your speed carefully within the 25 zone, and break out of it at 75 km/h when you're clear. Don't watch the green sign—even when your engine passes, the cars behind you are still within the zone. When the Track Monitor reflects the higher speed zone, you know it's safe to accelerate. Decelerate at 0.25 km outside of Shin-Matsuda, and unload at the platform for a perfect run.

Activity Crew Call: Shinjuku to Hon-Atsugi in the Summer

Operate commuter service in the morning rush hour from downtown Tokyo to the suburbs. Track maintenance may contribute to some delays.

ACTIVITY SUMMARY

Locomotive/Train:	2000 Series
Starting Point:	Shinjuku
Ending Point:	Hon-Atsugi
Time of Day/light:	8:15; summer/clear
Difficulty Level:	Medium
Distance Covered:	43.1 km
Estimated Duration:	One hour, five minutes

Activity Strategy

This is a very straightforward Activity, made challenging mostly by its length and the special speed zones resulting from track maintenance. You're running the early morning commute, which means that you'll have trains stacked up in front of you and in back of you. Since you're stopping so frequently, you also have trouble making up time if you fall behind, so you've really got to nail your speed transitions.

Numerous special speed zones exist all along the line. Although the briefing lists three, there are actually several altered speed zones along your journey, so you'll have to pay close attention to the Track Monitor and anticipate them, braking early to avoid entering the speed zones too fast.

Playing the Activity

You'll spend almost the entire activity accelerating at 100% throttle, decelerating at 100% brakes, or loading and unloading at the platform. You've even got to get your boarding skills down, hitting the Enter key as soon as you've come to a complete stop, and anticipating the all-clear buzzer for on-time departures.

TIP You've got three reduced speed zones due to essential maintenance, but you need to maximize your time at speed even when facing these restrictions. Treat them just like stations: speed as long as you can, and hit the brakes hard to slow down in time.

The first stretch of the line has a speed limit of 40 km/h until you are all the way into the Minami Shinjuku Station, which is one of the only stations along your way that isn't on your timetable. Accelerate to 80 km/h as soon you clear the 40 zone, and brake when you are 0.25 km away from the Sangubashi platform. The line is restricted to 40 km/h past the station, so it'll be an easy stop at Yoyogi Hachiman. You've got a short stretch of open speed zone after the station (see Figure 6.12), so put it to good use by accelerating to 90 km/h for a short while, braking again before the 75 zone near Yoyogi-Uehara.

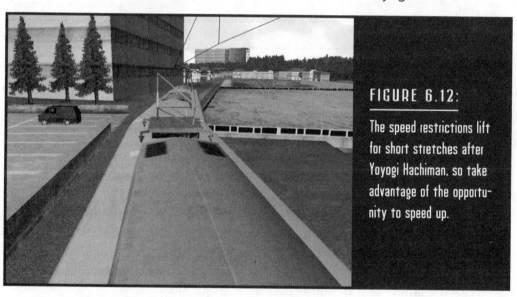

FIGURE 6.12:

The speed restrictions lift for short stretches after Yoyogi Hachiman, so take advantage of the opportunity to speed up.

There aren't any other surprises on this route. If you start falling behind on your schedule, try making up time between the following stations:

- Seijo Gakuen Mae and Noborito
- Mukogaoka-Yuen and Ikuta
- Tsurukawa and Machida
- Sobudaime and Zama

With a precise touch on the throttle and brakes, you should be able to maintain your timetable with little or no delay. Watch the signals, as you may catch some color if you manage to close with the train ahead of you on the line.

Activity Crew Call: Summer Holiday

With throngs of vacationers flocking south, your train has been added to the schedule to help relieve some of the crowding on the overtaxed transit system. Operate passenger service over almost the entire route, stopping at every station on the way.

ACTIVITY SUMMARY

Locomotive/Train:	2000 Series
Starting Point:	Shinjuku
Ending Point:	Odawara
Time of Day/light:	9:42; summer/clear
Difficulty Level:	Medium
Distance Covered:	82.8 km
Estimated Duration:	Two hours

Activity Strategy

This Activity runs the entire length of the Odakyu line, with station stops at every platform along the way. You'll be dealing with full loads at each station, so it's even more important here than ever to make accurate station stops. You should play the preceding Activities in this chapter before attempting this one, to get a feel for the timing of your braking before each station.

Playing the Activity

Expect to see color on this route, as the trains are practically running nose to tail today. This is essentially a full-schedule run from one end of the line to the other, so you should have a good, solid familiarity with the Tokyo-Hakone route before you attempt it. People are very heavy (believe it or not), so don't underestimate your stopping distance with the full loads you'll be operating with.

TIP Save your Activity with the F2 key every few station stops. This is a long route, and it would be horrible to lose 90 minutes of work if you spill your drink on approach to Shibusawa and blow through the station.

Since you're operating the whole route, it's best to refer to the Route Overview provided at the beginning of this chapter. Follow your progress down the system, noting the normal speed zones on the line, as well as the grades and curves. You'll still want to push your speed transitions to maintain your schedule (see Figure 6.13), using heavy applications of throttle and brakes.

FIGURE 6.13:

Open up the throttle as you depart each station for maximum time at track speed.

Between the last stations on the route, starting with Tokai Daigaku Mae, you can really make up time if you're very bold with your throttle. Accelerate at 100% throttle to just under the 110-km/h speed limit, and brake at the last possible moment, within 0.3–0.35 km of your next station. Observe the speed restrictions of course, which will be displayed in your Track Monitor. If you find yourself falling behind, try making up time between the following stations:

- Seijo Gakuen Mae and Noborito

- Mukogaoka-Yuen and Ikuta

- Tsurukawa and Machida

- Sobudaime and Zama

- Hon-Atsugi and Tsurumaki Onsen

- Tokai Daigaku Mae all the way to Ashigara

If you can nail your station stops, you should be able to complete this Activity with a perfect evaluation. Don't be afraid to break it up into more than one playing session by saving the game. You can also restore a save point if you blow a stop.

Activity Crew Call: Heavy Delay Day

A power outage on the line in the early morning has delayed several trains. Maintenance crews are still working on the problem, but the trains are up and running. Operate northbound commuter service and try to keep your schedule, despite the delays and traffic backups on the line.

ACTIVITY SUMMARY

Locomotive/Train:	2000 Series
Starting Point:	Mukogaoka-Yuen
Ending Point:	Shinjuku
Time of Day/light:	9:35; winter/clear
Difficulty Level:	Hard
Distance Covered:	13.5 km
Estimated Duration:	30 minutes

Activity Strategy

In addition to the delays, Heavy Delay Day has the built-in complication of running northbound, which is in the opposite direction of all the other Activities. Therefore, you won't have the same familiarity with the station approaches that you do when you run southbound. Pay more attention to station indicators than landmarks, which you will naturally use on familiar routes.

Special speed zones:

- 25 between Mileposts 9.8 and 8.5

- 25 between Mileposts 6.7 and 6.2

- 25 between Mileposts 5.6 and 4.6

Playing the Activity

Get off to a good start by using 100% throttle to reach 75 km/h on your way into the first station at Noborito. You will get up to speed quickly, so remember to cut the throttle early to avoid going overspeed. Apply 100% brakes when you are 0.17 km away from the platform's end. Speed up under full throttle again after you hear the all-clear, but be careful to stay under 75 km/h to observe the slow order on approach to Izumi Tamagawa. Brake approximately 0.12 km from the end of the platform for best performance.

WARNING Power outages this morning have already caused some of the trains ahead of you to experience delays, so you may see color as you watch the signals on your route. Leave your brake lever in the 0% released position while running to assure responsiveness if you need to observe a surprise signal.

A short run to Komae Station still requires careful speed management. Get up to (but not over) 75 km/h as quickly as possible, and maintain it with about 25% throttle as you head for the end of the long platform. Cut the throttle at about 0.2 km, and apply full brakes at 0.12 km. After loading, the next section of track has a 110-km/h limit, which gives you the opportunity to make up some time if you're falling behind by a few seconds. Stay on the throttle until you're just 0.25 km from Kitami Station, and then cut and put your hand on the brake. Quickly apply 100% brakes from 0.18 km to the end of the platform and you should pick up about six seconds on this leg.

Seiji Gauken Mae is another easy leg on which to make up lost time. The slow order zone is beyond the station, so feel free to accelerate to about 85 km/h, and then let the uphill grade slow you below 75 for the station's limit. Maintain a speed of about 73 km/h through the station, and then apply your brakes at about 0.11 km out. This is a short platform, so it's better to overshoot than undershoot.

The first slow order zone is immediately after the station. Accelerate to about 30, and then let your speed drop off naturally below 25. Don't be afraid to cycle the brakes lightly if you are overspeed while coasting into the slow order zone. Maintain your speed with periodic throttle bumps throughout the restricted zone (see Figure 6.14). It's very hard to arrive on time at Soshigaya Okura, so you may have to make up time again on the other side of the slow order. As you leave the station, compensate for the uphill grade by applying up to 40% throttle to maintain speed.

FIGURE 6.14:

A southbound train passes as we negotiate the slow order zone.

Chitose Funabashi is another short platform, so pull a little past the end of the pavement. As you clear the first slow order zone, you'll actually be in a 110-km/h zone, so accelerate as you move down the platform, hitting your brakes sometime before 0.04 km to the platform's end (depending on the speed you reach). This simple maneuver will grab you a few seconds as you transit the last 200 meters of the platform.

Use normal operating procedures until you approach Gotokuji. Speed up to 100 km/h after Kyodo Station, but apply the brakes hard when you approach the 90 speed zone. The 25-km/h zone starts immediately after it, at the front end of the platform, so keep on braking after you pass 90—ignore that benchmark completely. Remember to release your brake pressure as you approach 25 to avoid stopping altogether, and maintain 25 all the way to the end of the platform.

Two more slow order zones lay between you and the end of the line. Negotiate them as you did the first one, tapping your throttle when you drop to 23 km/h or less. Accelerate at 100% throttle to the speed limit as soon as the

Track Monitor says you've cleared the slow order, and hit the stations fast, braking at the last possible moment to settle at the end of the platforms. With concentration and skill, you can keep your delays well under a minute in this Activity, and you can even finish your run on schedule if you make up time after MP 4.5.

Off Duty

The commuter service on the Odakyu Line is a real taste of urban mass transit. With trains stacked tight on the line during heavy use periods, delays are a very real and ever present threat—efficiency is of paramount importance. After you've met the challenge of metro passenger service, take a tour on the historic Orient Express in Chapter 7.

Chapter 7

Operating Austria's Innsbruck–St. Anton Line

*T*he Orient Express route offers you another chance to operate a steam locomotive circa 1930, this time on the famous Orient Express line between Paris and Vienna. Unlike the Flying Scotsman, where the engine is the focal point, on this route the entire train itself is the subject of people's affections. The Activities on the route help capture the nostalgic romance of days gone by, when wealthy patrons traveled between France and the Eastern Mediterranean in luxurious comfort. This is probably the most challenging route in the game: the route itself is challenging, the Activities include several set outs, and steam operations are very difficult in their own right.

Route Description

Train Simulator's Orient Express route models the historic line from Innsbruck to St. Anton, Austria, as it was in the late 1920s. The real line offered uniquely luxurious passenger service between Paris and exotic Istanbul, between the Black and Aegean Seas. Additional lines also served London, Venice, and Rome, although the Paris-Bulgaria route was (and still is) by far the most famous. The Innsbruck-St. Anton portion of the route takes you through the beautiful Austrian Alps, showing off spectacular alpine peaks dotted with beautiful Tyrolean villages in sweeping, untouched valleys.

 WARNING By the time you take on the Orient Express, you should be familiar with both passenger and steam operations. The Orient Express route is one of the most difficult in the game, so it should be attempted only after you've mastered a few other routes. If you'd just like to enjoy the route, try running in Simple mode.

The Gölsdorf Series 380 is the only player-operative locomotive native to the Orient Express route. Designed by famed Austrian locomotive designer Karl Gölsdorf, the 2-10-0 engine is classified as 1E using the German system. Although it was originally designed for freight operation, the 380 was a natural fit for the steep grades of the Austrian Alps, with an impressive 12.1 metric tons of tractive effort coming from its 10 55.5-inch drive wheels (see Figure 7.1). The compound design means it uses its steam pressure twice before being exhausted.

FIGURE 7.1:

The Gölsdorf Series 380 saw widespread use as a freight locomotive, but served passengers well on the mountainous Orient Express line.

History

The Orient Express line from Paris to Bulgaria was completed in 1883. At the time, there was little in the way of consolidated rail service throughout Europe. Varying gauges of track (the distance between the rails) were used in different countries, forcing passengers to change lines and trains when traveling long distances. Most routes were poorly maintained, local mixed passenger and freight lines, and traveling over them was very uncomfortable. When the Orient Express service was inaugurated, it was a completely different approach to travel by rail in Europe.

Belgian George Nagelmackers created la Compagnie des Wagons-Lits (CIWL) after an 1872 visit to the US inspired him to create a line offering service across Europe in style and elegance. One of the trains between Paris and Istanbul was named The Orient Express, and quickly became synonymous with luxury, glamour, and adventure. During the period modeled in *Train Simulator*, the passenger manifest was practically the Who's Who list of international celebrities, nobility, and government leaders.

 NOTE CIWLT carefully maintains the surviving relics and memorabilia from the golden age of the Orient Express, and offers related materials on its website at www.wagons-lits-paris.com.

Every year, CIWL opened up service to a new destination across Europe, Asia, and the Middle East. With each new route, a train was christened with a name that would become a legend in its own right: Orient Express, Train Bleu, Golden Arrow, Transsiberien…these and many more fueled the romance of the rails. Whether because it was the first or because it was the best, all of the routes were collectively referred to as the Orient Express.

The Orient Express earned its reputation through its elegantly appointed dining and sleeping cars. Exquisite food served by impeccable attendants kept the passengers in the lap of luxury, including breakfast served in bed. Despite the comforts, the train was not exempt from the ravages of war, and the service was often interrupted by border disputes, trade restrictions, revolutions, and even world wars.

Today

Today, CIWL is a subsidiary of the ACCOR group, a world leader in hotels and travel services, and continues to maintain the legend of the Orient Express through its branded product line and historical archives. The public can travel the same route re-created in Microsoft Train Simulator on board the Venice Simplon-Orient-Express (http://www.orient-expresstrains.com/), which uses the authentically restored CIWL cars. Other nostalgia trains still ply the old lines through Thailand, India, and several other portions of the historic Orient Express routes.

Route Tour: Train Simulator's Innsbruck-St. Anton Route

The Innsbruck-St. Anton route lies in the very heart of the Austrian Alps (Figure 7.2). St. Anton sits within the Arlberg Pass in the Lechtaler Alps. 100 km to the east sits Innsbruck, at the base of the Bavarian Alps. The route shadows the Inn River as it winds its way up to Landeck, where it splits off to follow the Rosanna River, one of the Inn's tributaries. The line has about 700 meters of rise over its length. Almost 400 meters of the overall rise is in the last 30 kilometers or so, west of Landeck. This portion of the line can be particularly brutal in bad weather, and the Orient Express has been snowed-in countless times over its history.

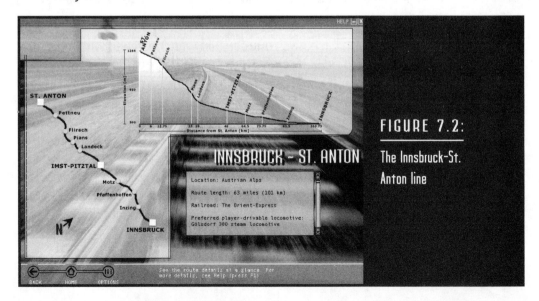

FIGURE 7.2:

The Innsbruck-St. Anton line

The portion of the route represented in *Train Simulator* basically consists of two parts: the Lechtaler Alps and the Bavarian Alps. The following sections take a closer look at each of these areas, and will serve as an aid in any of the Activities you may undertake on this route. The following table lists some of the stations you'll service on the line.

STATION NAME	MILEPOST LOCATION	NOTES
St. Anton	0.6	Western end of route
Schann	5.0	
Flirsch	8.0	
Pians	14.0	
Landeck	17.8	Rossana/Inn river junction
Imst-Pitztal	28.4	Large station
Otzthal	34.4	Large station
Motz	40.3	
Pfaffenhoffen	46.8	
Inzing	52.7	
Innsbruck	63.8	Eastern end of route

The Lechtaler Alps

St Anton is set in the middle of the Arlberg Pass through the Lechtaler Alps. To the west lies Switzerland, and beyond that the end of the line in Paris, France. The advantage of the pass is clear as soon as you are placed in the train at this station—the Alps tower above the station on either side (see Figure 7.3), so much so that you cannot see the peaks using the available views! St. Anton is often snowed in, so you'll be using your sander more often than not when you serve this station.

The route is all downhill from St. Anton. Other than a sharp turn just below the station (near MP 3), the line has moderate curves through to the Schann platform. Between mileposts 6 and 13 (Flirsch), the line is as straight as it gets, providing you with a good opportunity to make up speed in both directions. Beginning at Flirsch, you need to exercise great care, because the steepest grades modeled in the game start here and extend west over the next 3 kilometers. The grade gets less severe at Strengen, and a sweeping curve near MP 24 lets you know you're almost through the pass.

FIGURE 7.3:

The Alps are so steep and tall that it's sometimes impossible to see their peaks.

TIP Try the Steam Tutorial from the Tutorials screen before attempting the St. Anton-Innsbruck route. The Lechtaler leg is very difficult, and it won't be very enjoyable if you're spending all your time fighting your engine. The tutorial's straightforward lesson can help you with the basics of steam operation.

Once you reach Pians, it's relatively straight through the beautiful mountain landscape until you reach Landeck. A large, graded station complete with sidings, a maintenance facility, and tender supplies designates the end of the descent from the Lechtaler Alps and the Arlberg Pass. You can take on water if you need to, and you will often be called upon to do switching operations here.

The Bavarian Alps

On the eastern side of the line lies the Landeck-Innsbruck leg, characterized by flatter grades and wider valleys. Heavier traffic and a wider roadbed allow double-track here, so you'll often pass computer-controlled Gölsdorf Series 310 locomotives and their trains on this portion of the route (see Figure 7.4). Without the need to snake around mountainsides while maintaining a steady grade, the curves in the Bavarian section are much longer, allowing high-speed operation along the entire line.

FIGURE 7.4:

The eastern half of the route is double-tracked, and you'll encounter other trains along its length.

A relatively light downgrade extends all the way from Landeck past the Motz Station to about MP 68. You'll have to open up your reverser to maintain your speed on the approach to Pfaffenhoffen, and then bring it back again for the descent towards Inzing. Around MP 70, prepare to throttle up once again for a steeper climb to Inzing Station. The last leg is very nearly flat, and the curves are slightly sharper in this area owing to right-of-way issues in the populated valley.

The approach into Innsbruck is characterized by increasingly urban areas dotting the landscape. Innsbruck is the only major city in the Austrian Alps, and it becomes apparent that you are approaching a city as you travel east on the route. Over seven centuries old at the time of *Train Simulator's* portrayal, the city has a reputation as a cultural and vacation center (see Figure 7.5). It serves as the gateway to the mountaintop resorts on the west end of the line, which are renowned today as some of the best skiing destinations in the world.

FIGURE 7.5:

Innsbruck is the capitol of Tyrol, and the only major city within the Austrian Alps.

Passenger Activity Tutorial

This tutorial offers you a quick and easy introduction to the route. It's particularly helpful in getting a feel for the stopping distance and starting pace of the Orient Express. You'll be placed on a simple passenger run from Landeck to Pians on a clear spring day. You'll learn how to start and stop the Orient Express through the use of pop-up messages that guide you through two station stops for passenger service. While you should already be familiar with steam train operation before trying this route, the programmed introduction to the line and the engine is very useful.

Activity Crew Call: Bar Car Set Out

A minor loss of brake pressure in the bar car forces you to set it out at Shonwies Station. Unfortunately, the bar is currently hosting a VIP party. Replace the car with the Chinoise dining car that happens to be at Shonwies so that the party can continue.

ACTIVITY SUMMARY

Locomotive/Train:	Gölsdorf Series 380
Starting Point:	Near Pians
Ending Point:	Imst-Pitztal
Time of Day/light:	17:00; summer/clear
Difficulty Level:	Easy
Distance Covered:	14.4 miles
Estimated Duration:	30 minutes

Activity Strategy

You'll be putting your switching and coupling skills to work in this Activity, as you will make changes to your consist at Shonwies. The bar car is the eighth carriage back from your tender, and it is the only one without windows on the rear side of the car (see Figure 7.6). The actual number of the car is 0-19, which will be useful once you're ready to set it out in the yard.

FIGURE 7.6:

The bar car doesn't have windows on the back third of its side.

This is a good test of your external train handling skills. Many of the tasks associated with switching must be performed from outside the cab, so you have to rely on keyboard shortcuts to control your train.

Playing the Activity

You begin the Activity at rail speed, approximately 3 miles below Shonwies. Maintain your speed and get familiar with your consist using the external views. Proceed to Shonwies station and stop and unload at the platform as usual. The signal for the track east of the station (where you just came from) is red, so you'll have to do all your switching within the yard in front of you. When you get the all-clear whistle, roll the train up past the switch that leads to the sidings on the left side of the mainline. When your last car is approximately 50 feet in front of the switch that leads to the left sidings, call up the switching display with the F8 key. Click the down-facing arrow and watch as the colors exchange. The larger arrow pointing straight down the mainline was green before the switch, but now the smaller siding arrow is lit, indicating the switch has been thrown to lead you off the mainline.

WARNING Bar Car Set Out may not be the ideal Activity to introduce you to the Innsbruck-St Anton route; the Short Passenger Run and Royalty On Board Activities are more straightforward, shorter, and easier.

You want to set out the back half of your train on the first left-hand siding (see Figure 7.7). If you press F6 to bring up station and siding names, you'll see the siding is labeled Shonwies 2. Back your train up over the switch, and you'll be transferred over to the siding. Notice that the siding switch leads to the Shonwies 2 by default, so you don't have to throw that one. Continue backing at about 12 mph until your locomotive is on the mainline between the two siding switches.

FIGURE 7.7:

Use the F6 key to display the labels of each of the sidings.

Bring your train to a stop, and set the hand brakes on every car from the bar car (number 0-19) back. To do this, call up the Train Operations dialog box with the F9 key. Click a car to select it, then set the hand brake by double-clicking. When the hand brakes are set on every car being set out, uncouple the train behind the bar car. To do this, select the coupler between the 0-19 and 0-20 cars, and then double-click it to uncouple it. You'll be separated from the rear half of your train and ready to set out the bar car.

 TIP Besides seeing the car numbers in the Train Operations dialog box, you can also press F7 to display car names on the screen.

Pull your train forward until you clear the first switch, then throw the switch behind you from Shonwies 2 to Shonwies 1. Now when you return after setting out the bar car, you'll be all switched to pick up the dining car on Shonwies 1. Pull back onto the mainline, and this time pull all the way out of the yard until you're clear of the switch to the right-hand siding (Shonwies 4). Throw the switch behind you, then back up until you're completely off the mainline. Bring your train to a stop, set the handbrake on the bar car, and set it out.

Pull back onto the mainline again and throw the switch behind you so that it no longer leads right toward Shonwies 4. When the switch is thrown, back up onto the left siding once more, this time continuing onto Shonwies 1 thanks to the switching you did on the way out last time. Gently pull back to the dining car at 4 mph or less. You can use the coupling view by pressing 6 to get an overhead view of your coupler, which can help in the final moments of hookup. You'll automatically couple once you make contact. Use the Train Operations dialog box to release the hand brake on the dining car, then pull forward off the Shonwies 1 siding. As soon as your new dining car clears the Shonwies 2 switch, stop the train and throw the switch behind you. Now back up to the rest of your train and recouple it behind you. You are assembled and ready to continue on to Imst-Pitztal!

Pull onto the mainline, and as your last car clears the siding, throw the switch to allow mainline operation again. As a measure of safety and courtesy, you should always return all switches to the mainline after any switching activities. Get up to track speed and take your new consist to your destination for a successful evaluation!

Activity Crew Call: Royalty on Board

A princess has come aboard at Vols station, looking for comfortable and discreet transport to Zirl with an unknown gentleman. Such things are to be expected on the legendary Orient Express, and you must make sure the train lives up to its reputation.

ACTIVITY SUMMARY

Locomotive/Train:	Gölsdorf Series 380
Starting Point:	Vols
Ending Point:	Zirl
Time of Day/light:	20:00; summer/clear
Difficulty Level:	Easy
Distance Covered:	4.5 miles
Estimated Duration:	10 minutes

Activity Strategy

Provide comfortable and timely passage for the princess and her companion by keeping a very close watch on train forces. Accelerate slowly and smoothly, and manage your train's slack by coasting before applying very gentle brake pressure when stopping. Although you've got to make it to Zirl on time, watch your speed around the corners to avoid jostling your royal passenger.

Playing the Activity

Start rolling as soon as you begin the Activity. Head for Kimanten station, gradually building up to a track speed of about 60 mph. Settings of roughly 50 regulator and 50 reverser should get you accelerating well once you are rolling, though you'll have to adjust according to your current speed and grade.

 TIP The Orient Express is one of the longest passenger trains in the game, and it has the most slack. Be very gentle with your controls, because it's very easy to exceed passenger comfort levels by slamming the cars into one another.

Start stopping about 0.4 miles outside of Kimanten, so that you have enough time to glide to a stop on about 50% brakes. Work your way up 10% at a time, spending a full 5 seconds or so at 10% brakes. You should drift to an on-time stop if you managed to get to 60 mph efficiently (see Figure 7.8). Make your station call, and start down the line again when you hear the all-clear whistle.

FIGURE 7.8:

Going fast isn't the same as accelerating and decelerating quickly. Pay careful attention to your in-train forces.

The last station is more of the same. Slow carefully beginning a third of a mile out, and be careful to apply your brakes slowly. Once again, if you accelerated efficiently, you should have no trouble meeting your scheduled arrival time.

Activity Crew Call: Short Passenger Run

Operate the Orient Express along a small section of its run during the winter, making station calls along the way.

ACTIVITY SUMMARY

Locomotive/Train:	Gölsdorf Series 380
Starting Point:	Ozthal
Ending Point:	Pfaffenhoffen
Time of Day/light:	10:00; winter/clear
Difficulty Level:	Easy
Distance Covered:	12.4 miles
Estimated Duration:	30 minutes

Activity Strategy

The snow is the most significant factor in this Activity. Stand by with your sander (the X key) to improve your traction should your wheels begin to slip. Six station calls along the way will challenge you with the start each time. Don't apply too much power from the stop, or your wheels will lose traction.

Playing the Activity

You begin outside of Ozthal, headed for Haiming. The line is fairly straight throughout this section of the route, so you need not worry about speed on the curves. Roll out and accelerate to about 50 mph before beginning to slow about a third of a mile short of Haiming. Coast for at least 15 seconds before gently applying 10% brakes, and then increase your brake pressure to about 40% to stop at the platform. Remember the weight of the Orient Express (see Figure 7.9), and begin your station stops earlier if you have to.

FIGURE 7.9:

The Orient Express is heavy, and can take up to half a mile to stop comfortably.

The rest of the Activity is exactly the same. Broad curves and 2–4 miles separate small village platforms. Begin decelerating no closer than a third of a mile from the stations, and accelerate slowly until your slack is played out. Once the last car has started to move, you may begin accelerating at will. If you find yourself lagging behind schedule, try increasing your speed between stations rather than compressing your acceleration and deceleration phases.

Activity Crew Call: Murder on the Orient Express

A real whodunit during your run from St. Anton to Innsbruck leaves you as the primary assistant to a detective trying to solve the murder. Make changes to your consist as you complete the run to Innsbruck as directed by the detective.

ACTIVITY SUMMARY

Locomotive/Train:	Gölsdorf Series 380
Starting Point:	Near Silz
Ending Point:	Innsbruck
Time of Day/light:	17:00; autumn/rain
Difficulty Level:	Medium
Distance Covered:	24 miles
Estimated Duration:	1 hour

Activity Strategy

In this fun and challenging Activity, a detective will give you instructions along the way via pop-up messages that will alter your timetable and work orders. Follow his directions, and whenever you complete a task, continue on your regular route to Innsbruck.

Playing the Activity

You begin this Activity underway, just west of Silz. Because you are an express train headed down the grade from the resorts at St. Anton, you don't have any scheduled stops other than your destination in Innsbruck. All this will change a few minutes into the Activity when someone will commit a murder on board.

 TIP Watch yard signals carefully when switching. You'll usually only be able to operate one side of the yard, and if you blow a signal the Activity will end immediately!

Follow the detective's instructions to help solve the crime. He will direct you to set out some cars along the way, and make other changes to your consist as he sees fit. Use the F8 key to view the status of the switches closest to the front and back of your train (see Figure 7.10). Use G to throw switches in front of you, and Shift-G to throw those behind you. The Station and Siding labels (F6) will also be a great help to you, as this tool will help you figure out which sidings the detective is specifying.

The Activity ends with a surprise revelation, so rather than expose the entire storyline we'll leave it to you to discover! Simply follow the instructions for setouts, and get back on the mainline for Innsbruck whenever the inspector is not giving you specific instructions. Don't forget to use F8 to bring up the Train Operations menu when you're setting out a car. Also, it's important to maintain yard speeds under 15 mph to avoid jostling the passengers. Make all the proper setouts with the help of your dialog boxes and monitors, and you should complete this Activity with a successful arrest!

FIGURE 7.10:

Switches can either be thrown in the Switching dialog box itself, or by using G and Shift-G.

Activity Crew Call: Bride and Groom

Your train has been held at Landeck station for a newlywed couple. Their honeymoon boat is floating down the Rosanna River in a little over an hour, and you must race to get them there on time.

ACTIVITY SUMMARY

Locomotive/Train:	Gölsdorf Series 380
Starting Point:	Landeck
Ending Point:	St. Anton
Time of Day/light:	14:15; spring/clear
Difficulty Level:	Hard
Distance Covered:	17.2 miles
Estimated Duration:	1 hour

Activity Strategy

Despite the briefing suggesting maximum speed all the way up the mountain, you won't be able to rush this one any faster than your timetable permits. Thus, concentrate on making efficient, smooth starts and stops, and accelerating all the way to the next station.

Temporary speed restriction:

- 15 mph speed restriction, MP 11.5 to 9

Playing the Activity

You begin at the Landeck platform, headed for Perfuchs. Accelerate gently at first, taking up all the slack in your train. Once the last car starts moving (you can use the external camera to help you discern this), accelerate rapidly out of the station. As with every other Activity with the Orient Express, your stops must also be managed so that the train bunches up against the locomotive before you begin any heavy braking (see Figure 7.11). Make all of your station calls on time, and try accelerating a bit faster on the high end if you start lagging behind.

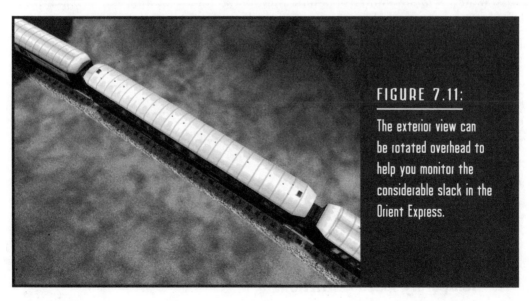

FIGURE 7.11:

The exterior view can be rotated overhead to help you monitor the considerable slack in the Orient Express.

The engineering project at MP 11.5 will slow you down for a mile and a half. Fortunately the zone is on an uphill stretch of track, which makes it easier to keep your speed under the limit. Make sure you avoid stalling the train, monitoring your projected speed very carefully in the Track Monitor dialog box. Remember that the rear of your train must be clear of the slow order zone before you can accelerate to track speed.

Activity Crew Call: Replacement Locomotive

The locomotive at the head of the Orient Express has broken down at Pians station and is out of service. Head out to replace the locomotive at maximum speed and hook up with the stranded train, completing its journey to Landeck.

ACTIVITY SUMMARY

Locomotive/Train:	Gölsdorf Series 380
Starting Point:	Strengen
Ending Point:	Landeck
Time of Day/light:	11:00; autumn/clear
Difficulty Level:	Hard
Distance Covered:	7.9 miles
Estimated Duration:	25 minutes

Activity Strategy

The first part of this Activity is a unique pleasure—just your locomotive and tender with special instructions to make the best time possible to Pians. While minding the 100-mph mainline speed limit, dash to meet the stranded train. Hook up with it gently, and complete its journey.

Temporary speed restriction:

• 15 mph speed restriction, MP 15.2 to 16.1

Playing the Activity

Throw caution to the wind and fly up the line to Pians. If you love speed, you couldn't ask for a better scenario: with no train in tow, dispatch has called upon you to make your best time to rendezvous with the stranded train. There's no slack to worry about, no comfort around the corners, and no weight to hold you back. Open up the regulator and let her go as fast as she can! You'll have to slow down at MP 15, but approach to within a half mile at full speed, and then apply emergency brakes at approximately 0.2 miles out.

Once you arrive in Pians, slow to 20 mph to negotiate the yard. Pass the siding switch, then throw it behind you by pressing shift-G, or click the lower arrow in the Switch display. Back up under 15 mph to negotiate the siding, then slow to a 4-mph crawl as you approach the stranded train. Monitor your coupling operation with the Coupler view (6), and try to stop your locomotive just as you make contact with the train (see Figure 7.12).

FIGURE 7.12:

Try to brake so that your locomotive comes to a stop just at the point of contact with the train.

As soon as you are coupled, set the train brake. Release the hand brakes on the cars by double-clicking them in the Train Operations menu (F9). Double-check all cars after you've released each individual brake, because a set brake could be very dangerous on the move. Once clear, gently pull out of Pians and head for your scheduled stop in Perfuchs. Take up the slack in your train with a gentle initial brake application, then apply moderate brakes to come to a stop.

TIP It will feel strange to have a train behind your locomotive after your high-speed, unladen run. Be sure to avoid jarring your passengers by using smooth transitions, and plan for all that extra weight in your acceleration and braking.

The last leg of your journey is uneventful. Make sure you're not getting any wheel slippage on your acceleration phase towards Landeck. You can either watch your wheels, or use the heads-up display via the F5 key. If you see Wheelslip Indicator, back off the regulator and reverser until it disappears, then reapply them at about 10% lower settings than the onset of wheelslip. Make another smooth stop at Landeck to complete the Activity successfully!

Activity Crew Call: St. Anton-Innsbruck in the Winter

Take the Orient Express down the entire route from St. Anton to Innsbruck in the middle of the winter, stopping at every station along the way.

ACTIVITY SUMMARY

Locomotive/Train:	Gölsdorf Series 380
Starting Point:	St. Anton
Ending Point:	Innsbruck
Time of Day/light:	7:30; winter/snow
Difficulty Level:	Hard
Distance Covered:	63.8 miles
Estimated Duration:	3 hours

Activity Strategy

This is one of the most difficult Activities in the game—the grand tour of a difficult route in the middle of a winter snowstorm. Ice on the rails dictates two slow order zones, but these are by no means the only areas of low traction. Go easy on the speed and brake very, very early to avoid losing control of your train down the grade.

Temporary speed restrictions:

- 15 mph speed restriction, MP 15 to 17

- 15 mph speed restriction, MP 29 to 30.5

Playing the Activity

This is it—the real test of your train-handling skills. Everything in this book up to this point applies on this run. You've got to manage your speed very carefully, using your mouse to waggle the brakes. Keep your train tight against the locomotive even on the downgrades, using very gradual acceleration assisted by gravity. Use the heads-up display to monitor your wheelslip very carefully (see Figure 7.13).

FIGURE 7.13:

Monitor your traction with the heads-up display, and reduce your control settings if you see wheelslip.

You'll want to start decelerating almost half a mile away from each station. Don't use more than about 20% brakes, or your wheels will slip. If they do, immediately back off the brakes until you regain traction. Make ample use of your sander in all transitions—whenever you are accelerating or decelerating.

NOTE You can still run at high speeds in foul weather: unlike a car on a road, your train will stay on the rails in the snow just as easily as you would on a dry day. The real challenge is speeding up and slowing down without losing traction.

You have plenty of time to make it between stations if you accelerate and decelerate at a reasonable rate. Try to make all of your station calls on time. If you are lagging behind, try pushing your acceleration a little bit, but don't compromise braking distance. You simply cannot stop any faster on wet rails, and it is important to maintain the safety of your dignified passengers. Even if you fall off schedule, if you manage to make all of your station stops you'll at least complete the Activity successfully.

Off Duty

With its extremely sensitive tolerances to in-train forces and tradition of passenger comfort, the Orient Express is by far the hardest route in the game. Success in the Orient Express Activities is truly a great accomplishment, and if you've done them in order, this marks the completion of the challenges that ship with *Train Simulator*. Your adventures on the rails are far from over, however. From here, you're ready to explore the incredible expandability of *Train Simulator*, and we'll run you past every milepost of expanding the game in the next part of this guide!

Part II

Game Tools

Hi, I'm Rick Smith, your guide for the second part of the book. I'm a game designer and programmer and I'm thrilled to have this opportunity to help you get started laying track.

In the final chapters of this book you will learn how to create and modify Activities, routes, and terrain. This will require mastering some tools and terminology. They may seem complex at first, but this portion of the book is intended to make these potentially complicated topics a bit more accessible.

Whether you intend to build a new route or add to an existing one, you'll learn how to place the scenery, roads, buildings, and animals along the way. You will also learn how to create new Activities for your own railways and add them

Chapter 8

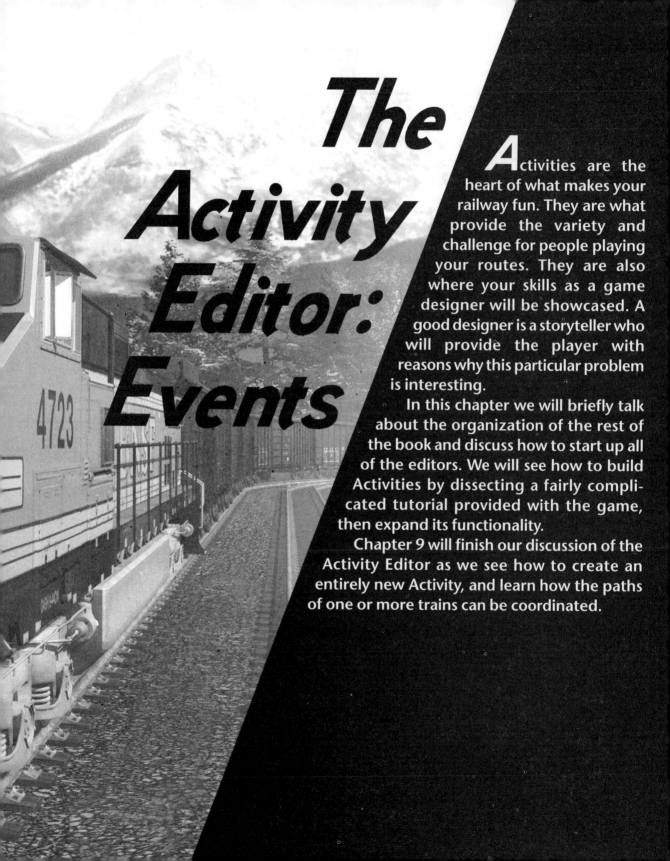

The Activity Editor: Events

Activities are the heart of what makes your railway fun. They are what provide the variety and challenge for people playing your routes. They are also where your skills as a game designer will be showcased. A good designer is a storyteller who will provide the player with reasons why this particular problem is interesting.

In this chapter we will briefly talk about the organization of the rest of the book and discuss how to start up all of the editors. We will see how to build Activities by dissecting a fairly complicated tutorial provided with the game, then expand its functionality.

Chapter 9 will finish our discussion of the Activity Editor as we see how to create an entirely new Activity, and learn how the paths of one or more trains can be coordinated.

How Best to Build a Railway

The most logical way to create a new railway in *Train Simulator* would be to first build the hills, rivers, valleys, and mountains. Next we would put in the route data, the tunnels, track, signals, stations, and the scenery. Finally we would worry about the specifics of the trains' schedules and work orders. Though this is logical, in this and the next chapters I will teach you how to build in the reverse order: Activities, routes, then physical geometry. Why?

The first reason is that if you build an Activity on an existing route you will immediately be able to use it in the game. But if you build the geometry first, you will have to learn how to create a route and get one working and then learn about Activities and get one working before you can see your terrain in the game.

The second reason is that in many ways the Activity Editor is the most complicated of the editors in *Train Simulator*. So when we discuss it, we want to make sure we have a solid base (terrain and route) to work from. If we first hone our skills with the existing routes, it will be easier to design our own.

If you would like to try making your terrain first, go right ahead! Once you have read the next section about how to start up the editors, the remaining chapters work independently from each other, and you can skip ahead.

Train Simulator's Editors

If you want to use *Train Simulator* editors to expand the game, make sure that you chose the full install when you first installed the game. If you find that the editors are missing, reinstall the game.

Starting Train Simulator's Editors

The easiest way to start up the *Train Simulator* editors is to go to the Start menu on the task bar. Choose Programs, then Microsoft Games, then Train Simulator, then Train Simulator Editors & Tools (see Figure 8.1).

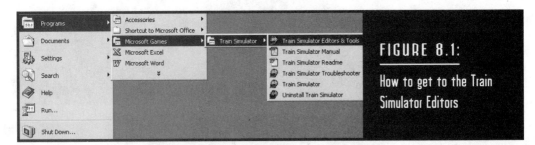

FIGURE 8.1:

How to get to the Train Simulator Editors

If you are using the editors a lot, you may wish to make a shortcut to your desktop. To do this, open up the Start menu as described previously, but instead of left-clicking Train Simulator Editors & Tools, right-click the Train Simulator Editors & Tools icon and hold down the right mouse button, then drag the mouse onto the desktop. Release the mouse button. A short menu will come up that has four choices: Copy Here, Move Here, Create Shortcut(s) Here, and Cancel. Choose the Create Shortcut(s) Here option. From now on you just have to double-click the shortcut icon to open the editor. If you ever want to get rid of the shortcut, just drag it to the recycle bin.

When you open the editor you will see the screen shown in Figure 8.2.

FIGURE 8.2:

The menu screen for the Editors

Train Simulator's Editors Defined

There are four editors that you can use; to activate them just click the menu item. You can choose from the Activity Editor, the Route Editor, the Route Geometry Extractor, and the Cab Editor.

- **The Activity Editor** enables you to build an Activity with weather effects, other rail traffic and specific schedules, and work orders to fulfill. Adding new Activities is a powerful way to expand the number of things to do. You can also fine-tune specific scenarios to match your level of interest, time, and difficulty.

- **The Route Editor** enables you to fine-tune the height data for your railway, lay track, and place buildings, roads, signs, signals, and other game objects. This is the easiest way to customize your railway.

- **The Route Geometry Extractor** will create a rough physical map of your railway. If you are modeling a real world route, it will give you geographic data of the real railway.

- **The Cab Editor** is a tool for the last step in adding new engines to *Train Simulator*. The Cab Editor is a bit beyond the scope of this book—we won't be covering its functions or creating 3D models of cars and engines and importing them into the game.

Other Utilities

In addition to these four editors there are a number of small programs that allow advanced users to import data into the game. These include makeace.exe (a utility for converting textures into a format that can be used by the game), TSUnpack (which unpacks Activity packages) and conv3dsd.exe (a utility for importing 3D objects into Train Simulator). We will not cover these programs in this book. Check the technical documents on the CD for descriptions of these tools.

The Activity Editor

This is the program that enables you to create new scenarios for *Train Simulator*. An Activity should tell a story or give the player a challenge that they have to overcome. Before you begin to build an Activity, know what kind of story you hope to tell.

 NOTE I use the terms Activity and scenario interchangeably throughout Part 2 of the book.

There are four basic types of Activities:

- **Passenger Service** is the most straightforward. You are the engineer of a passenger train and you must travel the route safely and as close to the schedule as possible. You also want to give your passengers a smooth ride. To make these Activities more interesting, the scenario designer will typically spice things up by adding difficulties such as animals on the track, malfunctioning signals, bad weather, and other traffic on the rails.

- **Road Freight** is long distance freight trains running on the main line. Typically they have a lower priority than passenger trains and so will have to stay on a siding when a passenger train is approaching. Often these trains are extremely massive; they usually have several engines to pull them along. It is difficult to keep such a heavy train to a low speed when going down steep grades. If you are carrying iron ore a few lurches and bangs are perfectly all right. However, some types of freight are more fragile and you will be expected to take greater care.

- **Local Freight** is just moving freight along branch lines. There is less traffic than with road freight, the consists are smaller than with road freight, and typically the distances traveled are much shorter. You will be much more concerned with moving individual cars to and from sidings for local industries.

- **Yard Freight** is building up consists from a rail yard. You will have to assemble a train out of individual cars, which may be scattered all over the yard. In some cases the order of the cars you pick up does not make a difference, but at other times you must build the consist in a particular order. This Activity is much easier if there are just a few cars in the rail yard. If the yard is congested, it is much more difficult to pull the needed consist together.

 TIP Advise your players to use F6 to turn on siding names and F7 to turn on car numbers when designing a yard freight scenario.

In the next section I'll introduce you to the Activity Editor by taking you step-by-step through building up a local freight Activity.

Expanding an Existing Activity

The Freight Activity Tutorial can be found in the Marias Pass Activities. It takes a little over five minutes to play through and if you have not played it you should do so now. During this Activity you pick up a car off the siding, then move your train a quarter mile down the track. Because this is a tutorial, messages come up several times with instructions for the player.

In this section we will add an extra freight car to the sidings and change the victory conditions so that a car picked up must be delivered to another siding further down the line. We will provide tutorial help messages warning the player not to pick up the wrong cars. We will change the victory conditions so that the player will lose if they pick up the wrong cars. Lastly we will have to revise the existing messages so that the user playing the new tutorial is given accurate advice.

Step 1. Starting Up the Activity Editor and Loading *freighttutorial.act*

Following the steps described in the section Starting Train Simulator's Editors, start up the Train Simulator Editors & Tools program and select the Activity Editor. You should be looking at the screen shown in Figure 8.3.

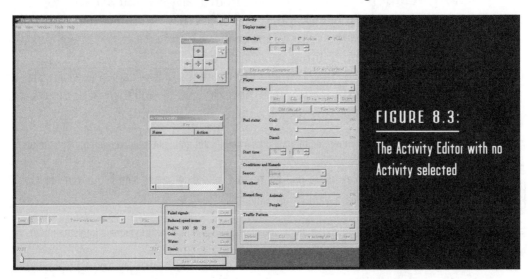

FIGURE 8.3:

The Activity Editor with no Activity selected

Go into the File menu and select Open…. You will see seven folders: two for Europe, two for Japan, a tutorial route, and two folders for the USA. Double-click the folder USA2. You will now see a dozen or so folders; the top one is labeled ACTIVITIES (see Figure 8.4).

Double-click ACTIVITIES. You will see the 10 or so Activities for the Marias Pass line. One of the files is called freighttutorial.act. Double-click this file to open the basic tutorial scenario, which we will modify.

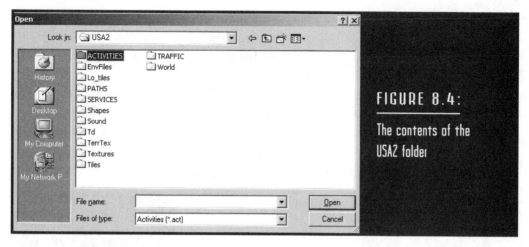

FIGURE 8.4:

The contents of the USA2 folder

Step 2. Moving to Where the Tutorial is Set Up

You should see a map showing the whole route with numbers and symbols overlapping each other (see Figure 8.5). This map is so busy that it's hard to see what's important. The first task is to find where the train and cars start, so look for a square window labeled Tools with five arrow buttons on it (as well as a plus and minus magnifying glass). Spend a moment pushing these buttons and watch what happens with the map. The arrows move the map around, the center button takes you back to the default view showing the whole route, and the magnifying glasses zoom in and out toward the center of the map.

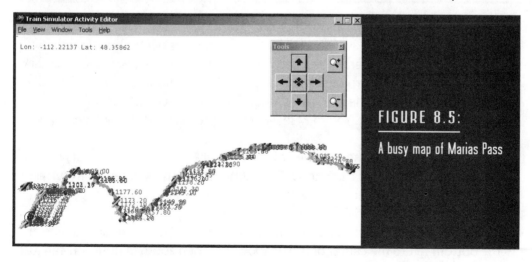

FIGURE 8.5:

A busy map of Marias Pass

There is a much easier way to use the map: left-click some white space and press and hold the mouse button. Now drag the cursor and the whole map will move quickly. You can zoom in and out by holding down the right mouse button and moving the mouse toward or away from you.

To get rid of the Tools window, go into the Window menu. One of the menu items should be the Tools window with a checkmark in front of it. Click this menu item and the Tools window should vanish. (If the Action Event window is in your way, you can get rid of it the same way.) Left-click the View menu to activate the drop-down menu (see Figure 8.6.).

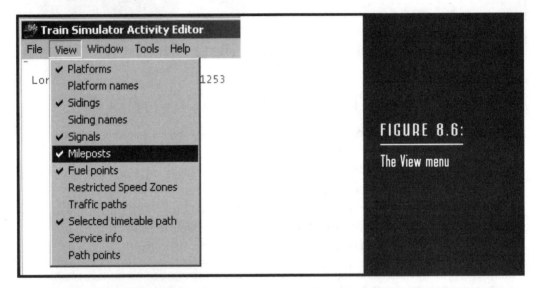

FIGURE 8.6:

The View menu

There are 12 different things that can be shown on the map, and currently about half are selected, as indicated by the checkmarks before the names. Open up this menu several times and click each of the names with a checkmark in front of it. This will turn off that item so that information does not show up on the map. When all the items are turned off you will see just the rail line covered with black dots. You may see a few purple circles at the bottom-left side of the map.

The black dots are the switches where the track branches. Black dots also mark where a section of track ends. The purple circles show where railway cars are sitting. Only one place on the map has any railway cars, and that corner is the location of the tutorial.

Use the arrow buttons or drag with your mouse to move the branch line at the bottom-left to the center of the window and then zoom in until you can just see that section of the track. You should now see something like Figure 8.7.

FIGURE 8.7:

The Kalispell branch line

You should see some small green circles with numbers as well as some larger purple circles. Please zoom in closer on the purple circles.

Step 3. Examining the Editor

Pause for a moment to study the rest of the editor before looking at the details of the Activity. There are six areas placed around the main map, along with a small floating window. We will look at these in clockwise order.

In the top-right corner is a box labeled Activity. This has some information about the Activity as a whole. Display Name is the name of the Activity that your players will see when they are choosing between the Activities during the game.

Under that is the Difficulty, which is just a way to indicate how hard it is to succeed at this Activity. Changing the difficulty value does not make the scenario any easier or more difficult; it's how you communicate the anticipated difficulty level to your players. Next comes Duration, which enables you to tell the player how long you think it will take to finish the Activity. This is an estimate—the player may do it in more or less time. Lastly, at the bottom of this box are two buttons labeled Edit Activity Description and Edit Activity Brief. The Activity description is the short text that describes what the scenario is about. The briefing is a much longer set of text that will tell the player what they must do when they start your scenario.

 WARNING Note that the Activity Briefing and the Activity Description are mandatory. The Activity won't save if these are left blank.

In the middle-right section of the screen is a box labeled Player divided into three sections. The top Player service gives information about the train that your user will be driving and the timetable (for passenger trains) or the work order (for freight Activities). Next is the Fuel status, allowing you to set how much fuel a player has at the start of the scenario. Lastly is the Starting Time, which is set on a 24-hour clock, so if you want to start at 3:00 PM you have to put in 15:00.

Below this is the Conditions and Hazards box where you can set up the season, the weather, and how often the player will see animals near the track. The animals don't show up automatically; you have to place some potential locations in the Route Editor. At the bottom-right section is the Traffic Pattern, which informs you of other trains that are running on the tracks during your Activity.

Under the main map are two unnamed boxes. The one on the left is used to check the timing when you have several trains running on the route. The one on the right enables you to set how much fuel and water are at a refueling stop and enables you to cause signals to malfunction. We won't look at these in this short tutorial; see the Microsoft Documentation for more information.

 NOTE You also may see a floating window labeled Action Events. We will discuss it later.

Step 4. Studying the Existing Cars

There are 19 green and gray circles inside of each other on the map (numbered from 0 to 18). (The gray circles are always the same size and show the location of the event regardless of the map's scale. The green circles show the radius of the event, and when you have zoomed out may become so small as to be invisible.) These are the location events that occur in the tutorial. Most of them will display a message when the player reaches them.

We turned off all of the map information to make it easier to see what's going on. Let's turn some of the information back on. Go to the View menu and turn on Siding Names and Service info. Now let's zoom in on the cars. Your screen should look like Figure 8.8.

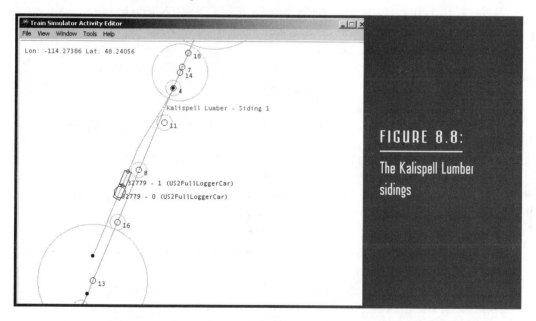

FIGURE 8.8:

The Kalispell Lumber sidings

We can see two cars on a siding. Each of the cars now has its number and its type shown in purple. What does not show up on this view is the engine and cars that the player will be running. We can look at the player's consist by choosing Verify Start State in the Tools menu. We will make some changes to the consist, so we will edit it as soon as we have made a new copy of the Activity.

NOTE In this game a service is made up of an engine and/or cars (a consist) and the path that the consist takes.

Step 5. Saving a New Copy of This Activity

We are about to start modifying this Activity, so make a copy that we can play with—this way we won't mess up the original scenario that comes with the game. *Train Simulator* will not Save As… unless you have made a change, so let's make a minor change to the game then save our copy.

Go to the Player rectangle on the middle-right side of the screen and change the start time to 10:05. Now go up to the File menu and choose Save As…. Give it any name you wish (I'm calling my version, Freight_Tutorial_2).

When the player starts the game and tries to play a Marias Pass Activity, he or she will see two scenarios with the name Freight Activity Tutorial. To fix that, let's change the display name of our tutorial. Go to the top-right area, labeled Activity, and change the text in the box labeled Display Name to New Freight Tutorial 2 (or some other name you like). Save (not Save As…) your scenario.

Now you have a private copy you can experiment on without hurting the original Activity. From this point forward we will be working with our new version and you can freely try out changes.

Step 6. Looking at the Player's Starting Service

Look in the Player box in the middle-right part of the screen. Click the Edit button, which is just under the text box that contains Tut6_Service. When you click the Edit button, the Service Editor dialog box appears. Let's take a look at the controls in this dialog box, shown in Figure 8.9.

The Display Name is the name that the player will see. It does not have to be unique but this is a good idea. (The file name that you give the Activity must be unique.) If you want to give the new tutorial a shorter Display Name you may, but I suggest that you keep the Display Name the same as the real one to avoid confusion. The Expected Player Performance tells the computer how tough to grade the player when reporting on how well they have done after they have completed the action. Starting speed is self-explanatory. Ending speed is irrelevant for the player's services but for computer controlled trains it allows you to say what speed it should be going when it leaves the route.

Let's skip the Consist section for a minute and look now at the Path. In the Path section click the Edit button just under the text box labeled Playtest_Freight1_Path. This brings up the Path Editor. The player's starting position is a blue dot with a green circle around it. The ending position is a blue dot with a purple circle around it. (You may have to scroll or zoom the screen to see both on the map at once.) In this view the cars and other information we have been looking at on the map do not show.

Service editor

Name: tut6service

Display name: Tut6Service

Expected player performance   75

Start speed: Miles per hour   0

End speed: Miles per hour   0

Consist:

GP38-2 lumber

| New | Edit | Use as template | Delete |

Path:

Tut6Path

| New | Edit | Use as template | Delete |

Stops:

| Stations | |

| OK | Cancel |

FIGURE 8.9.

The Service Editor dialog box

Left-click the ending position and drag it down the track a short distance so that the train has to travel a tiny bit farther than it does now. Then click the button labeled Leave Path Editor to return to the Service Editor dialog box. When you are asked if you want to save your changes, say Yes.

Your screen should again look like it did in Figure 8.9. Let's change the starting engine and cars for the player. This is called the player's consist. We could make a new consist and once it is made select it here, but for now let's just modify the existing consist. Click the button labeled Use As Template just under the text box labeled GP38-2 Lumber.

TIP If we click the Edit button, we will change that consist for every activity in Train Simulator, which may break scenarios that use that consist. By making a new consist based on the existing one, we can make any changes we want without affecting any other Activities.

The Consist Editor opens. Notice that the new consist has been given a new name (GP38-2 lumber1) by adding a number to the end of the existing name. You can change this name or leave it as it is. Let's add a new car to the player's train. Scroll the picture of the consist at the bottom of the window until you can see the empty car just after the lumber car. Left-click this car and drag it up into the Preview box. Your screen should look like Figure 8.10.

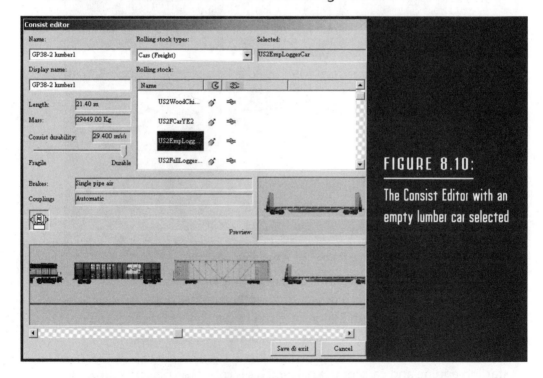

FIGURE 8.10:

The Consist Editor with an empty lumber car selected

At the top-right of the window the Selected text box now has the name of the current car in it. It is an empty logger. In the middle of the window is a white area called Rolling stock. Click the car directly below the US2EmpLoggerCar. It is a US2FcarRE2. The car showing in the Preview window changes. Left-click the grain car and drag it down into the player's consist just behind the engine. The new car is added to the train in the spot where you drop it. More cars can be added in this fashion.

WARNING This scenario has location events that expect the player's train to be a certain length. As you make the train longer, these will trigger at less appropriate times.

To delete a car you don't want in your consist, drag it to the little white car crusher icon that is just below the word Couplings, and then release the mouse button. The train will instantly update, showing you the new consist without that car.

We're done here for now, so select the Save & Exit button on the bottom of the window. We have finished looking at the player's starting consist, so click OK on the Service editor.

Step 7. Adding a New Box Car to the Siding

Let's make the tutorial a little bit tougher by adding an extra car to the siding. The player is not supposed to pick up this new car. We will place it behind the two cars the player should pick up, near the end of the siding.

TIP The new car can't be put on the very end of the siding; it must be placed a few yards away from the end to fit.

Adjust the map so you can see the siding clearly and move the cursor (without holding down any buttons) over the siding where you want to place the new car. A small gray circle should appear. Right-click the mouse. You should see the following menu shown in Figure 8.11.

Select the Place Consist menu item. This will bring up a small dialog box labeled Place Consist (see Figure 8.12).

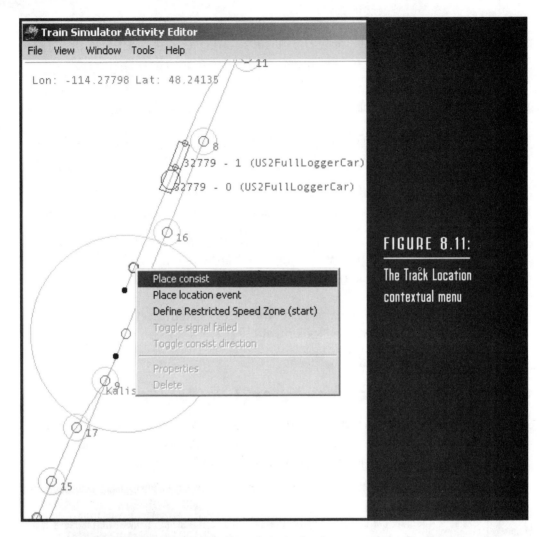

Train Simulator Activity Editor

File   View   Window   Tools   Help

Lon: -114.27798 Lat: 48.24135

11

8

32779 - 1 (US2FullLoggerCar)

32779 - 0 (US2FullLoggerCar)

16

| Place consist |
| Place location event |
| Define Restricted Speed Zone (start) |
| Toggle signal failed |
| Toggle consist direction |
| Properties |
| Delete |

9
Kalis

17

15

FIGURE 8.11:

The Track Location contextual menu

You can pick consists that already exist in the game, but for the sake of practice, let's make a new one. Push the New button; this brings up the Consist Editor dialog box (see Figure 8.10, earlier in this chapter). Select the Rolling Stock Type combo box; it should be labeled Engines (Electric). Pick Cars (Freight). In the Rolling Stock area of the screen, look through the various cars that you can pick. Grab one you like (I got US2Freight8) and drag it to the long blue box at the bottom of the screen. We have to give this consist a name. Call it Single_Boxcar in both the Name and the Display Name text boxes. You're done; click the Save & Exit button. A warning message will come up saying that this consist does not have an engine, and that we won't be able to start the player driving this consist. Click the Yes button to save it anyway. Click OK on the Place Consist dialog box.

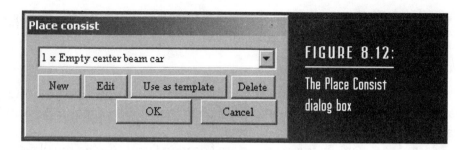

FIGURE 8.12:

The Place Consist dialog box

Step 8: Reviewing Changes and Trying Out Your Activity

We have now made enough changes that our Activity should look different from the basic scenario. Let's make one more change, then see what it looks like in the game. Go over to the Activity rectangle on the top-right of the screen and click the Edit Activity Brief button. This will bring up the briefing that tells the player what they're supposed to do. Change it so that it says that the player should only take the first two cars on the siding, then close the Edit box.

Go into the File menu and pick Save, then quit the editor and try out your new Activity in the Marias Pass scenarios. Notice that the extra boxcar appears on the siding. By going to external view (press 2 or 3 in the game) you can see the extra car in the player's consist.

Step 9. Examining the Events

There are three kinds of events: Location Events, Time Events, and Action Events. You've already seen Location Events (they are the concentric green and gray circles). They are triggered when the player reaches the radius (the green circle) around the event. Time Events occur when the game time reaches a specific triggering point. Action Events are triggered when the player performs an action. The following are actions that can trigger Action Events (in the order that they appear in the dialog box):

1. Stop at final station

2. Pick up passengers

3. Make a pickup

4. Reach speed X

5. Pickup Cars

6. Drop off cars at location

7. Assemble train

8. Assemble train at location

To see the Time Events or the Action Events you must open the windows that show them. These are turned on and off in the Window menu. (We will go over these types of events in detail later.)

Most of the events in this scenario are Location Events (when the player reaches this location, trigger something). Events are very important and we will come back to them several times in this tutorial, but for now, let's just look at some of the easier ones.

Location Events

Zoom out so that you can see several of the events. Move the cursor over the green and gray event circle with an 8 beside it. Right-click the event to get a menu like that shown in Figure 8.13.

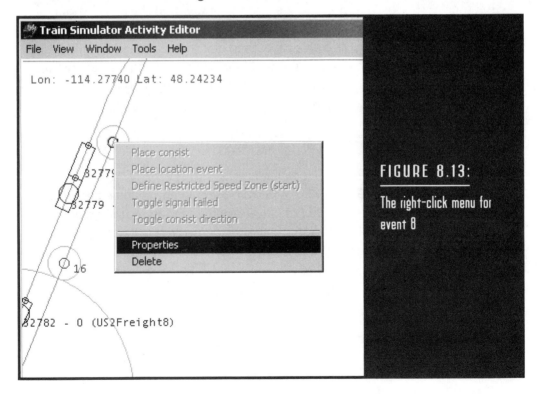

FIGURE 8.13:

The right-click menu for event 8

A mostly grayed-out menu will appear. There are two legal choices at the bottom of the menu: Properties and Delete. Choose Properties. This brings up the Location Event Properties dialog box, as shown in Figure 8.14.

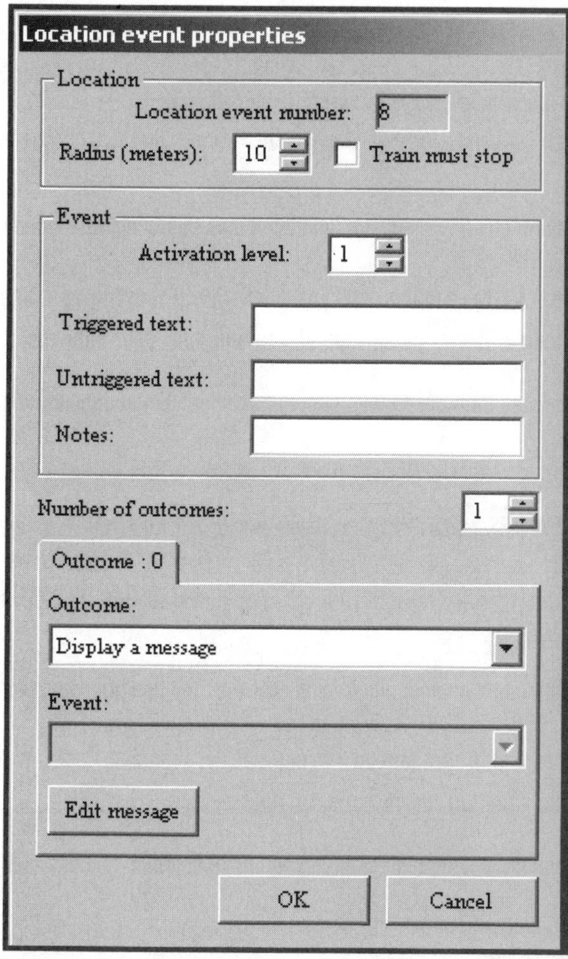

FIGURE 8.14:

The Location Event Properties dialog box for event 8

The top part of the dialog box is a rectangle labeled Location that shows the event's number, gives the radius that it can be triggered in, and enables you to say that the train must be stopped before the event will be triggered.

The middle part of the dialog box is the Event rectangle. The activation level is a way of turning the event on or off. Unless the event's activation level is 1 or higher, the event can't be triggered. The text boxes labeled Triggered Text and Untriggered Text are messages that will be printed out in the final report when the player is looking over how well they have done. The Notes text box is just a place where you can leave messages to other people who are reading these events and trying to figure out what is going on.

In the bottom part of the dialog box is the place for the result(s) of the event. This event has just one outcome (others will have more). Outcome 0 will display a message. Click the Edit Message button.

This edit box is where event 8's message is composed and changed. Let's make this message a bit more informative. Add this sentence to the message: "You can rotate the view by pressing ALT+ (left or right arrow)." When you are done changing the message, click the close box (the small box with the X in it) in the top-right of the Message to Display window. Click the OK button to exit this dialog box.

 TIP When you have edited the text make sure you click the OK button to close the Location Event Properties window. If you press Cancel you will lose your changes.

Time Events

Time Events are events that will trigger after a certain amount of time has gone by. This Activity has nine timer events. To see them, select the Window menu. One of your choices is Time Events window. Click it, and a small window will appear with the nine Time Events.

 TIP Occasionally the window can get moved off screen. By choosing Reset Window Positions in the Window menu they will move back to their default positions.

The first event is called "First Message." To change its name, double-click it (don't do this now). To look at the event, right-click it and select the properties menu item that comes up. A dialog box that looks similar to the Location dialog box appears. Look at the message that it displays, then look at the messages displayed by the first three Time Events.

 NOTE The first Time Events listed in the dialog box are not the first three reached in the game. They go off in timer order.

The second and third Time Events are designed to help the player get going, a good thing in a tutorial. However, we don't want NoMoving (the third message), which says that the player is having a hard time getting going, to come up if the player has already got the train moving. How can we turn it off?

The trick is that the events can affect each other. What the designer of this tutorial did is put a Location Event just in front of the starting position of the engine. When the player reaches it, it turns off the timer event NoMoving.

Close out of any dialog boxes and look at the 2D map. The first Location Event that the player will reach once they start moving is number 12. Right-click that event and bring up its properties. The outcome says "Decrease an events activation level by 1" and underneath it is a combo box labeled Event that says NoMoving. NoMoving is the name of the Timer Event that we just looked at (see Figure 8.15).

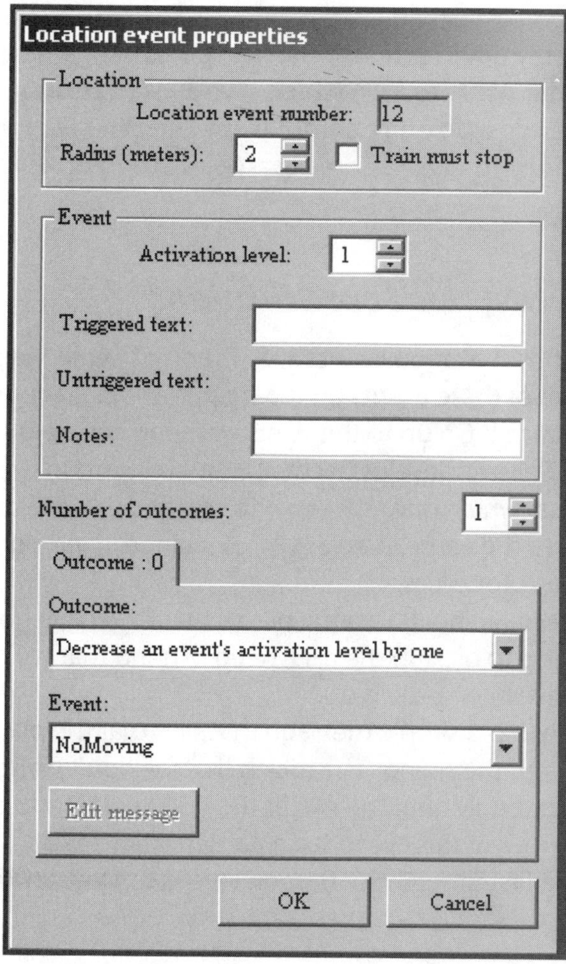

FIGURE 8.15:

Location event 12 will affect Timed Event NoMoving.

When you move your train forward a little bit, Location Event 12 is triggered. It lowers the activation level of the Timer Event by one. Now any event will *only* go off if its activation level is 1 or more, so the activation level of the Timer Event NoMoving goes from a one to a zero. This means that it won't play if the player has moved the train forward before one minute and 35 seconds have gone by.

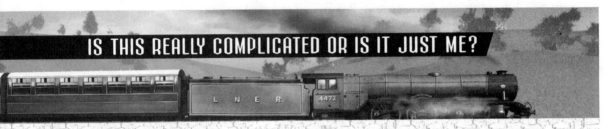

IS THIS REALLY COMPLICATED OR IS IT JUST ME?

By the way, the tutorial we are studying has far more events than you will likely put into most of your scenarios. Tutorials, which give a lot of context-sensitive advice to the player, tend to be quite complex. By the time we finish studying and changing this action, you will be an expert on setting up events.

Step 10: Working with Different Events

In this section we will look at how Location Events 4, 5, 7, and 11 work together. Rather than right-clicking each of these events on the map, there is a second way to see how they are organized. Go up to the Window menu item and select the Location Events window. This window lists all the Location Events in the scenario and shows their name, which makes it easier to remember what they do. Remember, double-clicking the name enables you to change it and right-clicking it allows you to view its properties.

The easiest event is 5, Passed Siding. It tells the player that they have gone past the siding and must reverse to pick up the cars. Keep in mind that we don't want it to run after the cars have been picked up.

Event 11, Forgot to Switch, has a simple message that says that the player didn't use the switch to get on to the siding. The trick is that we don't want it to run the first time we reach it, but only after the player has gone past it and come back. Take a look at the properties of this event. Its initial activation level is zero, so when the train hits it for the first time, the activation level is too low and it does not run.

Event 4, SlowToCouple, is the mastermind behind events 5 and 11. Open up its properties and study it (or look at the screenshot from Figure 8.16). Note that this event has three outcomes. Outcome zero displays a message telling the player not to go too fast. Outcome one decreases the activation level for the event PassedSiding (location event 5). Outcome two increases the activation level for the event ForgotToSwitch. When an event has several outcomes they *all* take effect if the event triggers. Event SlowToCouple (Location Event 4) has an activation level that starts at zero.

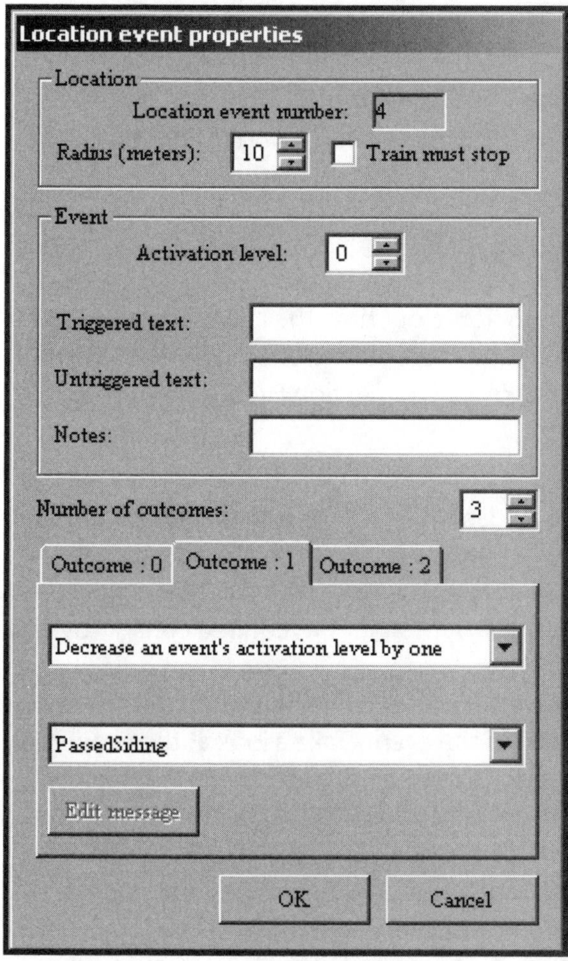

FIGURE 8.16:

SlowToCouple's properties

Event 7, StopAfterSiding, has two outcomes: It prints out a message and increases 4's activation level.

Let's follow what happens when the player's train rolls forward. It hits event ForgotToSwitch (Location Event 11) first but that event's activation level is zero so it does not trigger. No message is displayed. Then the train hits location 4. It starts with an activation level of 0 so it does not trigger. Now the train hits StopAfterSiding (event 7), which tells the player how to stop a train, and increases SlowToCouple (4) activation level by 1. The train goes on to PassedSiding (5), and gets a message that it's time to back up. The player starts to back up, and suppose for example that the player forgets to change the switch. The train hits 7 again. Location Events can only be triggered once. Since number 7 has already gone off, it isn't triggered again.

The train continues backing and hits SlowToCouple (4). Because its activation is now one, it triggers, doing three things: sending a message, reducing the PassedSiding (5) activation level by one, and increasing the ForgotToSwitch level by one. The user continues to back on the main line, hits ForgotToSwitch (11) which triggers because 4 turned it on. The player stops, reverses, goes forward and eventually hits PassedSiding (5) but this time it does not trigger because 4 lowered its activation level.

Step 11: Ending the Activity

With a little study you should be able to figure out how the rest of the events in this tutorial work. Let's quickly go over one more cluster of events—those that end the scenario. First, though, we'll take a look at Action Events.

Action Events

The Action Event window comes up by default, but if it has been closed, turn it on from the Window menu. There are only two Action Events in this Activity, PickUpCars and the Assemble Train message. The Assemble Train message event is triggered when the player has finished assembling the required consist (by dropping off the empty log car).

The PickUpCars event is the one we are interested in. It is triggered when the player's consist collects the cars named in the event. Take a look at the properties for this event. The dialog box looks much the same as the other events except that the triggering action can be chosen in a combo box at the top of the window (see Figure 8.17).

When the action is triggered there are four outcomes: a message appears saying that the player has succeeded in picking up the cars; the Location Event called SuccessfulEnd is raised one level; the Location Event SlowToCouple is turned off; and the Location Event TrackMonitor is activated.

Notice that there is a checkbox at the bottom of the window labeled Reversible and that it is checked. This means that if the player couples with the car and then manages to uncouple it, all four outcomes are reversed back to their original states.

Action event properties

Action

Pick up cars ▼

Car	Car location
32779 - 0	Kalispell Lumber - Siding 1

◄ ▶

[Add] [Delete]

Event

Activation level: [1] ▲▼

Triggered text: [_____]

Untriggered text: [_____]

Notes: [_____]

Number of outcomes: [4] ▲▼

Outcome : 0 | Outcome : 1 | Outcome : 2 | O ◄ ▶

Increase an event's activation level by one ▼

Successful end ▼

[Edit message]

Reversable: ☑

[OK] [Cancel]

FIGURE 8.17:

The PickUpCars Action
Event dialog box

One last thing about this dialog box. In the center area in the text box Untriggered is the message: "You did not pick up the cars in the Kalispell Lumber siding." This message will print out in the detailed report of how the player did at the end of the scenario. This message will only be recorded if the cars are not picked up.

The location event SuccessfulEnd is the event that actually ends the scenario. If it is not triggered, the train moves on a little farther to the Location Event GoneTooFar, which ends the scenario unsuccessfully.

Step 12: Don't Pick Up the Extra Car (Troubles and Difficulties...)

We have added an extra car to the siding but we don't want the player to pick it up. Spend a moment thinking about how you would organize events to enforce that rule and warn the player if he or she is making a mistake.

When I tried to do this I ran into a lot of trouble. At first I thought I would add a new PickUpCars event (for the car I don't want to grab) and use it to trigger messages telling the user not to pick it up. That idea worked perfectly except that the user would always fail the Activity because they failed to pick up that car in the PickUpCars event. The PickUpCars event automatically ties into the scenario's work order. Next I tried using a DoNotPickUpThisCar event. Unfortunately, cold hard reality soon showed me that there is no DoNotPickUpThisCar event.

Looking over the events that do exist, I found the Assemble Train and Assemble Train at Location Action Events. I tried the first one out and it worked (if you grabbed the wrong car you would lose the scenario). However, this did not give me any hook to which I could attach the warning messages. The purpose of a tutorial is to guide the user, and a rude message saying that the player has failed at the end without any warnings seems pretty harsh.

This is how I finally got it to work: I make a new Action Event called Drop Car on Siding, saying that the car that we are to leave alone must be placed on the siding. Because it is already there, that part of the player's task is done before the scenario even starts. This event turns off a warning message that tells the player to take the car back, and turns off a location trigger event that ends the scenario with a failure. I had a hard time making this work because I put the Location Events (the warning message and the end game) too close to the siding. The engine hit the locations but they weren't triggered because the bad car had not been pulled off the siding yet.

With the hints that I've previously given, see if you can set up the three actions so that the user will be first warned, then failed, if they do pick up the illegal car. I will give an answer later. It often takes a few attempts to solve a puzzle like this. This kind of problem solving is common in programming.

Step 13: Don't Pick Up the Extra Car (The Solution)

You need two Location Events, one to kill the scenario if the player messes up, and one to give a warning of impending disaster. Figure 8.18 shows where I placed my two Location Events. I created two new Location Events that show up as numbers 19 and 20 on the map.

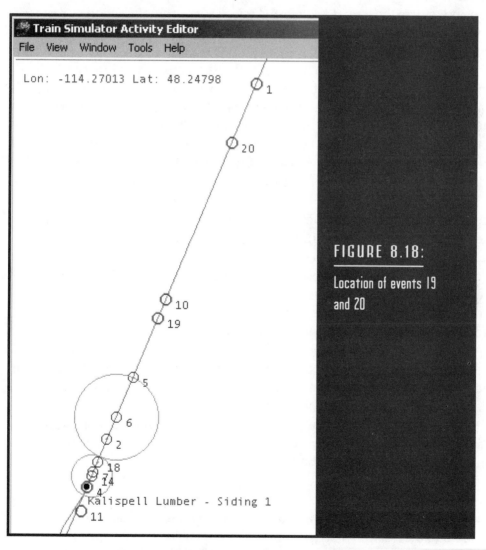

FIGURE 8.18:

Location of events 19 and 20

TIP I called Location Event 19 "Warning_TooManyCars" and 20 "KillScenario_TooManyCars". Take the time to give descriptive names to events because doing so can really help you to get things working properly.

I left a healthy distance between the events so the player would have time to stop and reverse the train. I also put them well away from the siding so that the last car actually has time to leave the siding before these events are encountered.

I clicked the New button at the top of the Action Events window and added a new Action Event. This event will be triggered when the new car we added (car number 32782-0) is placed on the siding. Because it starts on the siding, this event will trigger at once. However, we must tell the event what car is to be placed on that siding. To select the right car and siding, push the Add button on the Action Events dialog box. Two little dialog boxes will ask you to select the siding of the car that is to be placed there.

Our new event has three outcomes, the first two of which increase the activation levels of Location Events 19 and 20. (They start at zero, so normally they would never be triggered). The last outcome printed a message to warn people that this last car should be left on the siding. Lastly, I made the Action Event reversible so that if the player removes car 32782-0 then the warning message and kill event that has been turned off for the whole scenario will be turned back on. (This also means that if the driver realizes his or her mistake the problem can be fixed by returning the car to the siding.)

There is one last thing to do. Change the original Action Event called PickUpCars and turn it into an event that triggers when you Assemble Train. List the two cars that you must pick up (32775-0 and 32775-1). The Action Event should look like Figure 8.19 when you are done.

You may wish to look through the messages that the tutorial will give to the player and change any that are now out of date. Play-test your work and see what happens if you remove the extra car, or if you remove it and then put it back.

The only problem with the way it is set up is that when reporting on how the player has done, the message will say that the player successfully delivered car 32782-0 to the siding. This is a bit confusing but I believe it can't be fixed. We should likely mention to the player that the car to be dropped off on the work order was already done by an earlier train so they don't drop off part of their consist by mistake.

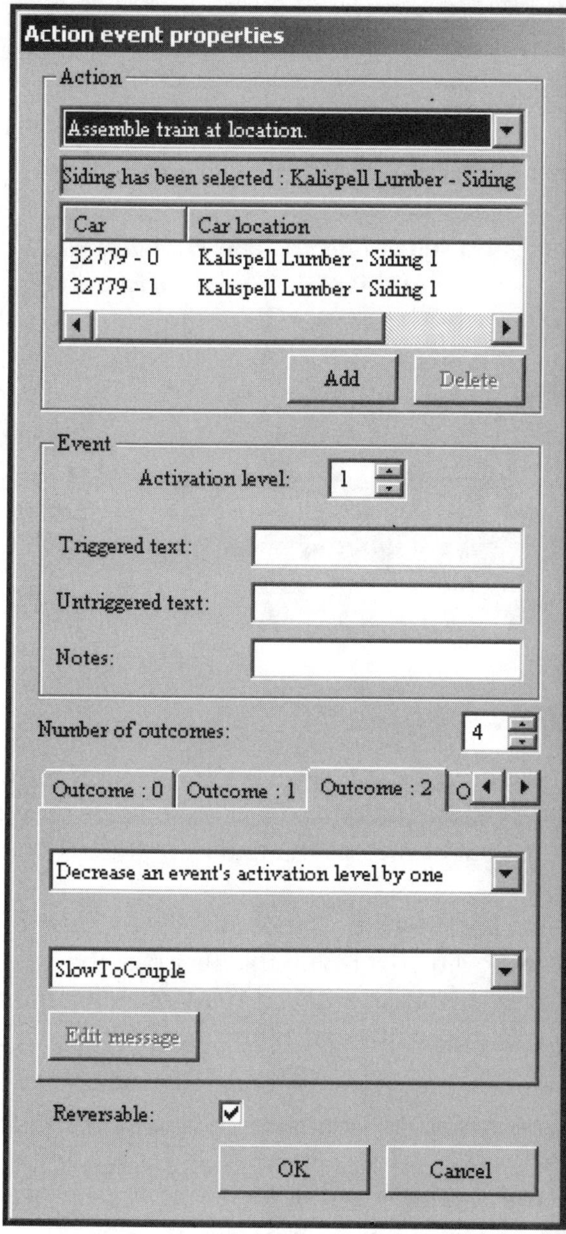

Action event properties

Action

Assemble train at location.

Siding has been selected : Kalispell Lumber - Siding

Car	Car location
32779 - 0	Kalispell Lumber - Siding 1
32779 - 1	Kalispell Lumber - Siding 1

Add   Delete

Event

Activation level: 1

Triggered text:

Untriggered text:

Notes:

Number of outcomes: 4

Outcome : 0   Outcome : 1   Outcome : 2   O

Decrease an event's activation level by one

SlowToCouple

Edit message

Reversable: ☑

OK   Cancel

FIGURE 8.19:

Cars that must be picked up in revised Action Event

ALTERNATE SOLUTION

Here's an alternate solution straight from Phil Marley, Designer, *Train Simulator*.

Set up an Assemble Train event and select *only* the cars that you want the player to end up with. Have the outcome of this event be an increased activation level on the Complete Activity Successfully Location Event. Now if the player picks up an extra car and tries to finish the Activity, the game won't let him finish. By using multiple outcomes on the Assemble Train event, you can issue warnings with other Location Events as well. The trick to using this technique is realizing that the Assemble Train event checks the *exact* consist of your train—so if you've got the right consist but have an extra car coupled on the end, it still won't accept it. This is the solution we used in our Activities and is the reason we didn't make a "don't pick up car" action.

Step 14: Move Them Doggies

When we pick up a car, we should drop it someplace. Let's take one of the cars that we just picked up and add on to the scenario so that it should be dropped off on the next siding. I will sketch out how to do this and leave the solution for you to work through.

First, both of the end scenario Location Events (both the successful and unsuccessful versions) should be moved 10 miles up the track past the other siding. The path of the player's service must be moved 10 miles up the track as well (see step 6 described earlier in this chapter for information about how to do this).

TIP To move a Location Event, click and drag it to the new location. You may wish to zoom the map so that you can move the long distance more quickly.

Make the successful end event's activity level one lower so people must drop off the other car before it will activate successfully. Add a new Action Event to the scenario where car number 32775-0 must be dropped off at the Columbia Falls Chip Spur siding. There should be two outcomes of this event: a message saying, "drop the car and go forward to end the scenario," and an outcome that raises the activity level of the successful ending event.

One problem with play-testing this change is that because the next siding is 10 miles away it takes an hour to reach if you stick to the 10-mph speed limit. What I did was turn off derailments and rocketed along at about 100 mph to speed up testing (this, however, is not the behavior we want to encourage in a tutorial).

Step 15: Polishing Things Up

There are two things we can do with an Activity once it is finished. Compute and save (in the File menu) will "pre-compute" the Activity so that it will load and run faster in the game.

Package Activity (also in the File menu) runs a program that will collect all the information needed to run an Activity and place it in a single file. This makes it easy to share your Activities with other people, or move them between different computers. When you click on this menu item, it will prompt you for a name, then store the Activity in a file that ends with a .apk extension.

Step 16: Further Improvements

The biggest problem with our current tutorial is the very long trip to where the car should be dropped off. This is too far for a quick tutorial. What we want is a siding just a short distance further down the track. In Chapter 10 one thing we will do is build a small hill on this route. We will build a siding off the main line that curves behind this hill, terminate the siding, and construct some industry beside it.

Summary

This is already a long chapter and we have not covered all the things that we can do in the Activity Editor. The next chapter will round out our coverage of the Activity Editor by building a new scenario. When we create new Activities, we will have to select an existing service or build a new one. Creating new services for player trains and computer controlled ones is a very important skill, and we'll learn about it next.

Chapter 9

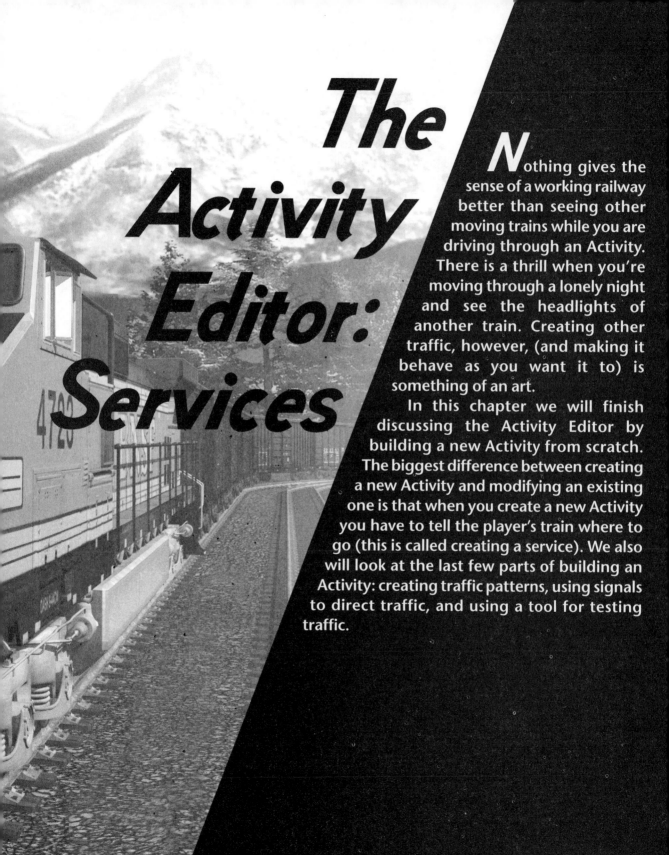

The Activity Editor: Services

Nothing gives the sense of a working railway better than seeing other moving trains while you are driving through an Activity. There is a thrill when you're moving through a lonely night and see the headlights of another train. Creating other traffic, however, (and making it behave as you want it to) is something of an art.

In this chapter we will finish discussing the Activity Editor by building a new Activity from scratch. The biggest difference between creating a new Activity and modifying an existing one is that when you create a new Activity you have to tell the player's train where to go (this is called creating a service). We also will look at the last few parts of building an Activity: creating traffic patterns, using signals to direct traffic, and using a tool for testing traffic.

Building a New Activity

This section briefly discusses how to build a new Activity rather than modifying an existing one. I'll first give a checklist of things to do to build a new scenario, and then go over the new topics in more detail.

Step 1: First Steps

- Start up the Activity Editor (see Chapter 8).
- Go into the File menu and select New...
- You will be prompted for the route. Choose one from the drop down menu.
- Choose a name for your new Activity.

Step 2: Setting the Activity Variables

- Create a display name for your Activity.
- Choose the Activity's level of difficulty.
- Edit the Activity Duration (this is just a suggestion to the player).
- Edit the Activity Description (this is mandatory, you must type something here).
- Edit the Activity Briefing (this is also mandatory).

Step 3: Choosing Weather and Hazards

- Choose the season and weather conditions.
- Set the frequency of animals near the tracks.
- Leave the traffic pattern as None until you have the rest of the Activity working.

Step 4: Choosing or Creating the Player's Service

- Choose from an existing service or create a new one.

 NOTE A consist is one or more cars coupled together. It may or may not have an engine. In this game, a service is a mobile consist with a path. Editing or creating a consist is straightforward and we have covered both in Chapter 8. Creating a path is done with the Path Editor that we'll discuss in detail in the following sections.

- Save the game.

- You should now try out your Activity in the game and make sure it is running properly.

Step 5: Adding Traffic

Once you have the basic service running you may add additional traffic. Other traffic is simply other services (consists + paths) that the player may see while doing the Activity.

Once other traffic is on the tracks, signals become much more important. Controlling signals is described in a short section toward the end of this chapter.

Step 6: Creating Data Files for the Activity

- In the File menu, click the Compute and Save menu item.

- In the Tools menu, click the Verify Start state

- In the Players box, click Edit Timetable and calculate the timetable for the activity.

- Go into the File menu and choose Save (or Save As…). You now have a completed Activity and can run it in the game.

Creating Paths

A path is the route that the train will take on the rail line (including changing tracks with switches, planned waits, and any reversals in direction). The basic idea of creating paths is to pick a starting point for a path. The computer will guess which direction you want the train to go in. If it guesses wrong you must manually change the direction. You will then follow along the path the computer guesses that you want. As you follow it, you may make different choices at switches. Each time you correct the computer's path it will guess again as to where you want the remainder of the path to go.

Eventually you will place an ending point. A path must have at the very least a starting and ending point. The path you pick out may also have reverses (where the train changes direction) and waiting points (where you must stop and wait for a time). Building paths is done in the Path Editor, which is covered in the next section.

Making a New Path

Let's make a very simple Activity where we will create our own path. Our Activity will have the player drive a passenger train from Washington to BWI airport, stopping midway at New Carrollton (see Figure 9.1).

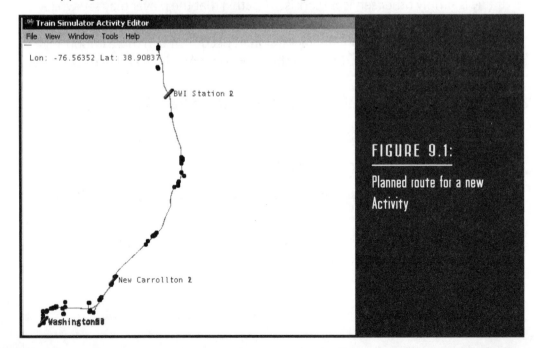

FIGURE 9.1:

Planned route for a new Activity

Creating a New Activity

We open up the Activity Editor and create a new Activity for the USA1 route. The name and display name for this Activity will be "test_of_paths". Give a scenario description and briefing and pick the season, time of day, and weather conditions (summer, noon, clear). For more details, see the steps given at the start of this chapter.

Picking the Player's Service

The first thing to do is decide on the player's consist and its starting location. In the Player section of the Activity Editor there is an area for picking the player's service. Click the New button in this area. This brings up the Service Editor dialog box shown in Figure 9.2.

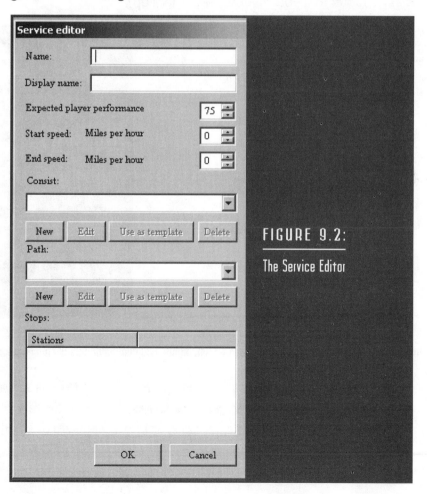

FIGURE 9.2:

The Service Editor

Fill in the blanks in this dialog box, giving the name, display name, expected player performance, and so on. For this tutorial there is no reason to create a special consist. Let's just go in and pick a standard Amtrak passenger consist. (For more information about picking consists, see Chapter 8.) The consist that you should find in the combo box is called: "Acela Express—standard trains."

Building a New Path

Now we come to the point of this tutorial. The next section in the Service Editor is Path. Click the New button. A pair of small dialog boxes will ask you to give a name and display name to your new path. Do so. This will hide the Service Editor dialog box and bring up the Path Editor (see Figure 9.3). Move the dialog box off of the window (you can't use any of the other parts of the Activity Editor so it doesn't matter that you cover some of them up).

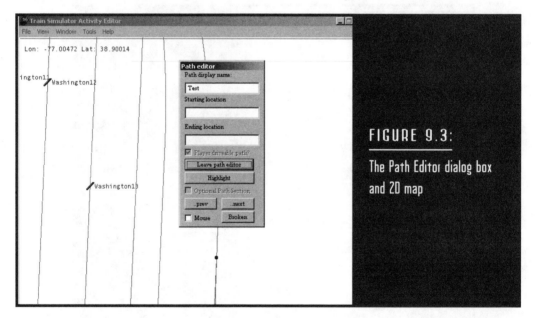

FIGURE 9.3:

The Path Editor dialog box and 2D map

TIP Except for dragging the start and end points a short distance in the Activity Editor (not past a switch), all changes to paths must be done in the Path Editor. If you want to change an existing path, you can do so by selecting it and clicking the Edit button.

We must pick the starting location for this train. Pick one of the Washington stations (I picked #12.) Now right-click the section of track, near a platform, that you've chosen. The contextual menu shown in Figure 9.4 will come up. A light green circle surrounding a blue dot will show the location of the start point for your path.

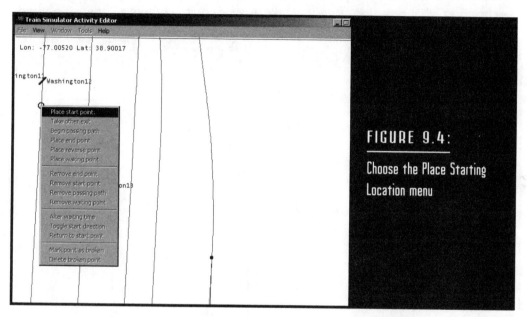

FIGURE 9.4:

Choose the Place Starting Location menu

The path itself is the line shooting up off the screen (it will be a green line in *Train Simulator* and stippled black in the picture in the book). Scroll the map up a short distance. You will see that every time the path crosses a switch there is a light green dot (in the black and white picture in the book, I've outlined the green dots in black to make them stand out).

TIP If you need to change your start point (beyond dragging it a short distance in the Activity Editor) you will lose your whole path and will have to start over.

By right-clicking the green dots, where the line branches, a contextual menu will come up that has in its menu options the choice Take Other Exit. By choosing Take Other Exit, you can change the path that your service takes. Examine the before and after screen shots in Figure 9.5 to see what it should look like when you change a switch. We must go along the player's path, choosing what directions they will take at every switch where a choice is offered.

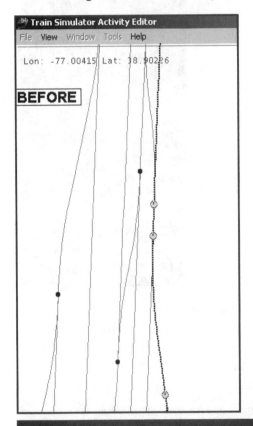
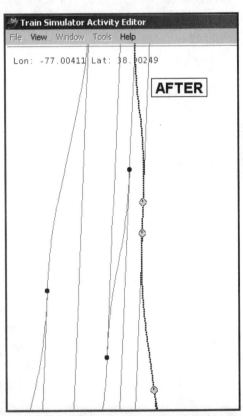

FIGURE 9.5:

Before and after changing the path

TIP Reversals of direction and scheduled waits must be placed in the order that the service reaches them. This is easiest, if you trace the route from beginning to end.

When you've gotten all the way to BWI Station, place the end point. The end point should be a little past the station and will be a green circle with a red outline.

TIP Be sure you are on one of the two outside platforms at BWI station, because the middle rail line does not have a platform. You won't be able to stop at BWI if you are on that line when you reach the airport.

There are a few things to remember about getting start and end points to match up with platforms. Turn on Platforms in the View menu in the Activity Editor. This shows the length of the platform as two green slashes across the track. Make sure that the path goes well past the end of the platform so the player will be able to complete the Activity (this will also allow you to put in an event reminding the player that they have to back up if you wish). Once you have finished building your path, click on the Verify Start State option in the Tools menu in the Activity Editor. This will allow you to study the start position of the train. If you want the train to start in a station, you may have to move the start point to a spot before the station in order for it to be properly placed, particularly for a long train.

Before we can leave the Path Editor we must name the starting and ending locations. These names can be anything, but we will put in "Washington" and "BWI Airport." The names that we type in will show up at the Starting At and Heading Towards boxes in the game so choose names that will help the player. If there is no station nearby, you can use mileposts. (If you later move the start or ending location, remember to update these names if needed.) We have finished with this path, so click the thin button labeled Leave Path Editor. This button is found in the center of the Path Editor dialog box.

Picking Stations

When we leave the Path Editor, the Service Editor dialog box returns. All of the stations on the path you've made show up in the Stops portion of the dialog box. You may wish to have a train go through a station without stopping at it. Check all stations you want the train to stop at (see Figure 9.6.).

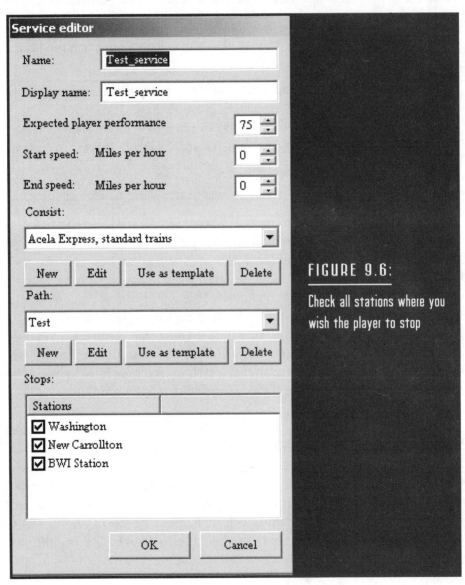

FIGURE 9.6:

Check all stations where you wish the player to stop

Recalculating Timetables

After selecting what stations the train will stop in, there is one final job to do. We must calculate the timetable for this route. In the Player box of the Activity Editor, below the New and Edit buttons for the Player Service combo box is the Edit Timetable button. Pressing this button brings up a dialog box with checkboxes for the various stations for which you can make timetables. Then click the Recalculate This button to build the timetables.

 TIP If you make a change to any of the paths in your Activity (either the player's or the paths for other traffic described in the next section), it may affect your timetable. After any path changes, recalculate the new timetable.

When this is done, we have finished creating a new path. Click the OK button in the Service Editor and then save your new Activity. Try out your work in the game and make sure that it runs properly.

Final Thoughts on Paths

To make the Activity interesting it is a great temptation for the designer to make the player's path very complex. Paths that wind back and forth, constantly switching from track to track, have some disadvantages. First of all, the player will have to slow down quite a bit to take the switches safely. Also, it's easy to lose track of exactly where you are in complex scenarios. This is especially true if the Activity's story does not explain the need for a complex route.

In such cases you may wish to have a few location events remind a player of what they have to do. (This is not strictly realistic, but real engineers know the routes better than your average player does.) Remember that a good designer's goal is to make a fun Activity and not a frustrating one.

Creating Traffic Patterns

A traffic pattern is just one or more AI services collected together. Practice making single services before you make a complex pattern. You must create paths for different services one by one and then collect them together into a traffic pattern.

NOTE In this portion of the chapter we talk about "AI trains" and "AI services." AI stands for Artificial Intelligence. AI trains and services refer to the computer-controlled trains that you create and direct.

In the bottom-right corner of the Activity Editor is a rectangular area labeled Traffic Pattern. Click the New button in this region. A pair of dialog boxes will appear, asking you for the name and display name of this traffic pattern. Enter "Test_Traffic_Pattern" into both dialog boxes. You will return to the Activity Editor, but the name of your new traffic pattern will now show up in the combo box in the region. Click on the Edit button, which will allow you to change your new traffic pattern. The dialog box for editing these is shown in Figure 9.7.

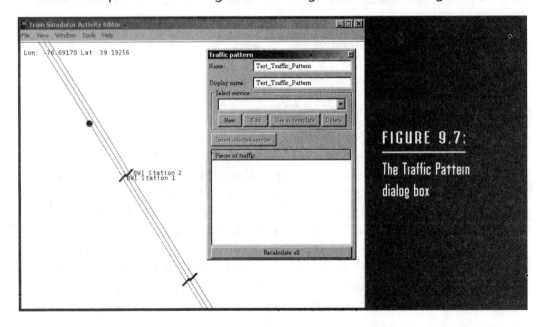

FIGURE 9.7:

The Traffic Pattern dialog box

Although this book doesn't include a tutorial on building up a traffic pattern, I suggest that you build one for yourself. Edit the test traffic pattern you built in the previous section, and add one or two trains that are running in the opposite direction on different tracks. (Since they are never on the same track as the player's train, there will be no complex signal issues as to who will be given control of a section of track.) When you have built one or two new services, go into the Select Service combo box and choose the new service you have just created.

Then you must press the Insert Selected Service button, which will add your service to the traffic pattern. You will be prompted for the starting time, so give a time close to the player's start time. Note that you can make one AI service and add it to the Activity multiple times with different starting times. This way, for the work of creating one service, the players could see several trains going past them.

 TIP You don't have to create a service to add interest on a route. An immobile engine and a few boxcars on a siding will give the impression that another train was waiting for the player, but a stationary train needs no traffic pattern. (Adding a new consist is covered in Chapter 8.)

After you have created the new traffic pattern, give it a try in the VCR Tool (described later in this chapter). You should see two or three circles crawling along the 2D map that looks something like Figure 9.8.

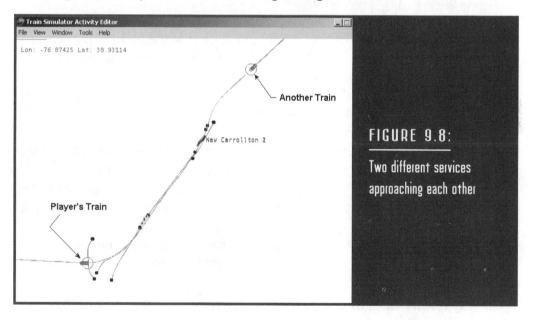

FIGURE 9.8:

Two different services approaching each other

How Signals Work in Train Simulator

In the next chapter we will learn how to place a signal beside the tracks. But, assuming signals are already placed along the track, how do we get them to turn on and off when we want?

In the real world, a dispatcher is in charge of the motions of all the trains for a section of line. He or she is responsible for making sure the trains do not collide, and that they are able to do their deliveries in a timely manner. To communicate with the engineers on the tracks, the dispatcher coordinates work orders and passenger schedules and uses telephone or radio to talk directly to the engineers. The dispatcher is also responsible for making sure that the trackside signals are correct. (Some signals also use automatic sensors.)

Sending a message event (see "Events" in Chapter 8) simulates last minute telephone messages and these are under our direct control when we create an action. But the signals are handled more indirectly.

Train Simulator has an automatic dispatcher, a program that runs in the background while *Train Simulator* is running. It looks at the paths of the other consists moving along the rails, looks at the player's path, and changes the signals to prevent a collision.

If you want the player's train to move along the tracks and see a certain set of signals, you have a tricky job ahead of you. Basically you must design the paths for all the other consists and by trial and error fiddle with things so that the timing is correct for the player to see the signals that you want. (Of course, if the player speeds or is too slow, your careful plan may fall to ruins.)

If there is a close conflict, the player is given priority. This lowers the chance that the player will have to sit still while an AI train uses a section of track in front of the player.

Here are some of the things that you can manipulate when you are trying to get the signals to behave in a certain way (roughly sequenced from most influential to least influential).

- **The start time of the AI and player services:** Whoever needs a section of track first is likely to be given the rights to it by the automatic dispatcher, so by starting an AI train after the player is already moving there is a good chance the player will beat it to a contested stretch of track.

- **The starting points of the AI trains and player trains:** By starting the player closer to this section of track, you can make it extremely likely that the player will reach it first.

- **Any scheduled waits in player or AI paths:** If an AI train always is farther ahead than you'd like, make it wait five minutes at a station or on a siding.

- **The starting speeds of the AI and player trains:** If the player is given a running start they have a better chance of winning the race to a section of track both need.

- **The expected efficiency at which the player or AI train drives their path:** This is set in the Service Editor window in the Activity Editor. (The field is called Expected Player Performance for the player's service and Default Performance for the AI services.) A 100% performance means flawless driving, with no slack or error in accelerating or decelerating, never going the slightest bit over speed, and never a severe jolt to the passengers or cargo. A 100% performance is impossible for a human engineer. By lowering the Default performance, the AI trains will run a bit slower.

Because this is a trial and error process, be sure to preview the impact of each change. Use the Verify Start State option under Tools in the Activity Editor and then use the VCR Tool to test run the Activity. (The VCR Tool is described in the following section.)

When you set up a signal beside the track (see Chapter 10) you set the default direction it allows. (For example, you may decide that the north track is for westbound traffic and the southern track is for eastbound traffic.) But the automatic dispatcher will ignore these default values if the paths you give it justify other signal patterns.

The VCR Tool Display

At the bottom left of the Activity Editor is a rectangular box that has no name. I have christened this the VCR Tool, because it has a Play and Stop button that enables you to watch a movie of the trains running in your Activity. The VCR Tool display is shown in Figure 9.9.

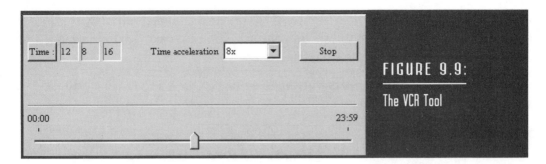

FIGURE 9.9:

The VCR Tool

To use the VCR Tool, make sure you are in the activity you want to test. Click Play on the VCR display. Usually you want to get rid of mileposts and most of the clutter that makes the 2D map hard to read. However, you will want to turn on the Service info in the View menu as this will give you information on the services moving in the VCR display. In particular it will allow you to tell apart the different services displayed.

 TIP When test-running the Activity using the VCR Tool display, grab the slider bar and move it close to the start time, or nothing will show up. (If your Activity starts at 10:30 AM, this display will be completely blank until start time). Another way to do this is to click on the Time button, which will bring up a dialog box that will allow you to set the time exactly.

Move the map and zoom in so you are over the service you want to watch. The trains will start moving, showing up as a series of small purple rectangles. To speed up the motion of the trains, you can choose a different rate of time in the Time Acceleration combo box.

Pay careful attention to which trains reach important junctions first. If an AI train is getting there too quickly, use the strategies discussed in the "How Signals Work in *Train Simulator*" section to slow it down. Remember that the players will not be running at 100% efficiency, so allow some slack time in the player's service.

The VCR Tool will give you a convenient guess as to what will happen but you should actually try the Activity to make sure it works properly.

Summary

It has taken two full chapters to outline what the Activity Editor can do. Chapter 10 covers the Route Editor, which is much easier to learn how to use, although it requires more trial and error to master. Fortunately the Route Editor enables you to do some simpler things as well, and it is designed so that you should quickly achieve proficiency; don't hesitate to get started.

Chapter 10

The Route Editor

When people think about building a new route for *Train Simulator* they usually think first about laying track, and have questions like the following:

- Where will the yards and sidings be?

- Which branch lines will be modeled?

- How much of the main line should be captured?

- How can I make the scenery look more realistic?

This chapter looks at creating small hills, laying track, building the track-side accessories needed for a railway, and creating buildings, trees and other scenery. It's not difficult to lay down the objects for a railway, but it can be time consuming, especially for longer routes. Fortunately it's easy to do a little bit at a time. If an area looks sparse you can always go back and add more features to it later.

Building a Route

Using the Route Editor is much easier than using the Activity Editor, but there are still thousands of different objects to use, and it takes a while to get comfortable with them all. I strongly suggest that you build a small route (only a few kilometers long) to try things out. Get familiar with as many different options as you can; for example, have the track wind back and forth between steep hills, then have it go over a ridge. Try laying track with normal pieces as well as with the dynamic track sections.

 TIP Getting two different sections of track to match up can be tricky. Generally you will be better off if you start at one end of the line, or in the middle.

It is bit tricky trying to get two different sections of track to match up. Generally you will be better off if you start at one end or in the middle. If you get stuck trying to do things one way, don't get frustrated. Just see if you can find a different way to do something similar.

How to Build a Route

This chapter assumes that you have the terrain tiles finished, either by using someone else's existing terrain or making your own terrain using the Geometry Extractor (see Chapter 11 for more information about this tool), I suggest you build your route in the following order:

- Create any hills you will add to the base terrain
- Lay the track, including bridges and tunnels
- Lay out the surface roads
- Place the interactive objects
- Place the static objects
- Place signals
- Edit ground textures

I will teach how to do things in an order a little bit different than the previous list. Although the list is the best way to build a route, it is not necessarily the best order in which to learn.

Route Editor Overview

To get started, launch the *Train Simulator* Editors and Tools as described in Chapter 8. When the menu screen for the four editors comes up, click the word bar that says Route Editor. A dialog box will appear, asking you which route you want to open (see Figure 10.1). Choose a route in the Combo box and the Route Editor will open.

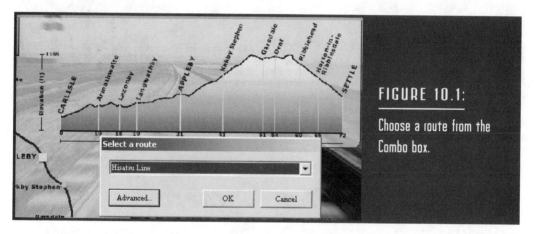

FIGURE 10.1:

Choose a route from the Combo box.

The main screen is a camera view into a section of the track. There are a number of windows scattered around the right side of this main window; each one enables you to manipulate different tools. Covering all of these tools in complete detail is a bit beyond the scope of this book, but this section will get you started and help you avoid the biggest pitfalls.

The different tools (in the order that we will review them) are as follows:

- The Route Editor Camera

- Creating terrain

- Laying track

- Adding scenery

- Adding railway accessories

- Changing ground textures

When you first open the Route Editor you might see something like Figure 10.2 (this will depend on what options you've chosen, naturally). The first thing you need to learn is how to move around in the Route Editor.

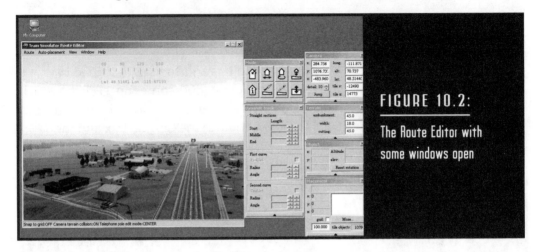

FIGURE 10.2:

The Route Editor with some windows open

In the Window menu you'll find a list of the different windows that you can open. To get a window to appear, check its name. If you want to hide a window you are not using, uncheck it.

The Route Editor Camera

The Route Editor Camera enables you to look at your route from almost any angle. Notice the red heads-up display in the top center part of the Camera View window. This lists the angle that the camera is pointing (zero degrees means that it is pointing north) and the latitude and longitude of the camera's position.

Use the keyboard and the mouse to move around and look at the route from different positions. (See Table 10.1 for a list of keyboard and mouse controls.) I suggest you spend some time exploring the routes that come with the game using these keys, which will give you practice moving the camera, not to mention a sense of how the development team built their routes.

TIP You can speed up any of the movement commands shown in Table 10.1 by holding the Shift key at the same time that you move the camera.

TABLE 10.1: KEYBOARD AND MOUSE CONTROLS FOR THE CAMERA

COMMAND	FUNCTION
Up arrow	Zoom camera in
Down arrow	Zoom camera out
Left arrow	Move camera left
Right arrow	Move camera right
CTRL + up arrow	Move camera up
CTRL + down arrow	Move camera down
Hold right mouse button down while moving mouse	Rotate the camera
Plus (+) or minus (-)	Change time of day (in 30 seconds or so the sun will make a circle around the virtual world)
Forward slash (/)	Toggles camera collision with ground (Defaults to On)

Even when holding down the Shift key, it can take a very long time to move to the other end of a large route. Fortunately, you can jump the camera to any point you want on a route by using the Camera Tool window (see Figure 10.3).

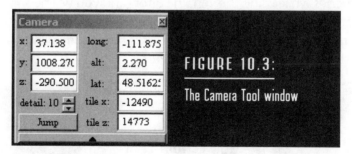

FIGURE 10.3:

The Camera Tool window

To jump to any location on the route, erase the current longitude and latitude, type in the new coordinates, then push the Jump button. To get the longitude and latitude of a spot at the opposite end of the route, write down the numbers for that location when you are in the Activity Editor (or when you are in the Geometry Extractor).

Beneath the x, y, and z coordinates for the camera is a number labeled Detail that varies from 1 to 10. When working in the Route Editor, leave this on 10. Remember that players may reduce the detail level of the route when they are running the game to get smoother rendering. By reducing the detail level, you can see what they would see.

In the Route Geometry Extractor the entire world has been mapped onto 2km by 2km tiles (these are called terrain tiles). The tile x and tile z coordinates show you which one of these $2km^2$ terrain tiles the camera is currently over.

Editing Terrain

The base terrain (made out of the $2km^2$ tiles) is created in the Route Geometry Extractor. The Route Editor does not change these tiles, but you can make small local changes to the base height that you get from the Geometry Extractor.

 TIP Minimize the number of hills and valleys you add. Every one of them slows down the rendering of Train Simulator.

To change the base height of an area you must activate the Edit Terrain Tool. To go into this mode, click the Edit Terrain icon in the Mode window (see Figure 10.4). You may also hit F9 to activate the Edit Terrain Tool. The cursor will turn into a round circle to remind you that you are now editing terrain. The Mode window is very important because it is the one you will use to shift between modes while using the Terrain Editor (and you will be shifting between modes a lot). Basically, each mode is a program that uses the mouse and keyboard in different ways to do different tasks. The Mode window allows you to choose which type of tool you want to use.

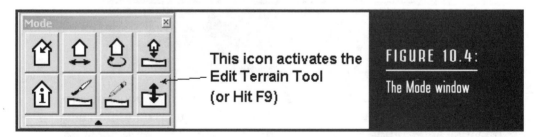

This icon activates the Edit Terrain Tool (or Hit F9)

FIGURE 10.4:

The Mode window

You may raise terrain by pressing the 8 key (keypad only). To lower terrain, press the 2 key (keypad only). Rather than raising or lowering terrain one point at a time, you can raise a rectangular area. Left-click and drag the mouse over a region and a red outline will appear, showing the area that you have selected. The terrain can now be raised or lowered as a group.

WARNING Any time you change the height, save your data at once! If you leave the Edit Terrain mode without saving, you will lose all your changes.

If you right-click, a contextual menu will come up that allows you to manually type in terrain heights. Usually it is easier to use the 8 or 2 keys (on the keypad). If you have an area selected, however, a menu item called Flatten is occasionally useful. Flatten takes the four corner points of your area and averages them so that all points in the rectangle are the same average height.

TIP If you want to make really big hills you can speed up the rate at which the height is changed by holding down the Shift key.

I find that the default slope of the hills is too steep. This slope can be changed with the Terrain Preferences dialog box (see Figure 10.5).

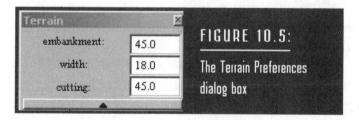

FIGURE 10.5:

The Terrain Preferences dialog box

In the Terrain Preferences window, the first number is the slope, in degrees, of the embankment. For a cut or an embankment, 45 degrees is fine, but a 20-degree slope would look better for most hills. The width represents how wide you make the top of an embankment when you raise the tracks above the local ground. The last number is the slope, in degrees, of any cuts through hillsides.

NOTE By pushing the W key, you can toggle on and off the Wire Frame mode. The wire frame may help you visualize the three-dimensional shape of the terrain, but I usually prefer to judge the slope and height in the normal rendering mode.

If you want to undo the last change you made when editing the terrain, hit the ` key (at the top-left corner of your keyboard).

 TIP If your railway is going through soft earth, make the slopes more gradual; if it is going through hard rock, the cuts can be steeper than 45 degrees.

Using the plus or minus keys to change the position of the sun helps you visualize the terrain because it gives you shadows to work with.

Laying Track

Laying track is essentially putting pre-constructed sections of track together. Each time you put down a piece, it snaps onto the end of any track close to it. There are many dozens of track pieces to choose from, and it may take some experimentation before you're comfortable with which track to use when and where each piece is found. You should study which pieces the designers used when building similar sections of existing railways—sometimes you can find the name of the perfect piece this way.

 TIP When track approaches a hill, just run it straight into the hill's side. Press the Y key and embankments and cuttings are made automatically—the ground adjusts to fit the track.

The Mode Window

Several different modes are useful when you're laying track, as shown in Figure 10.6. I'll briefly describe an example of how the various modes can be used, then discuss their use in more detail later in the chapter.

I usually start in Object Placement mode, select the track I want, and put down several pieces. For the sake of example, suppose I put down one piece too far away, and it didn't snap to the track. I go into Moving mode and drag the misplaced track beside the existing track. After putting down a few more pieces, the line begins to go up a slope, so I switch to Rotating mode and rotate the last piece of track so it is starting to slope upwards. At the top of the hill I want to find a very broad curve. I look over the existing track until I find a piece that looks about right, then go into Information mode to learn its name so that I can select it from the Track Selection dialog box.

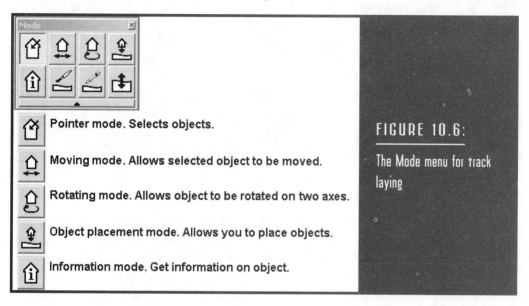

Pointer mode. Selects objects.

Moving mode. Allows selected object to be moved.

Rotating mode. Allows object to be rotated on two axes.

Object placement mode. Allows you to place objects.

Information mode. Get information on object.

FIGURE 10.6:

The Mode menu for track laying

As you can see, when dealing with track (and when doing other jobs, for that matter) you will shift modes depending on what editing tool you need at the time. Each of the modes (and how to move between them) will be discussed separately, but more often than not you'll be switching back and forth between them.

Route Modification Tutorial

Figure 10.7 shows a section of track a half mile away from the location of the tutorial that we modified in Chapter 8. I have added a couple of small hills just behind the trees. In this tutorial I'll make a siding that goes around and over the low hills and then stops. We will add some industry and fix the trees and other objects on our siding. Note the longitude and latitude of where we are working if you wish to try to do this yourself.

Notice three things: that the Object Placement icon is depressed in the Mode window, that the cursor is a white cross, and take a look at the Placement window. We will be using it in just a minute.

FIGURE 10.7:

Placement mode and white cross cursor

Object Deletion

Before we can add a switch for our new siding we have to make room for it. We will select a section of the line, and delete it. Go into Object Selection mode and move the cursor over the rails. The section of the track that the cursor is over turns red. Click that section of track and it becomes a wire frame (basically black and white). Press the Delete key and the section of track is deleted.

Object Placement

Click the Object Placement icon in the Mode window. The cursor should now turn into a white cross, as shown in Figure 10.7. Click the More... button in the Placement window. The Object Selection dialog box will appear (see Figure 10.8). Choose the category labeled Track Sections.

The track section selected in the picture is one track, 100 meters long, and completely straight. Click OK and move the white cross close to the end of the track. When we left-click once, a section of track will be added (it is visible in wire frame). Add one more section of track and then select a switch. (I used A1t45dYardLft.s—1 track, 45 degree, Yard Switch, left.) Once the switch is down, fix the main line by placing some more straight sections. I had to use some 10-meter-long straight sections to close the final gap.

Because I had 10-meter-long straight sections selected, I put a few of them off the switch. The track stayed flat, but the second piece disappeared under the ground (the hill I added had raised the ground a little bit). To fix this I selected the last piece of track I could see using the Selection mode, then I pressed the Y key and the program automatically made the cut for me.

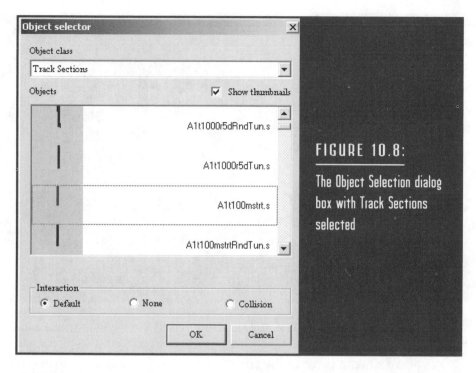

The Object Selection dialog box with Track Sections selected

TIP Press the F5 key for a short cut into the Object Placement mode.

My track began to run into a bunch of trees. I used the object selection tool to select these trees. They almost vanished, showing only a star-like symbol (the wire frame model for trees is pretty simple). Press the Delete key to remove them.

I then added a long slow curve. (I used A1t1500r10d.s—1 track, 1500-meter radius, 10 degrees.) It disappeared at once under the hills I was approaching (see Figure 10.9).

I knew that after the hills, the ground was a little higher (I had manually increased the height of that side of the ridge by 5 meters). With that in mind, I selected the long curve and while it was selected clicked the Rotation Mode icon in the Mode window. When I moved the cursor over the window the cursor turned into a little double loop (something like the old pictures of an atom). By holding down the left mouse button and moving the cursor up and down, I could rotate the track so it went uphill. When the track had a maximum slope, the other end became visible on the far side of the hills (see Figure 10.10).

FIGURE 10.9:

The long curve vanishes underground.

When the curved section was still selected, I used the Y key to make a cut through the ridge.

Let's add a straight piece at the end of our cut and then put on an end piece to terminate the siding. We have a 10-meter section displayed in the Placement window. Lay a section or three of the straight track. Now it's time to put the barriers that are placed at the end of sidings, but we need to know what those track pieces are called.

FIGURE 10.10:

The long curved section has hit the surface on the far side of the hill.

Finding Object Properties

Move down the track a half mile to the siding where we worked on the tutorial. Select the very last piece of track (so that its wire frame becomes visible). Now press the Information Mode icon. A dialog box will appear, showing information about the object that has been selected (see Figure 10.11). Go ahead and look at the other tabs, but all that's important right now is the name of the terminator piece. It is called "A1tBuffer.s". Now we know the name of the piece we need to end our siding. Go back to the siding we have been building and terminate the track by finding that piece in the Object Selector dialog box.

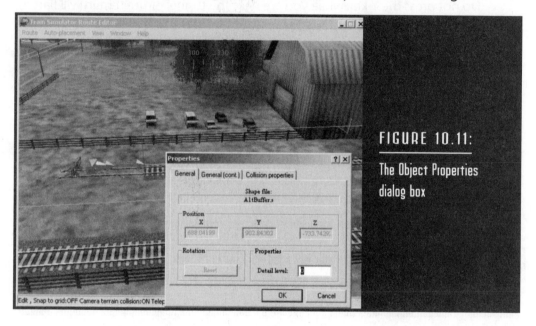

FIGURE 10.11:

The Object Properties dialog box

Marking the Siding

We have finished adding our siding except for one last thing. The route does not know about this siding so we won't be able to use it in the Activity Editor. To make a siding recognizable we must mark the section of track as a siding. This is done by placing a special object that will be invisible to the player, but that the Activity Editor will recognize.

To place the siding, go into Object Placement mode. Click the More button to bring up the Object Selector dialog box. Go into the Object Class drop-down box and choose Mainline Stations. Place the siding marker on the track (it will look like a pair of yellow pyramids facing each other, joined by a line). Click the Object Selector icon to get the pointer cursor and grab the end of the siding furthest away from the main line. Once it is selected, click the Move Object icon to go into Move mode. Now move the end marker down to the end of the siding. Right-click the siding to bring up its properties. A dialog box will appear, enabling you to give the siding a name.

Building Tunnels

To build a tunnel, approach a hillside with normal track. When you are about to enter the hillside, switch to tunnel track sections (they will have "Tun" in the coded name for the track).

Do not press the Y key while you are near the tunnel or the terrain will flatten out around it.

Laying Bridges

Placing bridges is tricky. The best way to go about this is to build up the ground so that it is flat, then place the track across it. Lower the terrain beneath the bridge to make your gully or valley. You now will have the rails shooting off into space unsupported.

Now build a bridge and carefully move it under the existing tracks. It can be very tricky to get the yaw, pitch, and roll of the bridge set correctly so do not rotate the bridge if you can possibly help it.

→ **TIP** From time to time you will need very accurate control with the mouse. By holding down the End key, motions are slowed, enabling very fine control.

To make a bridge of an automobile road going over the track, first lay the track, then build up the terrain for the overpass and place the road section. Rotate road sections until they go up and down as you like and use the Y key function to trim away extra land. Create the overpass and slide it into place under the road and over the rail line.

Dynamic Track

Dynamic track is track that allows you to place track that has a wide variety of user-created lengths and curves. It enables you to create virtually any shape track that you need. It is more difficult to use than regular track; beginners should become comfortable with laying normal track sections before working with dynamic track.

To be able to control dynamic track, open the Dynamic Track window in the Window menu (see Figure 10.12). To find dynamic track, go into the Track sections in the Object Selector dialog box. Dynamic Track is at the bottom of the list.

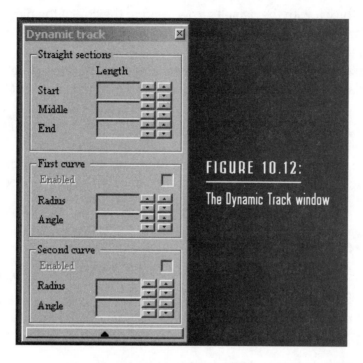

FIGURE 10.12:

The Dynamic Track window

Dynamic track straight sections are 1 meter long and have a direction (shown by the colored triangle associated with the track). For straight track the direction of the track does not matter. The Start, Middle, and End are the lengths of the map sections before, between, and after the two curves. There must be at least one meter of straight section between the first and second curves.

NOTE S-curves (where the track curves first to the left and then to the right) can cause derailments if they are too sharp. Ideally you want to have a car length of straight track between the two halves of an s-curve. If this is not possible make the s-curve as gentle as possible.

To lay down curved track, click the first Curve Enabled check box. When this is done, the Radius and Angle boxes will gain numbers. By using the up and down buttons to the right of these text boxes you can change these values. As the angle becomes smaller the track will begin to curve away from your starting point (to the left with the default arrows, and to the right if the direction of the starting box is reversed). To reverse the direction of the track, click the starting section and press the T key.

The track will always curve to the left. To reverse the direction of the track, select (again) the green triangle pointing at the curved section so it becomes a wireframe. Then press the T key. The arrow will switch ends so that the track has now been joined up "backwards." (The track still curves to the left from the point of view of the arrow, but to us, the curve has been reversed.)

At the bottom of the Dynamic Track window is an area called Second Curve. The Second Curve must have a straight section between the two sections of track and may curve in a different direction from the first curve.

Track Section Codes

The track sections each have a code that, once learned, can greatly ease track construction:

- A1t means that a piece has one track. A4t means that this piece has four tracks in parallel.

- Buf is a buffer for ending a siding.

- For curves, the track section has two numbers. 1000r means that the radius of the track is 1000 meters. 10d means that the arc of the circle covers 10 degrees. If you put 36 sections of track together that are 1000r10d you will make a perfect circle 1000 meters in radius. Note that a few track sections have Crv on them. This means curve and marks some old sections of track that were named before the current naming system was worked out.

- Ends are sharp curves that take the branch from a point section and straighten it so you have two tracks running parallel. (Or approaching it from the other direction, two tracks feed into a single line of track.) Study sections where one main line splits into two tracks running in parallel to see an example in the game of how they are used. (You may have to flip these curves to get them to lay the way you want. Flipping the track section is done with the T key.)

- Lft means the track curves to the left; rgt means the track curves to the right.

- Mnl is a manual switch junction point, which means that you can control it in the game. (Switches that are manually controlled have a little handle that is visible in the game.) Switches are used on sidings and in yards where the player needs to control the switch. However, they should be avoided on the main line when a pair of switches (called a point) enables the player to switch between main lines.

- Pnt is a point (another name for a switch). They are often used in pairs (back to back) to allow a train to switch between two parallel tracks. In the game, points are not intended to be under the driver's control; instead they are controlled by the Path Editor in the Activity Editor. Points are used on the main line because if manual control of these switches was allowed, the player could get into the path of a computer controlled train and cause the game to get stuck.

- Str means a straight section. With straight sections, the code 100m means that this section of track is 100 meters long.

- Wtr is a water trough (for steam locomotives).

- Tun is a tunnel track section.

- Xover is when two tracks cross each other.

- Yard means that the track section is intended to be used in a rail yard. In yards the curves are much sharper and all rail traffic should stay under 20 miles per hour. Sections of track with Yard on them should not be used on the (high-speed) main line.

Adding Scenery Objects

Scenery is what makes driving a train visually interesting and what gives the game the sense of speed. Dropping down scenery objects is very easy and if a mother or father is building a route, it should be possible to teach quite young children how to help out by placing scenery.

Placing Track-Side Objects

All track-side objects are placed the same way, but for this example I'll show you how to place a building.

Before you add an object, make sure the Placement window and the Mode windows are open. Click the Object Placement icon (the picture of the house with an arrow going down to the ground). The cursor over the map will turn into a white cross. In the Placement window, click the More... button as if you were adding track. When the Object Selector dialog box appears, pick one of the other list items (such as buildings).

When I place buildings I check the box that says Show Thumbnails. This shows a tiny picture of the object on the left side of its list box.

The top Building is Factory_Building; select it. Now click OK in the Object Selector dialog box. Move the X beside the siding that we created earlier. Left-click, and the factory will appear where the X is. The factory will be in wire frame. To see what it will look like drop another object or click the Selection icon in the Mode window and select something else. The object, when dropped, is selected, and selected objects appear in Wire Frame mode. By dropping or selecting another object, the new object becomes selected and you can see what the dropped object looks like without wire frames. Typically you will have to move or rotate the object to get it properly associated with your railway (see the following section on moving and rotating).

There are hundreds of objects and the best way to get to know them is to fire up the Route Editor and try them out. Note that some objects (such as the Trackside Object, Forest—US1DecidTree1) are not simple objects that you can see, but are actually codes to *Train Simulator*.

When you select a forest, you're really taking a huge rectangular box and making the whole area a forest. The density of the trees can be adjusted and the entire forest can be moved and rotated as a whole so that you don't have to place individual trees one at a time. The forest object will show up as three green cubes in the Route Editor. When it is selected (and you are far enough back) you can see the red outlines that show the limits of this giant object.

TIP You may be tempted not to bother with the small shrubs. However, having a bit of groundcover near the track adds visual variety and helps the user judge how fast the train is moving. Shrubs also can help make sections of forests look wilder.

Moving or Rotating Objects

While we have used the rotation tools to some extent in this chapter already, the following sections discuss them in more detail.

Moving Objects

When you select an object and then click the Move mode, the cursor turns into a little four-arrow direction pointer. If you look at it carefully, you will see a tiny xy beside it to the right. If you hold down the Control key this will turn into a xz and the top arrows will look flatter.

Train Simulator is telling you which two axes you can move the object in. Study the diagram in Figure 10.13. The x-axis runs along the bottom edge of your screen, the y-axis runs straight up along the side of the screen, and the z-axis moves directly into the screen away from you.

FIGURE 10.13:

The x-, y-, and z-axis during object movement

When you get the first Move icon, you can move the object left or right or lift it into the air or push it down under ground. When you hold down the Control key, you may move the object around on the game world, but it won't change its height. When moving objects you will usually hold down the Control key.

Rotating Objects

When you rotate objects you get an icon with a little xy or xz. However, the axes are different from those used with movement. Study the diagram in

Figure 10.14. The z-axis runs due north in the game world, the y-axis runs straight up away from the center of the Earth, and the x-axis runs due east.

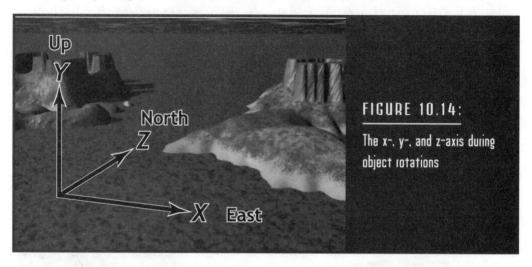

FIGURE 10.14:

The x-, y-, and z-axis during object rotations

To rotate an object, select it and click the Rotate Object Mode icon in the Mode window. The cursor turns to a vertical and horizontal loop with the letters xy beside it. Holding down the left mouse button and moving the mouse from left to right causes the object to rotate on the y-axis (so that the bottom of the object stays on the ground and the object spins). This is what you will usually want to do with objects.

To figure out what moving the mouse vertically does, move the camera around until it is looking at the object and pointing due north. (The red heads-up display should have a zero right above the object on your screen.)

With the object selected and north of you, rotate the object by moving the mouse up and down. The object will rotate on the x-axis (which points east).

Now hold down the Control key. The cursor shows a single flat loop and a tiny xz appears beside it. Moving the mouse from left to right will still rotate the object on the y-axis, but moving it vertically now will rotate the object on the z-axis (as if it was spinning on a needle that was pointing due north and south).

Ninety percent of the time you will want the bottom of your objects to stay firmly planted on the ground, so you must be careful to move the mouse left and right only, and not to move it at all vertically (otherwise your buildings or trees will start leaning).

Adding Railway-Related Objects

Railway-Related Objects are used to tell the game that certain Activities can occur at these locations. These are placed right on the track and visible objects may or may not appear because of them. There are a number of different types, each discussed in the following sections.

Animal Points

To place an animal point on the track, click the More… button in the Placement window, and choose the Hazards object class in the Object Selector dialog box. Inside the Hazards category is Deer_On_Track. When a deer is placed, a strangely colored octagon appears above a wire frame deer. When playing the game, the octagon is invisible and a deer *may* show up. The chance of meeting a deer on the tracks is set in the Activity Editor for that activity and defaults to 100%.

If you put down 20 deer locations, and if the chance of meeting deer is set at 50% for that activity, then 10 of your locations will have deer during that run of the scenario. However, every time the player starts the scenario, the 10 locations that the deer appear at are chosen randomly.

Platforms

There are two kinds of platforms in this game. One is just a long, concrete, track-side object that your players will see. This is placed normally, just like a building or a tree. The other is an invisible object that is placed directly on the track. This invisible object is used by the Activity Editor when you are building your scenario. It tells the game where the train should stop to pick up passengers.

The platform object is found in the Mainline Stations list in the Object Selection dialog box. When it is placed on the track, two green pyramids (end-to-end) are placed on the track. They have a green line running between them, which has an angled section pointing to the side of the train the people will get on and off of.

If you right-click one of the pyramids you can see their properties. This includes the name of the station, platform, whether people will enter on the left or right side of the track, the amount of time that trains should wait at this platform, and the number of people who are waiting. (By changing the number of people, the loading time will change.) There is also a control that will disable platforms by default. If this is checked, then the new activities that have passenger trains running along this track will ignore this platform unless the activity specifically tells the train's engineer to stop at it.

You will normally want to extend the length of the platform so it matches the length of the visible platform more closely. To do so, select one of the platform objects and use the Mode window to go into Move Object mode. Drag the selected pyramid along the track until it matches the visible object.

Fuel Points

Fuel points are objects that the player can interact with. They increase the fuel levels of the player's train when they come within a certain range of the point at a certain speed (usually zero).

The diesel pump is found in the Pickup Objects category of the Object Class combo box in the Object Selector dialog box (the dialog box from Figure 10.8). The fueling station is shown as a purple cube. This pump is used for a variety of refueling types including such fuels as coal, water, sand, and grain. By right-clicking the purple cube you can bring up its properties. The properties of the fuel point are self-explanatory.

Mileposts and Speed Limit Signs

Mileposts are vital real-world references. In the real world they are not always placed one mile apart and if you are trying to model a real world route, try to place them in their correct locations. Speed limit markers are simply mileposts that have their Set Speed option enabled.

To place a milepost, go into Place Object mode and click More… in the Placement window. In the Object Selector dialog box select Track Objects as the Object class. Near the bottom of the list of objects is the milepost. To place one, move the white cross onto the track and left-click. An octagon that looks much like a deer symbol with a shadowy milepost wire frame sticking through it will appear on the track.

To change the properties of the milepost, go into the Object Selection mode, select the milepost octagon, and right-click it.

 TIP You can select a milepost's properties and turn it into a speed sign if you wish.

Signals

Signals are just another kind of object. Placing them is simpler than getting them to do what you want, which is described in Chapter 9. To place a signal, go into Placement mode and hit the More… button to bring up the Object Selector dialog box. In the Object Class combo box select Track Objects. This list shows a number of different signals including US2Signal2.s.

Unlike the interactive track objects mentioned previously, signals do not have to be placed directly in the center of the track. They should be placed to one side, almost off the edge of the gravel at the side of the track. Signals should be placed down whenever a switch allows the possibility of two trains on the same track. If a point (switch) allows a train that is running beside you to move on to your track you need a signal before that switch for both tracks.

 TIP You do not need a signal on switches that service sidings, or on switches within yards. The engine that has permission for the line with the switch also has permission to move on and off of the siding. However, if the siding is used to park one train while another train passes on the main line, then that siding must be controlled by signals.

Long stretches of track where there are no switches do not need signals, unless that section of track is so long that the railway wants multiple trains to run on it at once. In that case, signals will be placed to prevent the trains from getting too close together.

A more in-depth discussion is beyond the scope of this book, but you will want to spend some time studying how the signals are laid out in the existing routes to get a sense of where they are needed.

Textures

A texture is a picture that is painted on an object to make it look better. The ground (and sky) in *Train Simulator* would be a drab indeed without grass, rough ground, rock, and clouds painted on it. This section looks briefly at textures and how they work in *Train Simulator*. To manipulate them we must be in the Terrain Texturing mode (push the button in the Mode window that looks like a paintbrush painting the ground).

Changing Ground Textures

Every 2km^2 geometry extractor (terrain) tile is split up into 256 smaller squares that have a texture that looks like ground, dirt, and so on. The default terrain textures differ depending on where they are. (For example, on flat ground the standard grass texture is used.)

To change a texture, first bring up the Texture Selector window by checking its box in the Window menu item. There will be a number of textures in the Texture Selection window, each with a number (see Figure 10.15).

FIGURE 10.15:

The Texture window and the main map divided off into black regions

TIP Press the F7 key to get quickly into the Terrain Texturing mode.

Click the Terrain Texturing icon on the Mode window. The world will become divided into large black squares (you may have to move the camera higher to be able to see them). Decide which texture you wish to place in one of the large squares and press the number key. The texture you selected will be placed in that terrain tile.

If the texture's orientation is not to your liking, you can right-click that square and the contextual menu in Figure 10.16 will come up. Choose the Rotate menu item and a sub-menu will ask how many degrees (in 90-degree increments) you want to rotate the texture.

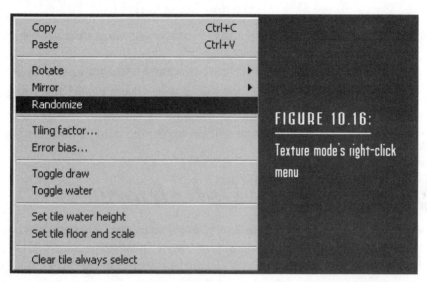

| Copy | Ctrl+C |
| Paste | Ctrl+V |

Rotate ▶
Mirror ▶
Randomize

Tiling factor...
Error bias...

Toggle draw
Toggle water

Set tile water height
Set tile floor and scale

Clear tile always select

FIGURE 10.16:

Texture mode's right-click menu

If you want to change several tiles at the same time, click multiple tiles while holding down the Shift key. Clicking a number key will place that texture into all of the selected boxes. To avoid repeating patterns, you can then choose Randomize in the Contextual menu, which will give the textures in all of those tiles random orientations.

Textures can greatly add to the visual variety that your train drivers see when they are traversing your route. However, they come at a cost: they require more computer power to render. You should be careful to only texture those tiles that will improve the experience of your players.

Setting Water Levels

Water levels in *Train Simulator* are based on the local tiles rather than on some global height that is the same for the whole route. This is good because it means that if your route shows some water at sea level you can also have a lake hundreds of meters above the ocean's level.

To set the water level, press the F7 key so you are in the Terrain Texturing mode. You will see a number of black squares. Select those squares that you want to be (at least partially) underwater and right-click to bring up a contextual menu. Once it appears, choose the Toggle Water item.

Next, right-click and choose the Select Tile Water Height option. You will be prompted to enter four heights. These heights give the water level across the terrain tile. (A terrain tile is one of the 2km² tiles from the Route Geometry Extractor.) If all four corners are the same height then the water is flat; if they are different the water slopes across the area of the terrain tile.

 TIP To find the height you want, move the camera where you want water level to be and look at the y number in the Camera window. This shows you the approximate values that you must type in.

Flags and Yard Definitions

In the routes built into *Train Simulator*, you will see giant blue flags with white crosses that have numbers floating above them. These are markers. They are created by *Train Simulator* automatically and are stored in the *.mkr files in the route directory. They are a visual aid only to help you find items in your route (an important junction on some route might be near marker number 17, for example). They may be turned on and off within the View Menu in the Route Editor.

In the built-in routes you may see green, square boxes with "Yard" written on them. These are usually placed around very complicated sections of track. They are used to define the area where the yard camera can be used. (This is a special top-down camera that is useful for locating consists and areas of track that may be hard to see from the cameras centered on the player's train). The yard camera can only move around inside the yard definition object, but if several overlapping yard areas are defined, the camera can move between them freely. Inside the game press the 7 key to bring up the Yard view (when you are in a yard).

Summary

Almost everything in the Route Editor is placed, selected, rotated, and moved in exactly the same ways, so don't be overwhelmed by its large number of items. It shouldn't be long before you can use the editor to do most things mentioned in this chapter. The key to this tool is practice.

In the final chapter we will look at how to make the base terrain tiles that make the large hills and mountains you see in *Train Simulator.* The Route Geometry Extractor includes a database of the heights of terrain over the entire world, which enables you to import the exact terrain height data that your favorite railway goes over.

Chapter 11

The Geometry Extractor

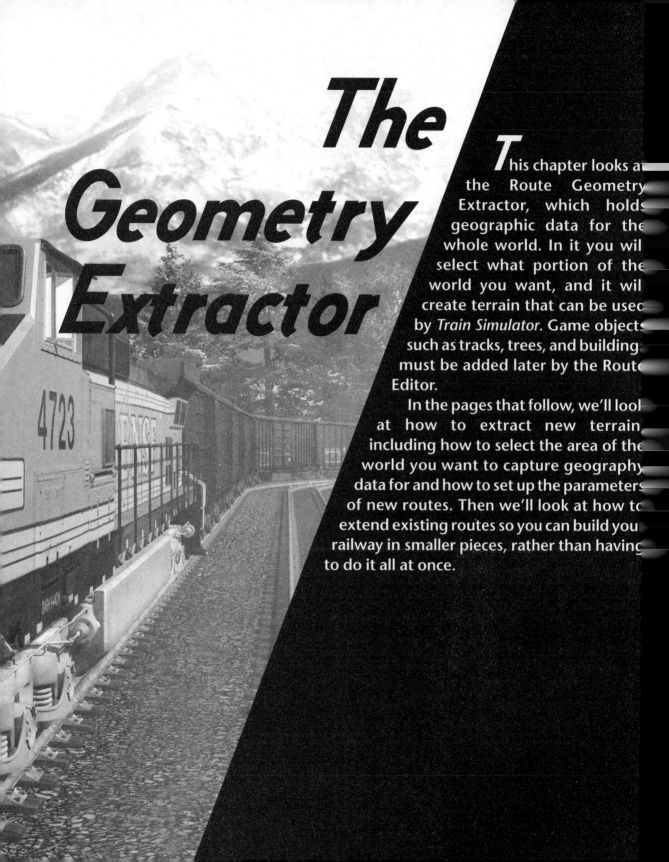

*T*his chapter looks at the Route Geometry Extractor, which holds geographic data for the whole world. In it you will select what portion of the world you want, and it will create terrain that can be used by *Train Simulator*. Game objects such as tracks, trees, and buildings must be added later by the Route Editor.

In the pages that follow, we'll look at how to extract new terrain, including how to select the area of the world you want to capture geography data for and how to set up the parameters of new routes. Then we'll look at how to extend existing routes so you can build your railway in smaller pieces, rather than having to do it all at once.

Extracting New Terrain

Before you can create a new route you must create the terrain that it will travel over. Once your new terrain is in the game, you must use the Route Editor to fill it up with rails, scenery, buildings, and game objects like stations and lights.

Creating a New Route

Once you have finished opening the Route Generator, there are two steps to making a new route. First you'll answer a few questions about your new route, then you'll generate the height data for your new terrain.

Entering Basic Route Data

When you click the Geometry Extractor Editor, a map of the world opens. Click File, then choose New Route. This will display the Create New Route dialog box (see Figure 11.1).

Enter the route's name. You will be able to change the name later if you wish. This name will show up in the list of routes when you run *Train Simulator*. If you wish, you can enter a description of the route by pushing the Edit Description button. Type in a description, then click the OK button to finish. (You'll be able to change this description later.)

In the field called Route's Folder Name and Unique Identifier, enter a short name that will serve as the new route's unique identifier. This will appear in the folder on route information when the new route you are creating is saved. Spend a moment picking a good name because it's not possible to change this name later.

A pair of checkboxes is next. The first is called the Distant Mountain Terrain and should be checked if your train is moving through mountainous terrain and you want distant mountains to show up.

 TIP Turning on Distant Mountains makes the terrain look better but will slow the rendering of the visuals. On flat terrain make sure this option is turned off so your computing power can be used to show other kinds of details.

Click on the Electrified Track checkbox if you want this route to be electrified. If you select this box you will be able to decide if the engines use overhead wires or a third rail and, if you use wires, what height they are set at.

Create New Route   ☒

Source Template

| rogram Files\Microsoft Games\Train Simulator\template | Browse... |

Route Name

| Test_Map | Route name seen by user
                    e.g. Northeast Corridor

| Test_Map | Directory name (name only; no path)
                    e.g. Usal

Edit Description...

Route Features

☑ Distant mountain terrain

☐ Electrified track

| 0.0 | Electrified cable height in metres (0 for none)

| 1.0 | Terrain detail scaling factor
               (e.g. 0.5 to double detail, 2.0 to halve detail)

Route Speed Limits

| 15.0 | Route restricted speed limit

| 80.0 | Route maximum speed limit

☑ Speed limit values are MPH (KPH otherwise)

Cancel   OK

FIGURE 11.1:

The Create New Route dialog box

With the terrain detail scaling factor field you can increase or decrease the amount of terrain detail that your route displays. You can set this value or use the default.

TIP Experiment with the different detail levels of existing routes and find the highest level that your machine will display smoothly.

The last questions you must answer are about the route's speed limits. You can accept the default values already entered or pick new ones.

- The Route Restricted Speed Limit enables you to designate the speed of trains in restricted speed zones. If you change this from 15 mph, be sure to warn your engineers in the briefings for that route.

- The Route Maximum Speed Limit is self-explanatory.

Click OK to leave the Create New Route dialog box. The Route Geography Creator will set up the proper files on your hard drive and will tell you that the route has been created. It will show you the file's location on your hard drive.

Picking the Terrain Area—Rough Area

Now pick File, then Select Route. This will display the Select Route dialog box with a combo box list of available routes. Open the combo box and select the route that you just finished creating. Click OK.

Click File, then click New Quad-Tree (see Figure 11.2). Every route in *Train Simulator* contains a quad-tree, which is a way of organizing the height data for the whole world. We don't need to know about the vast majority of the world for any particular route, so our job is to tell *Train Simulator* what parts we want for our route so it can ignore the rest.

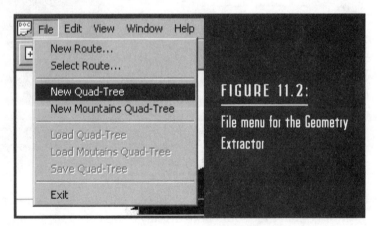

FIGURE 11.2:

File menu for the Geometry Extractor

A map of the world should appear. Right-click the map to bring up a contextual menu (see Figure 11.3). On this menu you can both zoom the region and zoom the window. You can zoom the window as many times as you like, but you can only zoom the region twice. To get the right area, zoom the window a couple of times so that your view is centered on the area you want to capture the data for. Only then zoom to the region.

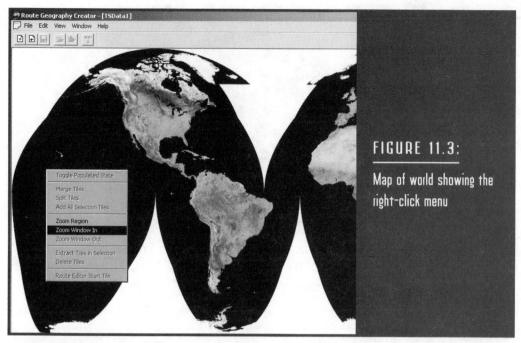

FIGURE 11.3:

Map of world showing the right-click menu

As you zoom in on the area of the map where you want to build your railway, you should see red lines showing real world railways. (If no red lines show up where you know railways exist, check that you have a "vector file" for the given region.)

TIP Before you zoom in to a region, make note of your current latitude and longitude. This information will help you to return to the location you're currently zooming in on.

After zooming in on the region twice, drag a box around the region where you want your new route to be built. Right-click in the selected area and then choose Add All Selection Tiles from the menu (see Figure 11.4).

An empty grid of black squares is created over the region you selected. The smallest squares represent the two kilometer square terrain tiles that are used in *Train Simulator's* Route Editor. The current squares with X's in them show the terrain that will be imported into your route. However, you probably have many squares that are a long way away from your railroad. See the screen shot in Figure 11.5 showing a portion of the CPR line in the Canadian Rockies.

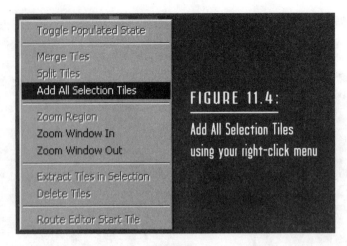

FIGURE 11.4:

Add All Selection Tiles
using your right-click menu

The more terrain tiles that you load, the slower *Train Simulator* will run. On very long routes you only want to keep information for 1 or 2 km on each side of your tracks. On shorter lines you can afford to keep terrain that is a bit more distant.

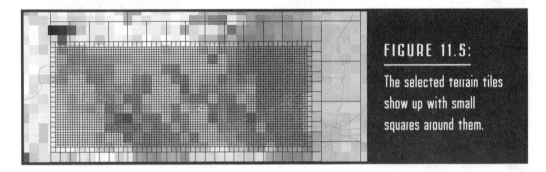

FIGURE 11.5:

The selected terrain tiles show up with small squares around them.

Picking the Terrain Area—Fine-Tuning

To eliminate squares that are too far away from your railway, right-click the square. When the contextual menu comes up, click the choice labeled Toggle Populated State. This will toggle the square to its reverse state. (So if the square had an X in it, the X will vanish. If it didn't have an X, an X will be placed in it.)

You may have hundreds of little squares to add or subtract X's from. You can left-click and drag a box around a group of squares and then toggle them as a batch. Left-click another spot to eliminate the box once you are done with it (see the example in Figure 11.6).

When you have X's in all of the smallest squares (2 km on a side) tell the program that you're done by going to the Edit menu and choosing Generate

Flagged Tiles. A message will tell you the number of tiles that must be generated, and the number already flagged. (If this is the first time you have done this for this route, the number already flagged will be zero.) The message box will ask you if you want to generate these tiles and you should answer Yes.

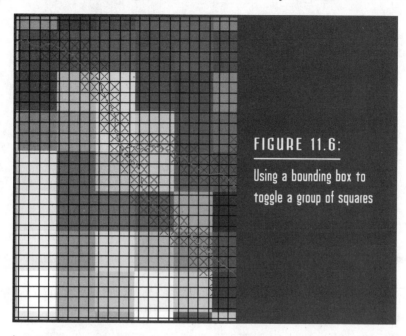

FIGURE 11.6:

Using a bounding box to toggle a group of squares

If a message appears saying that there is no DEM (Digital Elevation Model) data available for some or all of your route and do you want to proceed anyway, just answer Yes. (This is why the final terrain will look flat.)

On the status bar on the lower-left side of the screen you will see a count of how many tiles have been generated once the program has generated all of the tiles.

Compressing the Data

The route is done, but it can be made more efficient by compressing the data for areas that you have said you don't want. You should now go to the Edit menu and click Minimize Quad-Tree. A message will come up stating: "This will remove empty Quad-Tree nodes. Continue?" Click Yes. This will make the empty squares as large as possible, which will improve game performance (see Figure 11.7 for an example).

After you pick and optimize the terrain you want, save your work by going into the File menu and selecting Save Quad-Tree.

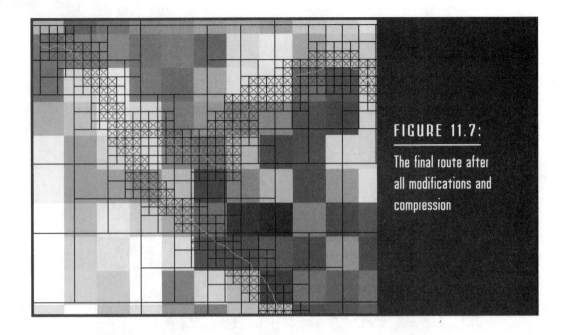

FIGURE 11.7:

The final route after all modifications and compression

TIP If you have some marginal squares that you are not sure if you want to keep or reject, you can save Train Simulator a little memory space by preserving the larger squares. (Notice how I've chosen to make larger empty squares whenever possible in Figure 11.7.)

Picking the Start Square

There is one last thing to do. When someone opens up your route in the Route Editor, the Editor has to know where you would like the camera to start looking. To tell it this, pick one of the squares with a blue X in it and right-click it. In the contextual menu, pick Route Editor Start Tile. (If later you want to change the starting position of the camera you can reopen this route using the Route Geometry Extractor and pick a new start tile.) Save your change.

Using Your New Route

Now when you exit from *Train Simulator* Editor & Tools and restart it, you will be able to go into the Route Editor and start placing tracks and other objects. When you open your new route the camera will point north a little above ground level in the center of the start square you picked. Unless you later want to add more terrain to your route (or trim some off) you will not use the Route Geometry Extractor again. Further modifications will be made in the Route Editor.

Editing an Existing Route

You also can use the Route Geography Creator tool to edit an existing route (one you have created or one included with *Train Simulator*) at any time. The nitty-gritty details of selecting which tiles to include are the same as building a new route, but you must take a slightly different path to get to the data.

Editing Existing Route Parameters

Let's say that you have bought a more powerful computer and you want to turn on mountain terrain. (Your old machine was so slow that you had to turn off many of the nice visual effects.) You want to go into the route you made a few months ago and change one of its parameters (variables) so that the distant mountains will show up when you run your route.

Opening an Existing Route

Launch the Route Geography Editor (refer to Chapter 8 if you're unsure about how to do this). Click the File menu and then pick Select Route. A dialog box will appear with a drop-down combo box that lists all of the existing routes.

Pick the route you want to edit from the combo box, then click OK to close the window. You'll see a map of the world. Click the continent that you're working with (example: North America) and right-click the map. A right-click menu will appear; pick Zoom Region (this will look like Figure 11.3, shown near the start of this chapter).

Editing an Existing Route's Parameters

To change the variables that are set for your route, go into the Edit menu and choose Route Values… This brings up the Route dialog box you saw back in Figure 11.1. Now you can simply edit any of the values for this route that you want to change.

Adding or Subtracting Tiles to Your Route

If your route is in a crowded area it's easy to lose track of which route is yours, because it's likely to be covered with red lines representing railways. To better see your own route, turn on the quad-tree for that route by going into the File menu and selecting Load Quad-Tree.

 TIP If you can't see the quad-tree squares or the red lines that show where railways are, try pressing the F6 and F7 keys to display the quad-tree and vector data.

If you want to do more than just change a few route properties, you will have to reload the quad-tree and edit which parts of the world will show up on your route. Select the File menu, then click Load Quad-Tree. This will show the quad-tree and the blue squares for your route. It should be possible to see which route is yours even if it's in a busy area. It should look similar to Figure 11.5.

You can zoom in the window a time or two by right-clicking the map and selecting the Zoom Window menu choice. (The screen is not centered on your click after zooming, so you'll have to scroll the window each time you do this. You may want to note the longitude and latitude of the route to help you.)

When you have the window zoomed in a bit and your route centered, right-click the route to bring up the contextual menu. Click Zoom Region again (you can only zoom region twice).

Zoom the window a couple of times until you can clearly see the smallest squares (the 2 km by 2 km tiles that make up the terrain in *Train Simulator*). Now you can add or subtract tiles from your route by toggling the X in each box, just as in the first section of this chapter. You can right-click any of these small squares and make it your new starting square if you want to change the start square for your route.

Be sure to generate flagged tiles if you've added any new tiles to the route. Then minimize your quad-tree and save your route once you've made your changes.

You should now be able to go into the route to which you've added terrain tiles, and start laying track and adding objects for the new part of it. (See Chapter 10 for more on laying track and scenery.)

Conclusion

You should now be able to get the geometry data for an existing route using the Route Geometry Extractor. You can fine-tune the hills and rivers, lay track, and place all sorts of game objects using the Route Editor. You can build new activities using the Activity Editor. *Train Simulator* has dozens of little programs that must work together to build routes so don't worry if you're still having some troubles with one part of the editor or another; there is a lot to learn.

If you own a 3D-modeling package and know how to use it, you may be able to import new 3D objects into *Train Simulator* and use the Geometry Extractor to place them. You'll have to check the Microsoft website for more information about this, as it is beyond the scope of this book.

We hope that you've an enjoyable time using *Train Simulator* and its editors.

Appendix

Train Simulator Community

*T*rain Simulator players can benefit from a wealth of Internet resources related to the game. These add-ons, customized routes, new engines and rolling stock, and several other resources improve the breadth, depth, and length of your virtual rails. This appendix features links to some of the more popular websites, and explains how to take advantage of some of the available supplemental materials. To find these websites, simply type the address into your web browser's address bar exactly as it is printed.

Official Website

This website is officially licensed by Microsoft to offer content related to *Microsoft Train Simulator*. As a result, it has the most authoritative and up-to-date information. This site is professionally run by the company that supports *Train Simulator*, so you can generally trust the content and downloads you find on it. The unofficial websites listed later in this appendix are run by individuals who are not affiliated with Microsoft, and the content there usually has not been specifically approved for use with the game.

Microsoft Train Simulator Official Website

Address: http://www.microsoft.com/games/trainsim/

The first stop on the Internet for a *Train Simulator* railroader should naturally be Microsoft's official homepage. Here you'll find the most important type of resource for the game available: software patches. After the release of the game, the development team stays hard at work supporting customers and addressing any software issues as they come up. Periodically, Microsoft may release updates to the game software that fix known problems. Sometimes Microsoft even adds or modifies game features. These fixes are bundled as downloadable program files called software patches. You should always try to download and install the current patch, so that your trains run at peak performance.

The official website also contains links to other sites, information about each of the routes modeled in the simulator, and supplemental content covering the game's development, features, and current events. Microsoft offers links to technical support on the website, and also maintains a FAQ, which lists the answers to many common questions about the game. If you have trouble with the game or need some questions answered, this site is the place to start.

Unofficial Websites

The following sites are run by fans of the game, or by companies offering supplemental materials for *Train Simulator* that are not endorsed by Microsoft. The sites listed here will have some of the most interesting information, as *Train Simulator* was developed specifically to support player add-ons and customization. However, keep in mind that not all of the downloads on these pages will be stable, and you'll find add-ons of widely varying quality. Read some of the information from the player-generated supplements on the community forums and websites to find the best downloads. Sybex does not endorse the content of any of these sites, and provides these links as a service to its readers.

MSN Train Simulator Fan Site

Address: http://communities.msn.com/TrainSimulatorFanSite

This fan site is hosted by the Microsoft Network (MSN). Here you'll find a real-time chat and a message board. These community forums enable you to get in touch with your fellow sim-engineers to swap ideas, get help, trade files, or discuss any aspect of the game. The site also lists current events and announcements, helping you keep your finger on the pulse of the *Train Simulator* community. If you want to get connected with other fans of the game, this is the easiest place to go!

This fan site also hosts supplemental material, including file swapping between fans. These folders are more robust than the game's homepage, but they are not necessarily produced by Microsoft. The site periodically sends out a member newsletter. You can also access the site without becoming a member if you don't wish to receive their updates on *Train Simulator* news and events.

Lastly, the MSN fan site offers an abundance of links to other train-related sites. Not all of them are directly related to *Train Simulator*—you'll find links to information about real-world railways, model railroading clubs, historical railroad links, and all other things related to the rails.

MS Trainstation

Address: http://www.trainstation.cjb.net/

This slick site features free hosting for *Train Simulator* add-ons, opening up distribution for people who don't have their own websites. As a result, you'll find some rare and exciting downloads here. It is also updated frequently with news, community links, and other interesting tidbits.

Subway Simulator Central

Address: http://hometown.aol.com/subwaysimcentral

Some of the most fascinating fan sites are those that are devoted to a particular niche of the game. Subway Simulator Central is focused entirely on urban subways, light rail, and commuter routes. Of particular interest is the comprehensive Route Database, which lists a great many related custom routes in a clear and useful table, and provides links to the home page of each route's creator.

Train Simulator Station

Address: http://tss.gametropics.com/

This fan site is professionally hosted, and gets updated regularly. You'll find an extensive mix of community support, add-on downloads, and news here. This site also contains a walkthrough section where they plan to offer suggestions for getting through the game's activities.

Trainsimu.com

Address: http://www.trainsimu.com/home/

This site allows you to customize its presentation, including the default language. Its dynamic programming also keeps track of the most popular stories, downloads, and forums on the site, so you don't have to search very hard to find what's hot. The forums are also very active, with very specific categories to help you to find the exact kind of information or discussion you're looking for.